ALSO BY PHILIP RIEFF

Freud: The Mind of the Moralist

The Triumph of the Therapeutic: Uses of Faith After Freud

Fellow Teachers: Of Culture and Its Second Death

The Feeling Intellect: Selected Writings

Sacred Order/Social Order: My Life Among the Deathworks

CHARISMA

CHARISMA

The Gift of Grace, and How It Has Been Taken Away from Us

PHILIP RIEFF

Foreword by Daniel Frank and Aaron Manson

PANTHEON BOOKS, NEW YORK

Library of Congress Cataloging-in-Publication Data

Rieff, Philip, [date]
Charisma / Philip Rieff ; foreword by Daniel Frank and Aaron Manson.
p. cm.
Includes bibliographical references and index.
ISBN-13: 978-0-375-42452-6
1. Charisma (Personality trait)—History. I. Title.

BF698.35.C45R53 2007 128—dc22 2006047490

www.pantheonbooks.com

Printed in the United States of America

First Edition

2 4 6 8 9 7 5 3 1

This book could not have been completed without the assistance of Philip Rieff's family, friends, and students. We wish to thank Dr. Kenneth C. Piver for guiding us through the maze of Professor Rieff's unedited manuscripts. We also wish to thank Dr. Mark Greene for his continued interest and support. This book could not have been published without the generous encouragement of David Rieff. He brought his unique perspective as author, editor, and son to these pages. We hope that this book would have met his father's expectations.

CONTENTS

FOREWORD

> "I don't need any guide, I already know the way. Remember this,
> I'm your servant both night and day."
>
> —BOB DYLAN

THE IMPORTANCE OF religious faith in Western culture has been a continuous and central concern in Philip Rieff's work. His first two books described how the religious culture of the West has been under critical attack for the last century, and how that attack seeks to "liquidate" the very possibility of faith. In *Freud: The Mind of a Moralist* (1959), Rieff argued that Freud's theories laid the intellectual groundwork for the assault on established moral order, and he explored the consequences of Freud's theories on faith and unbelief in Western civilization. In *The Triumph of the Therapeutic: Uses of Faith After Freud* (1966), he tried to anticipate what new social types would emerge beyond the old culture based on faith. He named that new character type "the therapeutic." In 1970, Rieff turned his attention to an investigation of the significance of faith over the entire extent of Western civilization, from the ancient Hebrews to the present day. He did not intend to dwell nostalgically on an irretrievable past, but to understand how genuine faith has been lost in modern times, and what has been lost in the process. Rieff analyzed this process through the lens of charisma, a concept that united his theological interest in the meaning of faith with his sociological interest in what constituted authority.

"Charisma" was originally an obscure concept that the great German sociologist Max Weber lifted from the work of the Protestant theologian Rudolph Sohm. Without Weber, the term would have disappeared in the oblivion of obsolete nineteenth-century theological polemics. Today, charisma has become a ubiquitous term that has, in Rieff's words, "been battered to death." The difference between its original meaning and its modern use is the subject of this book.

In Rieff's view, charisma has been transformed from the gift of grace into the gift of evil. Christ was once the prototype of charismatic authority. The modern charismatic is his polar opposite: a "purely political animal," a performer, whose actions, whether aesthetic or political, are divorced from ethical considerations. As a political leader, he is often criminal, destructive, and violent. Rieff believes that the political divisions of Left and Right are obsolete. The only distinction that matters is between those who seek to defend and restore a genuinely charismatic culture and the false charismatics whose authority is the authority to deal death.

Again and again in his work, Rieff returned to the thinkers who led the modern intellectual attack on religious faith. Nietzsche, Weber, and Freud are the supreme anti-religious theorists of the late nineteenth and early twentieth centuries, the "transitional geniuses" who announced the death of divine authority and who called into question the very possibility of faith and true charisma. They are the true heralds of "the therapeutic." They are also the theorists that Rieff admires the most. *Charisma* is Rieff's defense of the traditions they attack. It is his attempt, he told us, "to develop a theology that doesn't reject modernity. It was my intention to resurrect theology from within modern sociology."

By 1973, Rieff had abandoned work on this project, even acknowledging in *Fellow Teachers* the likelihood of failure. When we asked him why he had not completed this work, he said, "There was no constituency for the book. Something in America had changed. We live in an anti-theologic age."

Fortunately he changed his mind. He helped us assemble the manuscripts and supervised our editorial work. Four weeks before he died, we asked him again why he had not finished *Charisma*. "Perhaps I was wrong," he said. "There is always a constituency."

—DANIEL FRANK AND AARON MANSON,
JULY 2006

PART ONE

The Charismatic Foundations of Culture

CHARISMA

ONE

SPRAY-ON CHARISMA

IT ALL SEEMS PERFECTLY PLAUSIBLE; in fact, the item advertised on p. 2 of this book may be on the market now, having seen it prophesied in the *New Yorker* cartoon.

Is it not likely that since all action is now decided from the outside in that a spray-on charisma can will soon be invented? We shall have the recognition factors sorted out, and so by purchase smartly in the economy size, spray ourselves into something extraordinary. This is simply to say what Søren Kierkegaard said more than a century ago, that all inwardness is lost. In this book, I have tried to work through, critically, toward an understanding of how my inwardness was lost for me, and to recognize those chiefly responsible for the loss—our charismatics. The writing has not been therapeutic; on the contrary, that is the point. From the extraordinary way in which Max Weber, among others, canned charisma for us, I have learned that I am opposed to all therapies. The therapeutic is that terrible beast who has been slouching toward Bethlehem. The pity of our lives is that there are no charismatics to save us from him. We can hope for the spray-on charisma can, which will realize the ancient dream of making even the least of us extraordinarily attractive on the outside. The world is fuller than ever before of people who look like charismatics and try to act the part; like the early medieval sect of Waldenses, they insist on wearing sandals, some even in winter. If not to be like the founder, which was the original reason for wearing sandals, then to be recognizable, a little extraordinary, in lieu of the spray-on charisma can. I doubt that the Western world has ever been so full of innovators all hawking their changes, or so full of deviants, all asserting their rights. Where are the charismatics? The question is, more precisely, who are the charismatics? Who deviates decisively from the beaten path? Who opens a new road, a different way of life and revelation for men to go, even remain, for such openers of new roads are all but lost. Is he a guru, like Timothy Leary, for the guru, in its original meaning, meant, I understand, heavy, weighty, venerable. A modern guru, a figure like Timothy Leary or Norman O. Brown, carries the reverse meaning. He is deliberately weightless and preaches weightlessness to us. The modern guru represents the ephemeral, the fugitive, the contingent. It is in this sense that he is an exemplar, someone to follow.

Where are our gifted leaders, our charismatics? Perhaps the idea itself is an illusion and not only has no future, but has no past. My position in this book will be that there is no charisma without creed—there must be a conscious and intense established symbolic* in the field before there can be a standard that can be used to break through that field. Doubt, skepticism, infidelity, are not charisma, nor are they therapy, the two major terms I shall use throughout this book. Yet charisma proclaims something to be true and important. In Weber's idea, it announces a way, it lights the fire of a new interdict, it has the emphasis of infallibility, no less than that which it breaks through. But I ask again, where are our charismatics? Certainly, we have stunning numbers of people who copy the outward features of the charismatic. They insist on wearing sandals. But there is a great new perplexity in an anticredal order such as our own, because being therapeutics now there is no correlation between soul and body. All is body. Nothing material now emanates from the spiritual. We are mirrors still, but not mirrors of some spiritual or inner reality from which our appearance is derived. Rather, our world is as a theater, and in that theater, rather than the world as church, the program announces the end of all sacramental action; wearing sandals itself must be put in quotation marks—it is a role, a put-on, one of the many costumes that may be worn, one of the transformations and adjustments for which the therapeutic more or less consciously can prepare himself.

*A symbolic is a particular order of interdicts and remissions.

It is through Weber that charisma promises to be, and has become, a marketable item. But in the course of this book, I shall look at charisma as it has been considered before Weber and after. And the book itself intends to go beyond Weber's thought and to try to establish what a charismatic may be, if he is to oppose the therapeutic. Therapeutic and charismatic are proposed in this book as ideal anti-types. Thus, for Weber, the charismatic leader proposes a radical breakthrough, a transformation of those transgressive motifs proposed by him in his Protestant pathos as shadowing of a new normative order. The therapeutic, on the other hand, also proposes a radical transformation of transgressive motifs, but not as foreshadowings of a new normative order. Indeed, the key to understanding the therapeutic as the successor ideal anti-type of the charismatic is that he hopes for, as his own lifestyle proclaims, a society in which there is no normative order. It is further my intention to demonstrate how the modern Protestant and Weberian conceptions of the charismatic in fact lead toward this successor type, the therapeutic, and toward a transformation of transgressive motifs in a way that throws no shadow of normative order upon the future. My thesis shall be that the therapeutic is the ideal anti-type and real successor of the charismatic. I understand the charismatic as somehow in truth an innovative resolver of ambivalences by the introduction of new interdicts into our lives. The fire of a new no. The therapeutic is a releaser from the interdicts, a transgressive figure. The two are thus very closely related and it is their relation that is the chief concern of this book, and not an analysis of Weber, Marx, Freud, or any particular figure. They are pegs around which at times, given my lack of greater skills, I have hung my analysis. But they are important pegs, and they themselves have helped make the transition between the dominance of the charismatic ideal and the therapeutic anti-ideal.[1]

In this period of transition, our would-be charismatics are better understood as terrorists. The relation between the transitional, modern notion of charisma canned in the sense Weber, as I shall show, canned it, and terror needs some preliminary explanation. Perhaps the best place to begin is with the suggestion that holiness is entirely interdictory. A moral absolute thus becomes the object of all. Holy terror is charismatic; our terror is unholy. For our charismatics are engaged in no wrestlings of angels, but, rather, with the obeying of demons. Jacob was a charismatic when Laban and Jacob took mutual pledges before the God of their fathers; Jacob swears by the fear of his father, Isaac (Genesis 31:53). What is this charismatic fear? What is holy terror? Is it a fear of a mere father; in a phantasmagoric enlargement, Freud's idea is silly. Holy terror is rather fear of oneself, fear of the evil in oneself and in the world. It is also fear of punishment. Without this necessary fear, charisma is not possible. To live without this high fear is to be a terror oneself, a monster. And yet to be monstrous has become our ambition, for it is our ambition to live without fear. All holy terror is gone. The interdicts have no power. This is the real death of God and of our own humanity. It is out of sheer terror that charisma develops. We live in terror but never in holy terror. Those are the only alternatives, as I shall try to show in the course of this book.

A great charismatic does not save us from holy terror, but rather conveys it. One of my intentions is to make us again more responsive to the possibility of holy terror.

To lead into an understanding of the difference between the terror in our lives and holy terror, the difference between charisma and therapy, the two alternatives we have before us, the most convenient object is the thought of Max Weber on charisma. That will lead us also, by the way, into the deepest tension of modern sociology as a discipline functioning to dissolve all inwardness. We turn, therefore, first to an analysis of Max Weber's thought on charisma. Weber's sociology of charisma embodies at its greatest the polemical thrust of sociology, its intellectualism, its high function in the process of rationalization, that dissolution into meaninglessness from which such a discipline as sociology cannot save us. This intellectualism is coupled with a deliberate detachment from responsibility that goes under the name of science. Of course, such an intellectualism can be a conservative force, as Weber noted in the case of the priestly rationalizers of written sacred traditions. Or, it can be conservative through its defense of the high social status and institutional responsibility of the professional rationalizers themselves, the sociologists. But, even so, the interdicts are generally reduced by reason to magic, and the attack of sociology, like the attack of its Protestant predecessor, is on the very animus of charisma, as magic. Weber's entire treatment of religion is utterly suspect, and I shall try to unfold the suspicions. Weber is himself the culminating expression, I think, of the Protestant pathos, which turns into evolutionism and progressivism, with its mystique of breaks with the established order as the highest expression of the intellect and of soul. This Protestant pathos, this mystique of breaks with the established order, is less than a revolution and more than a reform. It is that relentless lusting after progressive social change that characterizes the liberal era and leads straight into the Marxist pathos, with its generalized species man, who turns into an apparatchik and party functionary. The truest reason for beginning with Weber is that in particular through his reworking of the idea of charisma, Weber made the most genuinely honest soundings, as Karl Jaspers said in his memorial address of the human spirit in the contemporary world. Weber achieved a form of such genuineness that his work became the adequate expression of truly original thought and fulfilled humanity. These soundings of the human spirit in the contemporary world need not remain unchallenged and opposed, and in this manuscript I have dared not only to learn from them, but to challenge and oppose them.

Weber's perspective on charisma is basically evolutionary; that is, charisma must develop into something else. It must transcend itself, it must unfold and become something more than it is at the beginning. That is why Weber begins with primitive religion, and sets that very primitivity as the basis for its own transformation. Weber's evolutionism carries implications that have become part of our own progressivist mythology, that is, the dominant, the shallow evolutionism of the nineteenth century that leads Weber to associate the interdicts, that fundamental motivational form of all culture by which men feel what it is they are not to do, as the very basis for the conduct of their lives, as associated with taboo and with magic, which in turn is to be succeeded by something higher, which to Weber is the "religious ethic." This dichotomy between the implicitly interdictory magical taboo and the higher religious ethic indicates the particular polemical thrust of the evolutionist model to which Weber remained loyal throughout his life. Since taboo is primitive, and the primitive is fated to be superseded, then the origins of charisma are themselves rendered quite ambiguous. Moreover, the social form, the distinctive communal institution within which charisma first expresses itself, seems to be in Weber (see for example his discussion of orgy, in the first chapter of his *Sociology of Religion*) ecstasy. Now, the social form of ecstasy is the orgy, which is "the primordial form of communal religious association." But the orgy is certainly a transgressive form; that is, it must be a reaction against something else, as what Weber calls an occasional activity. This must mean that the interdictory forms are prior in culture. Thus, Weber early, by implication, associates charisma, through ecstasy, with the opposite of taboo, that is, the social form of charisma, the orgy, implies that charisma is itself transgressive, and that what it is transgressive of is the established moral order. Thus, at once, we see two very important implications at the very beginnings of Weber's theory of distinctive charisma, 1) that charisma is itself, in its distinctive subjective condition of ecstasy, transgressive, and, 2) that there is by implication a form prior to these occasional transgressive forms, such as the orgy, in which charisma is expressed socially, which are the opposite of it and which the charismatic activity, that is, the orgy, breaks through. This is to say that the truly moral forms are interdictory. But this is at once to draw out the implications of Weber's own theory against the tendency of his own thought, and also to go beyond that theory by thus drawing it out. We still are left with the need of a more thorough examination of Weber's evolutionist bias, especially with reference to that pejorative term for the primitive interdicts, the taboos, which are specific and are to be superseded through generalization in religious ethic. We must first clear up the relation between the conception of taboo and our conception of the interdicts. As a primitive and magical mode of avoidance, taboo may be the first historical expression of the interdicts. Weber is in fact talking two different languages at the same time; he is using a term which located in a particular context of primitivity thus reduces the meaning of the term to that which is to be superseded. Weber's use of the term "taboo" is entirely pejorative. Evolutionism, whether of Weber's sort, or Sir James Frazer's, reduced the magical to a pejorative status. This was the tendency also of Protestant rationalism. What the primitive thinks cannot be satisfactorily summarized under the category taboo, precisely because the category itself projects a certain unsatisfactoriness, a certain supersession of that category. Taboo thus represents, in its relation to the whole discussion of magic in opposition to religion in Weber's dichotomist thought, a terminological imperialism which hides the true thrust of Weber's theory and also the meaning of charisma, which is transformed into a sociological category and thus serves to strain against that which it is, that is, an organization of avoidances and of salvations through avoidances. Taboo is an element of all those situations in which attitudes are expressed in terms of responses to danger. The particularity of response to danger is never dissolved in religious ethic. That is the key that destroys the Weberian dichotomy between the magical and the religious.

In understanding the liberal and critical attack on interdictory motifs, it is important to associate the distinction between magic and religious ethics, between crude and primitive religiosity and higher religiosity in terms of their discussion of taboo. From William Robertson Smith and the higher critics, through Weber and Freud, the liberal critics confused interdictory and remissive transference under the rubrics of taboo and religious ethics. Thus, Robertson Smith implies that avoidance behavior, the interdicts themselves, are the distinctive criterion between magic and religion, between the lowest form of superstition and religious ethic as between the crude and the sublime. Therefore, religious ethics constitutes a rising above interdictory motifs, the taboos themselves. The climax of this entire development may be said to be in Freud in that important brief passage of preface to *Totem and Taboo,* in which Freud locates the taboos as an entirely pejorative term for the interdictory motifs and says that although the totems have been defeated in modernity, the taboos have not. They have persisted. This complex of taboo guilt and magic is very important, too, in understanding the entire apparent renaissance in interest in magic among the young. That interest has been misunderstood—it is black, transgressive, magic, not the taboo, but its reverse, the magic of the transgression that is the dynamism of the so-called revival of interest in and the practice of magic. Robertson Smith, as Franz Steiner notes in his excellent lectures on taboo, "applied avoidance behavior as a distinctive criterion between the crude and the sublime. "For, it will be observed, no avoidance behavior," Steiner says, "is connected with cases of positive transmission, such as blessing." And for Robertson Smith, only the combination of avoidance behavior and contagion constitutes the low and primitive form of transmission. "It is the introduction of the category 'taboo' that makes possible a distinction that would otherwise be difficult to uphold," concludes Steiner.[2] But Steiner here confuses the issue. It is not at all clear how be himself intends us to take the distinction between those forms of so-called taboo which are, in fact, blessings, for example, from the higher being to the lower, and those from the lower to the higher, as in the case of barakas, or praisers of God. In the one case, the gift is received by God as homage; in the other case, it is God who blesses and this serves to identify the relation between man and God and God and man. On the other hand, in his example from contemporary Arab Bedouin usage, Steiner remarks that "the same Semitic root is found in the Arab word *baraka*, a word which, in contemporary Arab Bedouin usage, means the coveted power of a person. Thus, if a Bedu sees someone who is successful or skilful, or shows the *élan* of great vitality, or a stranger who, it is polite to assume, is furnished with superior skills or gifts of God, etc., he will approach and touch him with his hand to get what he calls his baraka. The Bedu in this case makes the same movement with his hand as the contemporary Jew when the scroll of the law is carried round the synagogue in procession and he touches it with reverence."[3] But there is considerable confusion here. What Steiner is referring to is charisma, but it would clarify the matter if the charisma to which he refers, the blessing, the baraka, is distinguished as between avoidance behavior or the interdictory motifs, and the positive transmissions of the blessings, for here, at one point, he appears to refer to remissive motifs, that is, the getting of certain great vitalities, and, on the other hand, to the interdictory motifs, the touching of the scroll of the law with reverence. So here, again, although a critic of the liberal thesis that associates taboo with the lowest forms of superstition, Steiner himself is not free of precisely this spurious anti-charismatic distinction between the magical forms, that is, taboo, and so-called religious ethics.

One has to understand charisma in terms of taboo as interdictory on the one hand, which include avoidance behavior, the positing of danger, and the transferences that occur which are charismatic in terms of avoidance behavior, and on the other hand, the remissive transferences which are the contrary of avoidance behavior and can be seen in contemporary interest in black magic and in therapies of transgression. One example of those therapies of transgression would be the therapist sleeping with his patient and having sexual intercourse in some form or other. Weber, in his Germanic use of categories as if they were established and true, simply depends upon this nineteenth-century liberal critical distinction between taboo and avoidance behavior, or the interdictory motifs specified as the lowest form of superstition, and religious ethics in a rather abstract and universal form. In this respect, Weber is a perfect example of the Protestant pathos as it is fed into the modern mind among the educated classes and into sociology. Yet Steiner does grasp the main point. The main point is that what he calls "positive and negative transmissions of taboo are not merely contemporaneous by accident: they are interdependent"[4] (pp. 64–65). "Any ritual or practice," he goes on to say, "embodying belief in negative transmission, strengthens attitudes toward positive transmission. What is remarkable about the two kinds of transmission, surely, is the way they combine to create a universe of properties, ordered only insofar as these properties are active, and they can be comprehended as active only in terms of transference and contagion. Only by conceiving these properties as active human relationships can one conceive structured social life in terms of them. If we today had to study a living society of that type, our attention would be given to this interplay of active properties."[5]

We are seeing in contemporary society a situation in which the deliberate transgression of interdictory motifs, the deliberate flouting of avoidance mechanisms, is creating a reaction which is toward the reestablishment of those interdicts. It is the rejection of rejection, by transgressive movements, of the entire notion of dangerous situations that has become the special object of fear and hatred in modern society. The liberal defense of these transgressions must inevitably bring liberalism itself crashing down, for in that defense, the liberals are defending the destruction of avoidance mechanisms which are necessary to the practice of liberalism itself. Steiner here can be quoted, to put the matter in another light. "In this connection," he writes, again referring to Robertson Smith's liberal distinction between magic, with its avoidance responses, as somehow pejoratively primitive, and religious ethics on the other, "a distinction between 'respect' for gods and 'mere terror,' a distinction worthy of much critical attention in a different context—becomes quite irrelevant. Terrors *not* connected or associated with the central religious experience (of the interdictory motifs) are inconceivable."[6] "The moral universe of active properties," as Steiner calls it, "is organized on monotheistic principles" (p. 66). In certain societies, Steiner argues, "negative transmission proper" (that is, what one may call interdictory transmissions), "is possible only in a society in which there is but *one* source of prohibition, that is, the absorption of prohibitory functions by the one God excludes, in the case of the Hebrews, at least, the positive magical use of the unclean," (that is, remissive techniques of gathering vitality and power and thus averting danger).[7] Robertson Smith, in his discussion of amulets as unclean things, is constantly confusing interdictory and remissive motifs. Thus, he writes that "the more notable unclean animals possess magical powers. The swine, for example, which the Saracens, as well as the Hebrews, refused to eat, supplies many charms, and magical medicines."[8] But Steiner replies rightly that "such an association of the unclean and the magically potent yielded by the comparative method, is inapplicable to the Hebrew bible." Steiner writes: "Absorption of all taboos by the One God, not only *indicates* His power: His power *consists* in this. The stipulation of all avoidance behavior in terms of the law of the One God is therefore a far from primitive feature"[9] (p. 66). Robertson Smith concludes his case against uncleanness with a passage that is a perfect expression of the transgressive thrust of liberal criticism. He writes, "The irrationality of the laws of uncleanness, from the standpoint of spiritual religion, or even of the higher heathenism, is so manifest that they must necessarily be looked upon as having survived from an earlier form of faith and society. And this being so, I do not see how any historical student can refuse to classify them with savage taboos."[10] This makes irrationality a proof of primitiveness and is such a strange procedure that Steiner does not think that it is necessary to refute it. But in fact Freud continues to instance irrationality as proof of primitiveness and so does Weber. What we see now, rather, is that irrationality is a proof of sophistication. The true savage god who is now taking power in our society is not the savage god of the taboos or *the* one God who has absorbed all the taboos. Rather, the true savagery comes after the success of the liberal and critical attack on the supposed irrationality of the laws of uncleanness and on the assumption that all prohibitions are somehow primitive and unjustifiable. Taboo is not at the origin of religion, or if *it* is at the origin of religion, then, as Steiner rightly points out, taboos or interdicts are being created continuously up to the present day. It is the thrust against the interdicts that is giving the savage god his true opportunity. The critical nineteenth- and early-twentieth-century interest in taboo as a pejorative term for the interdictory structure of taboo in social organization has now resulted in a transgressive attack on all the interdicts, precisely among the educated classes.

TWO

THE FIRST VANGUARD OF OUR INHERITED CULTURE

REMINISCING OF TOLSTOY, Gorky writes:

"Someone remarked that Shestov was a Jew. 'Hardly,' said Lev Nikoleavich, doubtfully. 'No, he is not a Jew; there are no disbelieving Jews, you can't name one . . . no.' "[1]

The modern world is full of disbelieving Jews. Yet, in Western history, the Jews have been *the* credal people. In the past 150 years, they have sought new creeds, and finally to escape from all creeds. The tragedy of this effort to escape their credal character is a red thread running through modern history. By our time, Karl Marx, yet another Jew committing identity suicide in the name of yet another new covenant, the Revolution, confronts the Jew of eternal law. And beyond the socialist movement is the therapeutic with its largely Jewish leadership. This latest leadership in moral revolution is not surprising. So many among our revolutionaries against morality are Jewish because so much of what was basic to our moral discipline is Jewish. The recalcitrance of the Jews to their credal vocation is nothing new; they were chosen; they did not choose. In this sense, they are the model of all credal vanguards, feeling their saving interdicts as a burden and yet superior precisely in their sense of also being a burden. It is against the background of the suffering and condescending God of the gentiles, a successful Kenosis in the sense that Jesus' grace cannot be achieved, that we have to understand the Jews as a people burdened by a long memory of their own suffering under the doctrine of a grace they must achieve.

Because a credal vanguard is chosen, it cannot avoid being carried away, toward ends it would not choose. This is the point of the great "upon the eagles' wings" speech in Exodus 19:4: "You yourselves have seen what I did in Egypt. I bore you upon eagles' wings and brought you unto me." "Here we have," concludes Martin Buber, "election, deliverance and education; all in one."[2] The Jews were far from eagles. Moreover, having been so carried up out of slavery, Israel had a debt to discharge, the debt incurred by its election to credal nationhood. This is a very special, debt-ridden superiority. The only way to discharge this debt was to confirm their election as "a kingdom of priests and a holy people" (Exodus 19:6). This is more a sign of their debt than of any innate superiority. A credal vanguard can only work to become what it is appointed to be; the terms of its appointment give it a partial and particular character from which it can escape only by suffering the supreme punishment of that escape: the loss of its identity, the achievement of being nothing.

The charisma of the Jews, that tremendous and yet peculiarly ironic corporate confidence of Israel in its own limiting symbolic, which closes a whole range of possibility, revolves around God's promise that he always "shall be present," standing by them. At the same time, this confidence itself is very demanding, and puts the vanguard in its place—for all its negative capability: to obey renunciatory demands. It is in this sociological sense that the Mosaic creed is demagicized; that creed prevents those acting upon it to consider they can actually do what they will with their bestowed capabilities. To the first vanguard of our inherited culture, the exodus out of Egypt is the rejection of earth magic. Egypt is the land of magic, of power constantly increasing. So long as a people understands its own limits, it rejects the supreme temptation, the quest for power. Societies seeking power, even over death, are all Egypts, at war with all Israels. Modern societies evidence many Egypts and no Israels. To be an Israel, society must cherish a symbolic of limits. In the sociology of credal organizations, to be free of limits, even in the name of that organization, is to be faithless. Faith is the general term of obedience to particular interdictory contents, whatever circumstances arise in the role of soul-making; only under this obedience are souls made. God is at the side of Israel *only* so far as Israel was faithful.

The finding, by the power-hungry, of gods to put by their side is exactly contrary to the symbolic of the first vanguard. "God" was not a shibboleth of power. Once the Mosaic God was present, the Jews had to study first what they may not do to each other. The interdictory form became the basis for individual and political existence. Such proclamation of the right and restricting conduct of life, for an entire people, must have been a tremendous experience, for it is entirely unlike the "natural" inclination of the human—to take advantage of every opportunity. Buber insists that "such discoveries or conversions are not born at the writing desk." Rather, it is the kind of experience, of opposition to things as they are, that "stands at the threshold of every genuine historical religion."[3] In such an experience everything is made strange—reality is explained differently and men feel the demand to try to behave differently as an irresistible force. Israel took a new road, an exodus out of the established symbolic and social structure that is informed by earth magic; that exodus from the enslavement of circumstance describes the charismatic situation. To say that charisma arises out of distress tells us nothing about the quality of that distress, as it must look, after it has been subjected to the constraints of charismatic authority.

On the other hand, Egypt is the scene of the greatest of all transgressions in yet another sense: in Egyptian culture, the attempt was made to "chill and congeal" the very structure of possibility.[4] It is in this sense that Egypt is the first culture, elaborately demonstrating its inherent thrust toward the maintenance of things exactly as they are. That Nile culture was an effort of men to organize power into a perfectly stable system, with everything received from the king. The first culture was a state, with all power sucked to the center and everything, including ghosts, assigned their duties. The mummy is the image of Egyptian culture: everything is to be preserved, even in its death. The great seated figures of dead kings are seated, as Buber noted, "never to rise again." Here, Buber says, is "the greatest effort made by human beings to give secular duration to a spiritual substance by introducing form into a material substance."[5] Egyptian culture was the fixing of all possibility, including death, in certain forms. This is an entire society aspiring to be exactly as it is, in love with itself.

A credal society can never fall in love with itself. Ego can never measure up to its ideal. The interdictory forms can never be identified with the political order, according to the faith of Israel.

In the faith of Israel, God alone possesses openness of possibility; therefore, according to this symbolic, God is dangerous to men in his essential character. In the story of God's attack on Moses, God is defined also as power, as all-powerful: it is God who "claims the entirety of the one he has chosen; he takes complete possession of the one to whom he addresses himself."[6] God, and God alone, can be the terrorist of man. And man is obligated to resist, put up a fight, wrestle against this terror in order to get his own infinite claims out of his system and become fully devoted. In the Jewish symbolic, resistance to God is actively admitted, as a propaedeutic to the covenant in the flesh, made as a sign of conciliation with God. This resistance is a testing time, when the authority to whom one is turned turns into a horror itself. The truths of resistance begin as an expression of doubt and incapacity on the part of the credal personality. The origin of the identifying ritual of Israel is as a defense of self from being overpowered by the terror of possibility. In the story of Moses' mission, taking him and his people out of Egypt, God appears to turn against him, trying to attack and slay him. The ritual act is a defense against the demonic—as that which is overpowering—and against even God, so far as having "absorbed everything demonic,"[7] God is himself all-demanding, overpowering. Whether God is attacking Moses or his wife, Zipporah (perhaps on their bridal night), he is, in his demonic activity, the creator as destroyer. Circumcision, as a rite, is the tactic by which Moses' wife limits that power which is demonic and would destroy her husband—or, perhaps, from the beginning, her husband's relation to herself. One exegetical tradition supposes that Zipporah is about to be raped when she devises a bloody ruse that will "let Moses be."[8]

Now, we cannot miss the plain fact that circumcision is a kind of bloody defect, an injury, a cutting off of a significant part of the body. This ritual is an assault upon the body image of a man. It implies that only in the sense of bloody defeat does man know the danger of power, and forewarn himself, by a permanent sign of aggression, against himself. Israel is to be known thereafter by the sign of this forewarning against power, precisely in its phallic aspect, where it is most personal and direct in its assault upon the person, so as to annihilate him as anything except the satisfying object of another will. The near-killing of Moses, precisely by his God, and its ritual deflection is a paradigm of the tension between ritual and power. But Moses is always in mortal danger, so long as he is appointed by God as his messenger. By the appointment, Moses is put in mortal danger precisely even in his merely human personality. He and his family, and his mission for the group, are all in danger of being stripped down to a naked struggle for power.

In his unusual depth of intuition, Buber verged upon what I consider the correct interpretation of ritual as a defense against the destructiveness of power, so far as power is a kind of demand that pulverizes, whether in sexual or religious acts, human personality and subordinates the self to another—most profoundly someone wholly other. "It is part of the basic character of this God that he claims the entirety of the one he has chosen; he takes complete possession of the one to whom he addresses himself."[9]

God thus becomes a problem for man. In his demonic aspect, and total claim, as the ancients of Israel knew, even God must be resisted. The moderns of Israel, especially the literary moderns, have accepted the terrible idea that they themselves can become as gods, to other persons, especially in the sexual encounter. Thus, in the modern novel there is a vengeful destruction of all limits on the sexual relation, its utter transformation into a coming struggle for power between one person and another. Norman Mailer's *An American Dream* is in this sense a perfect anti-Jewish nightmare, another grotesque effort by a nice Jewish boy to be un-nice, an attempt to murder the God of human limits. It is not surprising that a "death of God" theologian, in his identification of the religious with the destructive and anti-cultural, should announce that "the only first-rate religious fiction today is being written by Norman Mailer."[10] The deritualization of social life invites struggles for power. Far from being an enlightening process, the destruction of ritual in Western culture is a major symptom of its demonic character, opening up the possibility of some persons feeding themselves upon the destruction of others. Here, indeed, sex and politics converge in anti-credal movement, a convulsive fury of systematic destruction at once sexual and technological. The God of Israel is part terrorist, demanding even the killing of a son. To Isaac, this God remained a "terror" (Genesis 31:42). But it is only when men deify themselves, by taking life, that they themselves become terrorists, make a terror of life, stripping men of their relation to God by stripping them, both as killer and victim, of their humanity.

Kierkegaard's meditation upon Abraham and Isaac is our best evocation of the motif of power disguised as ritual. Then the one ritual left to man is the ritual of murder, which is at once the beginning and end of all possibility, a perfect fusion of anarchy and order. What Buber calls "divine demonism" is one thing: a consciousness of the power of God also girds the human Jacob to fight (resist) his own destruction, to protect his limits, himself. But when men take all power unto themselves, then the demonic loses its divine character. For then men no longer grasp their own limits; they become destroyers and worship only under the principle of power, which can only be fulfilled by breaking up ritualization as defensive similitudes of power in the struggle against power. The cool, analytic rejection of ritual, as "uncivilized" and "irrational," is one with the hot, romantic yearning to bring down the roof of civilization. The rationalist rejection of ritual is one element in the large compound of anti-culture. The other element is the deritualizing of intimate relations, the dissolution of all manners and reticence, so that men leap upon one another, to achieve their own persons in the submission, unto death, of another.

Kierkegaard understands how even under the most devoted self-sacrificial piety and humanity in one's role, to the degree that role has authority there lurks the demonism of power, even in an apparently ritual act of submission, like the sacrifice of Isaac. His understanding of

Abraham is of a man doing reluctantly what he must do, hurting more than Isaac is to hurt. Abraham's "venerable countenance, his broken heart, has made his speech the more impressive. He exhorts [Isaac] to bear his fate with patience, he has let him doubly understand that he the father suffered from it still more."[11] But all this is literally a hypocrisy, which is broken by Abraham's own surging desire: to break far beyond his role and authority as a father and to satisfy his surge of desire to be truly monstrous and truly himself if only he were free of his submission as a man to God, in whose name he is to "sacrifice" Isaac. The sacrifice is to himself, to the idol of his desire after desire. The would-be God, his God-free self, breaks through the hypocrisy of the loving father, powerless to stop the real sacrifice—of the son to the father. Kierkegaard imagines that Abraham has for an instant turned away from Isaac, and when again he turned toward him he was transformed, unrecognizable to Isaac, not his father but a visibly wild, unrestrained man. Abraham's "eyes were wild, his venerable locks had risen like the locks of furies over his head."[12] This is the inner image of the man of power. However such a man looks on the outside, within he is wild and his head a striking force of destruction, "locks of furies." The body imagery is of a man transmogrified into a demon, all destruction embodied even in his terrible revelation of the truth about himself, and his piety, to Isaac. For his piety is a pose, a role within which he cherishes the abolition of that role. Abraham is something else again, something he has rarely had a chance to be except under the cover of his devotion to a higher power. Now he reveals to Isaac that he himself is that higher power, an idolater of his own endless desire. Between men the imagery of desire is the cut and thrust of the knife; between men and women it would have been the cut and thrust of the phallus. But the act remains the same, an act of power, the ultimate act of desire in the destruction or absorption of the other. In the Christian symbolic, this power act of sexuality was hedged in, compensated, by the doctrine of one flesh and the submission to the procreative purpose of sexuality. "He seized Isaac by the throat, he drew the knife, he said: 'Thou didst believe it was for God's sake I would do this, thou art mistaken. I am an idolater, this desire has again awakened in my soul, I want to murder thee. This is my desire. I am worse than any cannibal; despair thou, foolish boy, who didst imagine that I was thy father. I am thy murderer, and this is my desire.' "[13] Then Kierkegaard falters, for he is too closely identified with Abraham, who is then let out of his power-seeking by a ruse, so that Isaac will think him, rather than God, monstrous. Both Abrahams are correct: God is monstrous and so is Abraham in his real desire to kill, to express thus his most primal urges to destroy even what he himself has created, his son. Abraham would not be an ordinary and limited man, no more than would Søren Kierkegaard, who uses spirituality to "live as though dead," without the satisfactions of sex (Regina) or power (status as an official Christian, a pastor). The point is that Abraham has himself come into collision with his God-relationship and wishes to be by himself. All men are on this same collision course.

Spirituality, as Kierkegaard knew, is a way of opting out of the fight to be a man of power. It is to "live as though dead," i.e., without power. But spirituality so threatens ordinary men, who want their fill of things, to conquer and digest, that they demand "the death of the man of spirit," or rush upon him "to put him to death." This is how it came about, concluded Kierkegaard, that Christ was crucified.[14] There are two kinds of death-dealing: God's and man's. When the spirit strikes, it kills the assertion of the body, self-assertions. When the body strikes, it kills the assertion of the spirit, God's assertion.

The defense of ritual (repetition) against power has nothing to do with the supposed antithesis of social organization and individual self-assertion; it is rather a question of what is demanded of the individual: that he accept, in ritual, that he is engaged in a contest that only permits him, at best, to play at victory and defeat or that he accept, in power, that he is engaged in a contest that permits him to win precisely in the defeat of others.

If men try to be as gods, then men are dangerous to God as well as to themselves. Opening all possibilities, men are always in the wrong—that is, against God. The god-terms, interdictory and remissive in form, are therefore exactly the opposite of beings projecting human wishes, which are entirely transgressive—"instinctual," in Freud's neutral language. The God of Israel was something other than an immense shadow cast by human intention. Indeed, there is a question whether a culture can exist, humanly, without god-terms that are other than projective. As it turns out, a projected God is the most indifferent one on earth, utterly unrelated to man—unless he is a God in opposition—and in that case his projection is not a sign of dependence, which is really what is at issue. It is as man becomes guiltless, as he can find no opposition to his infinite sense of possibility, that he becomes godless. The god-terms of the Jews as a credal nation were the permanent opposition that enabled them to be loyal to their own limits, to their own humanity and not to a subversive universalization of it.

The symbolic proclaimed in the Ten Commandments, of an exclusive relationship to the god-terms, consists in prohibitions of "that which must henceforward be left undone."[15] These interdictive instructions drew the Jews out of the welter of individual possibilities and established their *corporate* identity, their covenant.

As a credal organization, the Jews took the covenant form: a binding of an entire group to certain renunciatory demands upon them. Negative cult follows covenant, as a symbolic act by which all can experience, in common, the renunciatory demands.

The covenant is not an unconscious but a credal order, one which combines submission to the revealed will of the ultimate interdictory figure with confidence in the special relation between God and man stipulated in the creed itself. In the conflict between instinct and experience, on the one hand, and the interdictory ideals on the other, those under the covenant share a preference for the latter; it is this shared preference that makes them civilized. The preference is at once shared and deeply individual, allowing scope for a variety of response and for choice of practice in the particular situation. This combination of shared and individual preference is a way of stating the structure of public morale.

No higher morale can be conceived than that created in the charismatic institution of the covenant. This high morale is best seen in the great war addresses of Deuteronomy 20:1–9. These are great war addresses of selection, in which the individual had to make his own choice of whether to follow Yahweh into battle. In principle, of course,

Yahweh's battles are always victories, in advance, for what Yahweh elaborated in the covenant is just and right; only men can fail the credal relation; the credal relation can never fail men. So in the covenant, the supreme authority is there, victory is assured, the response of self-confidence is at the same time confidence in supreme authority. Under a credal order, there can be no struggle between self and authority. Where there is not this supreme confidence in authority—or, what amounts to the same thing, where there is no confidence in a supreme authority—the individual will lack confidence in himself.[16] Without such supreme confidence, the individual might drop out and not take the risk of death in battle. I quote from Deuteronomy 20:1–8, the passage which explains the meaning of discipline in a credal organization:

> When you go forth to battle with your enemies and see the horses and chariotry and an army larger than yours, do not be afraid of them, because Yahweh, your God who brought you up from the land of Egypt, is with you. So, when you draw near to battle, the priests shall come forth and address the people and say to them, Hear, o Israel, today you are going into battle against your enemies. Don't let your hearts turn soft, do not be afraid, and do not be shaken, and do not be terrified of them, for it is Yahweh, your God, who is going forth with you to fight for you with your enemies, to give you victory. Then the officer shall speak to the people, Is there any man who has built a new house and has not dedicated it? Let him go back home, lest he die in battle and another man dedicate it. Is there any man who has planted a vineyard and has not yet enjoyed its fruits? Let him go on back home, lest he die in battle and another man enjoy its fruits. Is there any man who has arranged to marry a bride and has not taken her? Let him go off home, lest he die in battle and another man take her. Then the officer shall go on and say to the people, Is there any man who is afraid, whose heart is soft with fear? Let him go home, so that he does not make the heart of the others melt by his own.

These considerate, supple rules of who should fight the Lord's battles and who need not indicate the relation between self-confidence and the confidence in a supreme authority. Considerateness of the individual is evident; bridegrooms need not fight. More important is the concern of the disciples' group that everyone in the ranks should place complete reliance in Yahweh, the supreme authority. Self-confidence is inseparable from submission to the credal order, and through that order, to the supreme authority expressed in that order.

It is important to note that, in the development of Western culture, the meaning of discipline cannot be separated from its credal animus. The *conformity* of action in mass organization is anti-credal. Deep individuality cannot exist except in relation to the highest authority. No inner discipline can operate without a charismatic institution, nor can such an institution survive without that supreme authority from a relation to whom self-confidence derives. Without an authority deeply installed, there is no foundation for individuality. Self-confidence thus expresses submission to supreme authority.

Covenant, then, as the symbolic order of credal authority, carries, in ancient Israel, the nuclear meaning of discipline. Charismatic artifacts, such as the Ark of the Covenant, function as behavioral emblems. In the relation between Israelite warfare and the idea of the covenant, we see a much different relation between war and charismatic authority than the one offered in Weber. The lines of determination run in reverse directions. In Weber, it is war that determines charisma; Weber can speak of "war charisma."[17] In the history of the Israelites, and of other cultures, it is the charismatic authority that determines the nature of war—and, moreover, also limits the nature of warlike behavior. "War charisma" means the dissolution of charisma, I think. When there is no longer the limiting authority of charisma, war takes on a dynamism of its own; this, precisely, is the anti-charismatic experience of modern warfare. Released from the constraints of charismatic authority, Western culture can engage freely in its own destruction.

For all the confidence of Israel in its covenanted identity, the covenant is itself a response to sheer transgressiveness. Only when the Israelites turn away from Moses and his mission does he receive the covenant. Covenants are ways of trying again. And from this new drawing power, Moses gathers a second and weird strength, yet without magical characteristics. Things go his way. Catastrophes pile up and give him his chance to persuade both oppositions—both internal (his own masses, for the elite is already his) and external (the ruling group, Pharaoh). In the world as a vale of soul-making, circumstances are enough to create wonder and astonishment; no causal explanation can destroy our wonder. There is no security in our knowledge because there is no limit on possibility. Hitler was an astonishment, no less than the Exodus. No age is without wonders, so long as men continue to be immensely surprised at the change in their circumstance. Against circumstance, we have only the interdicts with which to elaborate true protection. Since science is not an interdictory form, it cannot protect us against ourselves. On the contrary, science is earth magic, subversive in its capacity to inflate men to the size of the original Adam. Science needs its own Sabbatarian movement, an insistence upon what it is not to do, a time and sphere of constraint. The insoluble social condition of the scientists is that they are uncovenanted, without an interdictory form.

With the covenant, all Israel made its charismatic perception, a common interpretative pledge. A *social contract* called off the war of instinctual anarchists, each against all, ending the negative utopia of unlimited aggressiveness[18] in a rational legal order. In contrast, a *covenant* ends in a credal order; it is a bridge conception between the interdictory motifs and their institutionalization. The covenant articulates the charismatic meeting point of authority from the top down, and of obedience from the bottom up. The covenant is the classical articulation of charisma. To keep the covenant is to follow a charter for knowing what not to do. With the keeping of the covenant there develops the essential practice, that renunciation of "instinct," which is the essential form of all social organization. Indeed, covenant theology is the ancient rhetoric of identification.

How curious that the Jew, Freud, so dependent in his explanatory myth of origins on reference to the social contract, never attends to the covenant, the "charter" of Israel, that nation of moralizers to which he himself belongs. Such an exploration would have brought him nearer the empirical structure of social reality. The covenant, among Freud's own people, is no "myth" of social origins.

In a credal society, what is suppressed is kept conscious and the inclinations to break the interdicts, too, are kept conscious. Thus, the price of renunciation is not paid in neuroses but in a realization of guilt. The discipline of inwardness becomes a public and shared condition of inadequacy to the terms of the covenant. Experience assaults the covenant and life becomes a test of faith. In this test, the self-critical powers are sharpened; observation is transformed into a moral sense. It is with the invention of this supranatural sense—for it is not in nature, where the constraints are more nearly automatic—that we can speak of the charisma of perception. The covenant of Israel was a charisma of shared perceptions, first of all what not to do. In the covenant, the ideal becomes an extension of divine authority into human practice.

THREE

COVENANT AND CHARISMA

IN FREUD'S EXPLANATORY MYTH of social organization, the dynamics of guilt are never reconciled with his uses of the liberal myth of origins, the social contract, which is presented as a rational agreement among the masses-sons to cease their individual struggles to become men of power—except over their own women. The social contract is thus a rationalist alternative to charismatic organization. Yet, in the historical psychology of the Jews, what may be called social contract is combined creatively with the dynamics of guilt in the idea of the covenant. In their mythologizing efforts, neither Weber nor Freud took seriously the idea of the covenant.

This corporate articulation of something greater than self-respect organizes the dynamics of guilt. In the making of a covenant, guilt is the main mechanism. A covenanted culture cannot exist apart from a sense of guilt, for the most obvious fact of experience is the difficulty it presents in keeping a covenant—more important, the temptations it presents not to keep it.

The covenant was the way in which the charismatic quality was verbalized, the contents of which thus penetrate and organize the common life. The covenant may be considered the particular and deliberate expression of moral order through negation and denial. Breaking the covenant becomes an expression of guilt; equally, keeping the covenant was an expression of guilt; the covenant itself is a charismatic recognition of the ambivalences felt among the keepers of the covenant. To honor the maker of the convenant, the god-term, is to prefer him and his representatives precisely in their charismatic quality of the self; to respect the covenant more than the self is an articulation of that renunciation of "instinct," which is not only the essential form of all social organization, but also indicates the essential form of culture. Indeed, culture is the elaboration of respect for something other than the self, a creative preference for something that is not self. This achievement of something greater than self-respect, the preference for a holy other, constitutes the dynamics of guilt. In the making of a covenant, guilt is the main mechanism. Culture, if it is credal, cannot exist apart from a sense of guilt.

The other major point here is the meaning of the discipline of inwardness, with special reference to the disciples of the charismatic who mobilize those within their reach for fresh renunciations of instinct. This is the essential function of the discipline of inwardness and, therefore, of discipline itself, and the major way in which new institutions are created may be said to be through the discipline of inwardness as communicated by the disciples of the charismatic, who, in turn, mobilize others for fresh renunciations of instinct.

Failing to see that discipline, and, in particular, that the early disciples of the charismatic, must be, first of all, the renunciatory discipline of inwardness, Weber opposed discipline to charisma—and thus opened up in an insoluble way the false problem of institutionalization. In fact, he associated the waning of charisma with the development of discipline, understanding discipline as rational and external. For Weber, the content of discipline is nothing but the consistently rationalized, methodically trained, and exact execution of received orders. All critical capacity is unconditionally suspended; the actor is unswervingly set for carrying out commands. Superego and instinct reunite. The perfectly disciplined one will do whatever he is commanded to do.

Yet the opposite seems far more profoundly the case; the force of discipline does not eradicate personal charisma, nor does it eradicate stratification by status groups. On the contrary, discipline may be postulated as the extension of personal charisma and as a support of stratification by status groups, it is only because, through discipline, fresh renunciations of "instinct" are mobilized. Discipline thus is a bridge conception toward the institutionalization of charisma. No discipline of inwardness can lead to that consistently rationalized, external, exact execution of received orders Weber had in mind. The superego will not be so externalized. No discipline can survive the loss of inwardness. Rather, such discipline as Weber imagined necessitates the elimination of inwardness, a loss of the entire quality of respect, so that there is nothing to renounce. Weber's references to Spartans, to Jesuits, to officer corps, spell out his confused theory of discipline as opposed to charisma. Yet he declares that "discipline as such is certainly not hostile to charisma or to status group honor."[1] He does not understand how such apparently external discipline as the methodical and exact execution of received orders, the consistent and unswerving carrying out of commands, must be, if it is to be a discipline related to charisma, communicated by mobilizing fresh renunciations and extending those renunciations to larger numbers of people.

There may, in fact, well be another kind of discipline which is opposed to the charismatic quality, in which you have a discipline resting rather on externalization, on opportunism, on the constant accruing of instinctual satisfactions, but this discipline is far different from the classical order of discipline to which Weber refers. He himself, being a modern, has confused the two. Discipline is a mobilizing of fresh renunciations; that is the true spiritual exercise expressed in disciplinary institutions. This absence of internalization, characteristic of the Weberian conception of discipline, seems to me to indicate again Weber's modernist hostility to charisma.

In Freud's analogizing of the primal father, his mythical conception of the totally external man, the man of power, on the one hand, and his conception of the religious founder, Moses, the man of faith, on the other, Freud expressed his own hostility to charisma, at least as powerfully as Weber. That hostility is entirely dependent on Freud's historic postulate that inwardness itself, i.e., faith, is analogous to neurosis. Freud's treatment of inwardness on the analogy of neurosis constitutes a devastating attack on inwardness and on all the disciplines of inwardness which are, to Freud, seen in the perspective of our own time in late primal history, neurotic. No greater attack on inwardness has ever been mounted in our intellectual history; none has been more effective; none has appealed to men's constant desire, their most basic desire, which is to open up possibility. It is as a result of this condition—this intellectual and spiritual condition—of the attack on inwardness as neurotic and on the disciplines by which inwardness is constituted institutionally that the torment of the infinite has grown so much more powerful and movements of terrible liberation have increased the intensity of their destructive action. In their very different ways, both Freud and Weber have mounted major assaults on the possibility of the charismatic, and, in fact, have helped greatly to close off that possibility in our own time.

Against both Freud and Weber, we need to reconsider the meaning of discipline, not in opposition to charisma, but as the vehicle of transfer between the extraordinary inwardness of the charismatic and that charisma of perception by which we all become charismatic. At the very least, we need to distinguish between discipline as it may be exercised in what Weber refers to as a "*mass* organization" and that discipline of which we are capable in opposition precisely to mass organizations. The meaning of discipline, as an extension of the charismatic quality and of a particular charismatic message, can only develop in organizations that are small and elitist, spread through circles of disciples, if you will, through cell organizations. The moment that the effort is made to organize on a mass basis, then one is talking about a contrary meaning of discipline, in which the essence of discipline is the achievement of the gratification of "instinct," rather than a renewal of its renunciation. The gratificatory discipline of mass organizations, politically repressive and morally permissive, characterizes modern totalitarian movements; these latter are no less movements of liberation from inwardness than their apparent opposites, modern anarchist movements. Here we can now see, with startling clarity, how little our established political distinctions between left and right, conservative and radical, revolutionary and reactionary, matter nowadays. Rather, any remaking of political distinctions will have to ask, first, whether there is in fact a discipline of inwardness, a mobilization for fresh renunciations of instinct; or whether there is only the discipline of outwardness, a mobilizing for fresh satisfactions of instinct. Such a distinction will divide contemporary men and movements more accurately; then we shall find fashionable liberals and fascists on the same side, where they really belong.

I turn now to the idea of the covenant as a historical example of the meaning of discipline.

Some scholars believe that there is no relation to be discovered between such features of Israelite warfare as the requirement of sexual abstinence before the battle, and the credal constraints of Israelite society. Understood, however, as an interdictory enactment of the meaning of discipline, relating the individual to an ultimate interdictory figure, sexual abstinence becomes one tactic toward the achievement of inwardness. It is, after all, the most elementary renunciation of instinct. As a preparation before war, abstinence thus takes on meaning as the compensatory act, opposing the meaning of war as the opening of all possible transgressive acts.

There is a definite link between the requirement of sexual abstinence and credal organizations. Celibacy is a disciplinary enactment, intended to guarantee that an organization maintains a credal character, that it remains near its charismatic resources. In contrast, the social contract is not a charismatic symbolic, and Freud's use of the social contract as a mythic explanation for the origins of morality and social organization indicates that he inclined to a rationalist hypothesis of the external nature of basic constraints in any society. Men bound themselves to each other and limited each other's instinctual imaginations of everything by charismatic symbolics, like the covenant, not by some rationalist device like the social contract. Freud imagines what must be, in his own terms, a total contradiction, "rational primitives," sitting down as if to reason together, publicly admitting the futility and horror of the war of each against all, and, instead, working out a social contract. Thus, in one of Freud's two contradictory explanatory myths, not guilt but reason is the source of all morality, religion, and social order. This Freud, the liberal rationalist, is at war with that other Freud, the Jew, who, in his own mythic account of how his ancestors acquired their character, spurns precisely the rationalist pseudo-scientific myth of social contract in favor of an origins myth that is, in effect, an explanation of the primal history of all social order out of a covenanted guilt very different from a social contract. Yet Freud never actually examines, in any detail, precisely that credal expression which is the ancient charismatic institution which is the covenant.

But, lacking Freud's theoretical instruments, it is Weber, far more than Freud, who fails to relate the meaning of discipline precisely to inwardness. That meaning is there to be found, in Freudian theory, in the dynamics of instinctual renunciation. Failures have their own symptomatic meanings. Like Freud, Weber accepted what confronted both as the uniquely *modern* fact: the breaking of meaningful relation between discipline and credal organization. The geniuses of both, Weber and Freud, are themselves, in their separate ways, symptomatic expressions—intellectual rationalizations—of the very different twist then beginning to shape the organization of man: the anti-credal character. Weber saw that character in his role as a *bureaucrat*; Freud saw him as, at once, doctor and patient: what was later to emerge as the *therapeutic*. Both are harbingers of what they analyze, for neither, as theorist, offers what theory should offer: a meaningful discipline, effectually incarnate in charismatic authority. Freud's *therapy* and Weber's *neutrality* are prophylaxes against the return of that repressed charismatic authority latent in all men. The modern genius, in all its anti-charismatic analytic disguises, preaches an end to "primal history." Neither preached the end very happily. Yet neither could order, in what they considered their intellectual honesty, a return of the repressed; yet both took rather grim views of a culture cured of all charisma—except, possibly, the false charisma of power and its desire.

Neither hoped for much from covenants, or their secular offspring, law. Indeed, law is becoming mere legality just because law, to be compelling, must be thought true; and to be true, law must derive from those repressive oppositions to possibility, that very breaking of law, that criminality definitely opposed by the authority of charisma. Thus, for example, in ancient Israel, Deuteronomic laws make explicit the underlying assumption that wrongdoing constitutes an offense to the divine overlord, to the supreme authority; an offense against the Lord is a threat to the group, and for both reasons, and in that order, must be compensated against by the profoundly social act of punishment. Evil is the enactment of closed possibility. But, although closed, the possibility is always there, waiting to be freed from the preventive disciplines of obedience. Therefore, "evil" is always possible; it is there, in what must be denied. Law is a codification of denials. Law itself must lose effect, and criminality gain a peculiar eminence, wherever the dynamics of guilt, behind the denials, have been sapped by "rational" criticism. Finally, everything that is, or might be, is rational; everything that cannot be can be criticized into existence. Superego can be talked into deep alliances with id, under the name of Reason. The weakest of all legal theories, bound to destroy the law as a codified expression of charisma, is the rationalist one of people deliberately establishing such prohibitions or such regulations as suit their convenience at a particular time. Such "progressive" and "consensus" theories of law as now dominate our most persuasive legal minds are an advanced phase of disintegration in the binding authority of law. The lawyers' conception of law would make it derive, not from charismatic authority and embodied in charismatic institutions, but rather as a specification of popular opinion. Such a conception indicates a principled disinclination to remove that evil from our midst which is the soul and substance of law. If charismatic authority is ever to be reestablished, or, more precisely, if law is to again dominate, then perhaps a principled regression to primitive doctrine—a life for a life, an eye for an eye, a tooth for a tooth—is necessary; only thus, perhaps, will we work through the therapeutic phase and again establish a moral order beyond the dis-ease that therapy itself can only affirm by its analytic anti-charismatic intelligence. The very nature of therapy affirms the dis-ease endemic in an anti-charismatic culture. It is in this precise sense that such a cure can itself be called, with equal truth, the dis-ease.

In that form of law deriving from the authority of charisma, a community will not tolerate a retaliation greater than the actual injury done; but this is to say, first, that a community will not tolerate a retaliation that is less grave than the injury done. Such a disproportion between injury and retaliation may compound crime with injustice. For justice, understood under the signs of charisma, is a retaliation proportionate to the injury. Thus, for a death—death; the only exceptions should be exceptional indeed. Where there is an evil, it must be removed, lest it spread, like a contagion, the transgressive possibility itself. The only just removal of a transgressive act must take the form of an equivalent retaliation. The progressive failure of modern law to maintain just retaliatory principles is tantamount to a failure to recognize the equivalence of criminal and transgressive acts. Thus the law itself, breaking loose from its charismatic moorings, contributes to the transgressive movement, especially endemic among the "educated" (i.e., *therapeutically* educated) classes, against even the residual authoritative charismatic capital remaining in our culture. The widespread loss of a sense of evil reflects the loss of charismatic authority, to the absence of any sure feeling that something may not be done; that some act constitutes, in any but the "legal" sense, an offense; that, by the contagion of opening possibility, a transgressive act threatens the group and, thus defined as crime, must be rooted out. Without covenanted energies, deep inside its necessary, modern casuistries,[2] our laws cannot help us govern ourselves. The establishment of an offense as criminal must be in relation to the authority of charisma, against the inwardness of men—against what used to be called "conscience." Lawful retaliation against a transgressive act is, in conscience, necessary and right; and, moreover, it may work to ventilate transgressive impulses among those involved, directly or indirectly. But as inwardness is turned out, as law becomes mere legality, the law itself must weaken. Punishment gives way to rehabilitation; rehabilitation gives way to decriminalization. The present galloping decriminalization of law is itself one sign of a loss of charisma, of inwardness turned out and thus destroyed. The lawyers themselves advocate decriminalization, as a strategy against the revealed impotence of law. But, more important, the lawyers belong among those educated, professional classes who have rejected a culture founded upon deep renunciations of instinct. "Decriminalization" of the law is a logical expression of that celebration of possibility by which law, made outward as mere legality, becomes itself an instrument of moral revolution. The true, modern, enlightened solution for a rising rate of crime is the redefinition of crime. Indeed, transgressive criticism has its own logic: the new evils to be rooted out from our midst are the forms of renunciation themselves. The interdictory motifs, in every specific, become, according to the transgressive logic of an endless criticism of all inwardness, not the language of our salvation—or, at least our willingness to abide by the laws—but the language that causes evil. The problem of evil is thus to be solved by breaking the repressive tyranny of good.

There is a sense in which the liberal lawyers' campaign to "decriminalize" the law follows the lead of educated opinion; for the educated themselves hold the law in contempt, as a matter of principle. This is to say that the guiding principle of their education has been the therapeutic dissolution of inwardness—of that graveness of character upon which depends the very existence of authority.

The majesty of law is thus thrown down by a breaking of the systematic relation between law and normative order. Weber, for one, makes the cardinal error of opposing charisma and law because he failed to understand that interdictory motifs characterize both—and both precisely in their relation to each other. Weber's error culminates in his theory of modern domination through mass organization as the alternative to charisma.

THE CHARISMA OF PERCEPTION

The modernist concept of "public opinion," with its polls, as the rationalizing instrument of externality, hides much more than it reveals. Occasionally, the polls are confounded. The publicity of opinion cannot be trusted. People have hidden capacities, still to outwit both the techniques of "sampling" public opinion and manipulating it. The concept that opposes public opinion, charisma, is still, perhaps, recoverable by all men, the charisma of perception.

Our occasional outbursts of charismatic perception, our rejection of official lies, massively broadcast, indicates some hope that we are still capable of reconstructing a credal culture, even a deeper and more beautifully constraining one than any we have experienced before in our history. This reconstruction would be the consummation, rather than abolition, of primal history. For this to happen, however, both our legal and educational systems would have to reverse themselves, state capitalism would have to regulate very strictly its economic doctrines of consumption, provoking needs, and we would have to be taught, from the outside in, to practice precisely what is now universally preached against: the renunciation of "instinct"—which, translated into social reality, is sheer possibility. We would return to a new world of sacred scarcity. Until some such practice of renunciation is installed, there can be no charisma of perception, and all recognitions must continue to be manipulated recognitions of phonies.

But there can be no charisma of perception, universally attainable by all people, until again there are charismatics, guilts, and god-terms, reeducating us, credally, to a saving guilt. There is an instructive passage in Amos (3:1–2) on which all those should study who wonder how to break the hermeneutic circle that encloses our now widely accepted emptiness. With awful solemnity, through Amos, the personification of all renunciatory motifs declares: "You only have I known, of all the families on earth; therefore, I will punish you for all your iniquities." Why "therefore"? The "therefore" is a function of the true, oppositional, accusative, and personal nature of moral knowledge. God knows what we can be, what renunciations we dream as well as act against. God's knowledge of our persons is our personal knowledge of each other, and of ourselves; that personal knowledge is the universal charisma of perception by which any man might, if he were not to deny such knowledge, recognize, now and then, his true better. But that better could only be more like what he, the recognizer, ought to be. The charismatic can only be one's ideal self. To recognize such a person is to be indebted to him for his existence, for his presence in one's self. Thus there can be no charisma of perception without guilt. And, because the achievement of that which elicits recognition constitutes high culture, there can be no high culture without guilt—i.e., without a sense of indebtedness to those (and to the acts of those) whom we feel, deeply, we do not enough resemble. The great arts of a high culture are conveyances of this saving, renunciatory sense of what we are not but, stimulated by those arts, yet hope to be. All true works of art point out directions of renunciatory self-transformation. Of course, in any culture at the end of its charismatic fund of opposition to possibility, a work of art may be transgressive, opening up possibilities that it is the object of the art to shut down. For example, the case histories of perversion that pass for modern literature and theater, by failing to *transform* private into public, are not *art,* but transgressive assaults upon the public, mounted in public. An anti-credal play could be a man opening his fly, and inviting his audience to do the same. In such an artistic condition, there can be no disobediences. No act needs justification because it means nothing whatever—like a Pinter play.[3]

For there to be a culture, there must be the possibility of disobedience. It is in this sense that culture may be said to begin with man's first disobedience. But, then, there must be something—and someone—to disobey. The interdicts are, therefore, no less ancient than possibilities; order is not junior to disorder; high culture is not some late bloom on the compost heap of instinct. In my understanding of it, high culture has very little to do with aristocratic or upper-class prerogative, the prerogative of having fun, of enjoying oneself in exquisitely elaborate and varied ways. Rather, high culture depends upon recognition of charismatic authority; high culture itself is the elaboration of the charisma of perception.

In this sense, the early Christian communities were a high culture precisely because of the recognition of charismatic authority. It is very important to divide the conception of high culture off from the sophisticated production of entertainments; rather, high culture is related to the development of inwardness and that, in turn, to the capacity to recognize charismatic authority, which is the charisma of perception. All high cultures, then, are cultures of the superego, and neither the expression of instinctual pleasures nor the pleasures of instinctual displacement.

The relation between high culture and pleasure is an exceedingly problematic one, and, moreover, very recent in its development. As the elaborate seeking out of pleasures, high culture destroys itself; art and learning become forms of emptying out charismatic authority. Indeed, art and learning are transformed into ideologies of the therapeutic movement. The monuments of civilization become testimonials to power. Charismas of perception are rationalized into publicity machines; and with this rationalization, all hope dies of a democracy that is not a dictatorship of the empty by the phony.

What we now call "high culture," in the Arnoldian sense, the exquisite search after pleasure (admittedly refined pleasure), is, by our time, a theatrical domination of neurotic symbolisms, as a phase in the transition to the reign of the therapeutic. Wherever charismatic authority can make its presence felt, high culture must oppose the life of pleasure; such cultures depend upon the development of inwardness—the renunciation of instinct or possibility. High cultures may be creative; they are certainly tense—nervous. For the necessary mechanisms of guilt are generated by recognized failures to heed charismatic authority. That recognition of failure is far away from what Weber meant by "recognition," but it is the true nature of "recognition," as we can see (and have seen) through the prism of Freudian insight into the "origins" of all culture, morality, and religion. Charismas of perception—recognitions—are admissions of guilt, the very stuff of creative humanity.

Just these recognitions weave themselves into all personal knowledge: that is what Kierkegaard rightly intended by his declaration that subjectivity is truth and truth is subjectivity. All deeply personal truths are oppositional; they divide the self. Guilt is therefore an element in all personal knowledge.

Personal knowledge itself, as another name for recognition, means the charisma of perception. This was the only knowledge, so called, and what we now call knowledge, so far as it is not identical with that recognition of charismatic authority and therefore was not the charisma of perception, would not in such cultures (that is, cultures of charismatic authority) be called knowledge. Much of what we now call knowledge is in this sense anti-charismatic.

One of our problems, as moderns, is to so delimit the search for objective knowledge that it does not utterly destroy in each our inwardness. In this context, the therapeutic education of children is a threat to their inner existence. The young may well be a caste of last men, simply overcome with delight—and some promising intuitions of horror—at their own emptiness. Their knowledge is a terrible thing. Having been taught so by their elders, the young call true knowledge whatever blocks the recognition of charismatic authority, while, in the ancient world, true knowledge was identical with the recognition of charismatic authority. Therefore, we have two conceptions of knowledge, one in which "to know" is identical with the charisma of perception, and the second, or modern, conception of "to know" is that in which it is opposed to the guilt of recognition, i.e., blocks the charisma of perception. Professional students of knowledge seem to me especially subversive. I have already discussed Weber's doctrine of recognition as itself a subversion of the charisma of perception. The doctrine of knowledge which he himself practices constitutes an anti-charismatic activity, his "understanding" sociology.

The highest authority is a subjective knowledge of God. The highest knowledge under the authority of the therapeutic is the objective knowledge that there is no God. The first kind of knowledge, by its ever-presence, limits the very sense of what is possible; the second kind of knowledge must assert—and act on the assertion—that everything is possible. The first kind of knowledge can never be demonstrated by intellect; rather, it is known by the entire body, and in practice; the second kind of knowledge is the knowledge that the body itself has, released from that practice of inwardness that controls the knowledge of the body. The first kind of knowledge is constituted by the performance of the will of charismatic authority, which is itself a form of the renunciation of possibility and is therefore easily understood and common to the experience of everybody; while the second kind of knowledge is that knowledge which is demonstrated in the resistance to any form of charismatic authority and therefore to the struggle against all forms of renunciation. The second form, therefore, is fundamentally anti-authoritarian. The first form of knowledge is the knowledge of the charismatic; the second form of knowledge is the knowledge of the therapeutic. The knowledge which is finally knowledge of God, in its practicality and social and cultural effect, is opposed to that knowledge which is knowledge that God does not exist. The latter is negative with respect to God; the former is negative with respect to human possibilities. More precisely, therapeutic knowledge may be understood to be negative in the sense that it is a renunciation of renunciations.

What constitutes therapy, in principle, is its effectiveness as the renunciation of all renunciations. Knowledge derived from the authority of charisma is no intellectual acceptance of renunciations; rather, ordinary everyday charisma, the practical personal knowledge of all, is the personal practice of renunciation. We learn on our bodies. The play of intellect is constantly subversive of high culture and of the condition of inwardness. The Don Juan of the mind—and all Don Juans are such users of the body by the mind—is a therapeutic. The final ambiguity in Weber's doctrine of the recognition of charisma is precisely that such recognition of charismatic authority is the medium through which we create our inwardness and thus, by limiting our consciousness, become charismatic in our perception. Finally, to recognize charismatic authority is to know what is commanded by that authority; without what Weber calls "recognition," the charisma of perception, we are bound to go wrong, in the wrong knowledge to do what is not to be done and not do what is to be done.

FOUR

PROPHETIC CHARISMA

THE "GREAT REFRAIN IN ISRAEL'S HISTORY," Buber writes, is "prophet versus King. What one prophet after another did on the stage of history," he continues, was to penetrate it, to turn it aside from the direction given by the otherwise unalterable thrust of power. It was for the prophet "to stand forth against the ruler with words and signs of rebuke." The credal "word was a demand in the name of God."[1] For a ruling power to ignore that demand simply meant that the warnings of catastrophe carried in that demand would be fulfilled. This is the difference between mere prediction and prophecy. One is itself a moral demand, an inducement to do and not do; the other is not an affirmation or denial, as such, of the rightness or wrongness of an action, but a foresight that is not itself the spearhead of a demand of action. Prophesizing is utterly different from prediction. It is itself an effort to induce a right decision, or correct a wrong one. Prophecy is a form of struggle for the future, in order to avoid what is otherwise inevitable.

The moral demands of the prophets are made first upon themselves; their credal expressions are at once bodily expressions. This union of credal and bodily motifs is in accord with the Hebrew position that soul has no existence apart from body. There are no disembodied changes conceivable to these vanguard figures. The penetration of God's new word meant that the entire structure of the body was affected. Ezekiel's visions of God were literally hair-raising (Ezekiel 8:3).

Transformative theories are total; there is no immaterial spirit, no dualism, no disembodiment as in the Greek and Christian traditions of transformations. The spirit is a force capable of acting through any of its parts. It is in this sense that the soul is "in the flesh" and that, equally, "the flesh stamps the whole of the character of the soul."[2] Moral change, for the first vanguard, is also a bodily change. Corruption is never *merely* spiritual. "The whole head is sick/ and the whole heart faint. From the sole of the foot even to the head,/ there is no soundness in it" (Isaiah 1:5–6). The Psalms regularly sing this unity of moral and biological properties (Psalms 63:1; 84:3).

No vanguard inspiration occurs in which soul is affected and body is not, or body is transformed and not soul.

But this puts in a different light the "ecstatic" or "deviant" character of the first vanguard. They are sensitives, special locations of divine initiatives invading the total personality. Others might say that "the prophet is a fool, the man of the spirit is mad" (Hosea 9:7). It is an accusation precisely of the sensitivity of vanguard figures, literally, to a transformative symbolic. Jeremiah knows what it is to become such a figure. "My anguish, my anguish, I write in pain!/ Oh, the wells of my heart!/ My heart is beating wildly; I cannot keep silent" (Jeremiah 4:19). That so compelling a drawing power should leave "symptoms" is surprising only to those who expect man to live on his own surfaces, or split the symbolic off entirely from the physical existence of men. Then any change appears "neurotic" or even "psychotic." It is a modern prejudice, aided by what is left of Greek and Christian (and gnostic) dualism.

But the Hebrew vanguard figure is acutely aware of the literal character of a crisis. He sees the opening of closed possibilities and cannot but try to warn the less sensitive. He is not so protected by the distractions of everyday life that he can ignore what is going on around him as a defense against its reality. "Whenever I speak, I cry out./ I shout, 'Violence and Destruction' " (Jeremiah 20:8). Such figures are at best a bore to their defensive and less realistic contemporaries. If the vanguard figures persist in teaching the lessons of the crisis, they become fools, even madmen. Those most comfortable, and most defensive before the realities, are the first to denounce the sensitives as fools and madmen, for they are the most threatened. Therefore, the most observable conflict in a crisis occurs between those who are called "crazy" for their realism and those who defend their sanity by accepting things as they are, however those things may be. The positively insensitive are themselves defending precisely the order of life that the prophets know to be deadly. The vanguards are subject to the terror of representing something new, of manifesting a way out of the present. Those trapped in their contemporaneity are frightened, and contemptuous of these figures; it is the vanguards who, in their sense of the horrors of the present, appear to be suffering abnormal experiences—especially to those encased rigidly in that to which the vanguards react experientially. But the prophets, too, are men—and as men resist and fear their own selves as carriers of a transformative drawing power. To evaluate the prophet consciousness as "ecstatic" and "abnormal" is to imply a certain siding with the insensitives, on the side of things as they are. Here, too, is one explanation of "false prophets." The false prophets are those who show the various behavioral and physical characteristics of prophets but carry no transformative symbolic. They are pseudo-vanguards, with "a lying spirit" (1 Kings 22:20–23) who can use the symbolic for their own purposes, as professionals (Jeremiah 14:18). They know the lingo. "Thus saith Yahweh" (Jeremiah 23:25–26). But how are people to distinguish between true and pseudo-vanguards? To declare that a false prophet makes "people trust in a lie" (Jeremiah 28:15) is scarcely helpful. The truly transformative seem no less "mad" than the false. It appears that the answer to the agonizing Deuteronomic question (Deuteronomy 18:21) "How may we know the word which the Lord has not spoken?" must be postponed until history bears out or does not the nature of the message (Deuteronomy 18:22). *There is no psychological test for membership in a vanguard, or for vanguard figures.* Indeed, the writers of Deuteronomy knew that false prophets may have history supporting them. The real test is one difficult for any modern to understand: whether the vanguard figure submits to the higher power or expresses his own. Those who "speak visions of their own minds" are really men of power, putting themselves in place of the god-term; however little they may be conscious of what they are doing, these false prophets are serving their own selves, the "deceit of their own heart" (Jeremiah 23:26). Thus self-moving, they move people for themselves. Prophecy is no therapy, no self-satisfaction for the true prophet. On the contrary, the credal personality does not find speaking in the terms God has dictated to him a personally satisfying or happy function, on the one hand, or a "neurotic" symptom on the other.

The credal personality knows he is in danger, precisely in the tension between crisis and his message. He would prefer not to "speak anymore in [God's] name"; he is "weary with holding it [i.e., the transformative symbolic] in, and I cannot" (Jeremiah 20:9). The credal personality is never a political leader; he never takes power, and he is vulnerable precisely because he confronts power as it is. Jeremiah knew his situation perfectly, and can only warn those who might kill him, judicially or otherwise, of the implications of their act. But his submission to God gives him no power except moral. He is helpless before a compulsion of which he is well aware; it is not unconscious or neurotic. "The Lord God has spoken; who can but prophesy?" (Amos 3:8). Having spoken, he exposes himself to a reaction against which the only effective shield is thus taken away: silence. "The Lord has sent me to prophesy against this house and this city all the words you have heard. . . . But as for me, behold, I am in your hands. Do with me as seems good and right to you." But then Jeremiah makes it clear to the un-transformed what is at stake. "Only know for certain that if you put me to death, you will bring innocent blood upon yourselves and upon this city and its inhabitants, for in truth the Lord sent me to speak all these words in your ears" (Jeremiah 26:12–15).The prophets do not "predict" the future; they seek to transform the present, of which the future is all too likely, otherwise, to be a continuation. In a world from which god-terms are removed, Hebrew prophecy has become incomprehensible except as a psychological assertion. But this assertion is what the prophets explicitly denied. The first credal personalities are not asserting themselves; they are the opposites of the men of power, who in one degree or another populate the world. "No prophecy ever came by the impulse of man, but men moved by the Holy Spirit spoke from God" (2 Peter 1:21).

The Hebrew prophets knew that there may be many prophets. God says that in such an age "your sons and your daughters shall prophesy,/ Your old men shall dream dreams,/ and your young men shall see visions" (Joel 3:1). An age of crisis thus opens up, through such vanguards, the possibility of its own resolution.

But prophets do elect themselves in one important sense. However disturbingly God speaks to him, God speaks to his understanding of what is right and wrong with things as they are. Credal personalities are men of extraordinary understanding. It is in this sense, then, that their understanding is deepened and transformed, given drawing power. For that drawing power is precisely understanding made visionary. "If there is a prophet among you, I the Lord make myself known to him in a vision, I speak with him in dreams" (Numbers 12:6). Such visionary understanding is not to be acquired through learning, but through being open, in one's understanding, to interdicts that resist the assaults of both experience and "Reason." With such a devotionalizing of understanding, as Weber knew, understanding itself becomes transformative in a sense opposed to all prophetic understandings.

Are the prophets traditionalists or revolutionaries? The question is false. They were both traditionalists and revolutionaries. To call back a rebellious Israel to the God who had chosen it for his vanguard is at once a traditionalist and revolutionary task. That the symbolic consisted mainly of indictments of Israel for breach of covenant turns the first vanguard almost into legalists or purists. But, to observe the covenant in the present is precisely more than a matter of obeying the old letters; such an obedience cannot be in the fantasy of a return, but by confronting new events in that spirit which would be a restitution of the covenant.

That spirit has nothing to do with religious nationalism. While, in the nonprophetic traditions of Israel, Jehovah is made to support Israel right or wrong, the prophets break this relation between God and national power. That is the key: the covenant becomes a structure of moral demand, to which power itself is subordinate. Amos declares that Jehovah would destroy Israel for its breakings of the covenant to be an elected people. Exodus 19:6 already is a vanguard symbolic: "You shall be to me a kingdom of priests and a holy nation." And, before that appointment, the absolute commitment entailed by the relation, so that Israel becomes an instrument of something beyond itself, not in its own possession. On the contrary, "You shall be my own possession among all peoples" (Exodus 19:5).

This first vanguard is anything except self-possessed. The transformative idea of Israel as in the possession of something wholly other than itself, a commonplace in Deuteronomy (7:6; 14:2; 26:18) and in Leviticus (25:23), implies that Israel must act so as to make restitution for what it is, a people constantly struggling to escape this sense of being possessed by a purpose that is not its own, not made by itself but appointed to it, as the prophets are appointed, too, against their will. To be a "holy nation" meant the discipline of a code by which such a nation could live (Leviticus 19:2; 20:7; 25:55). What this vanguard knew was that all people, from the beginning, "at Adam . . . dwelt faithfully" with God. "They transgressed the covenant" and did not live as they should (Hosea 6:7). The key to vanguard formation, and to high culture, is this transgressive sense—a consciousness precisely of not being a vanguard, of breaking the covenant. That Israel has "transgressed my law" becomes the guilt out of which vanguard culture is created; where there is no guilt, there is no aspiration toward the achievement of limit. Where there is no motif of transgression, there is no symbolic of transformation. The prophet's saw transgressive acts all around them, in everyday relations between Israelites. Injustices are themselves transgressions of the covenant. And, as the transgressors remain all too human, so, too, do the vanguard figures. Never does a credal personality, in the Bible saga, merge with that which he represents.

Prophecy in its interdictory form once organized our high culture. Never has the interdictory form been more powerfully or beautifully specified than in the messages of the canonical prophets of Israel.

The personal call of a prophet described something special about the message he carried in his office, some motif in the message that the war and cultic prophets, the court prophets, the expert diviners of those bad times could not convey in their divinations.

How precisely the prophets proposed their inherited culture as the historical and utterly authoritative source for all disciplines of obedience to the renunciatory command. They were, in fact, defending their culture, what everybody knew, the entire "identity" of the nation threatened by national transgressions. God speaks through Amos: "Therefore will I punish you for all your inequities" (Amos 3:1–2).

In our culture, prophetic charisma once depended upon a "personal call"; but more precisely upon that call coming direct to the prophet through the presence of a supreme figure of authority, capable of punishing all those who commonly break the known and accepted interdicts. In our credal society, at its first foundation, punishment was the angry response of personal authority, confirming the discipline of obedience in the face of indiscipline. To punish is the most authoritative force against the sheer transgressive force of the human capacity to do everything that can be done. Micah put this common charismatic rejection and denial of possibility in language precisely for ordinary men. Yet his language is now quite extraordinary.

Micah puts the commonality of charisma as faith, under the renunciatory command of authority, with stunning and simple brevity. First: guilt actual, "for the Lord has a case against his people and will argue it with Israel." The anxiety of how to respond to the case against oneself. "What shall I bring when I approach the Lord?" How shall I act before God on high? The answer is faith, in commands already available: "God has told you what is good; and what is it that the Lord asks of you? Only to act justly, to love loyalty, to walk wisely before your God . . . the fear of whose name brings success" (Micah 6:2–8). To walk humbly with your God once carried the full discipline of obedience in a single phrase. Personal loyalty demanded that acceptance of good out of evil, and of evil out of good, that Friedrich Schleiermacher and others, with sinister intellectualizing, called the sense of absolute dependence upon the "Infinite." The God of the nineteenth-century Protestant intellectuals was not Micah's. They were trying to explain more than obey. On the basis of these intellectualizations, later symbolists of our culture developed a therapeutic transgressive behavior that assigned the Infinite precisely to man. For ancient Israel, this dangerous infinity, this endless possibility, belonged to the supreme authority figure himself, and to nothing else; by the twentieth century that infinity, still deified, was rediscovered in two very different places: first, in Science, which could deny nothing permanently; second, in the psychoanalytic doctrine of the Unconscious, a faculty basic to our egos, which, by definition, lack the gift of denial from which charisma once derived. There is no *No* in unconsciousness. With the end of charismatic authority, in the age of science and psychoanalysis, justice, love, and faithfulness lost their meanings as elements in any discipline of obedience. Society now truly shakes at its foundations; hostility to culture as such becomes more than conceivable; such hostility was inconceivable in the culture of Israel, for it would have found no object. "Israel" was constituted as a covenanted people. The "personal call" was a call to obedience of what everybody knew; the faith/guilt culture of ancient Israel was constituted by breaking of the covenant, both individually and nationally. "A word stole to me in my ear perceived the whisper of it in disquieting thoughts amid visions of the night when deep sleep falls on men, dread seized me and trembling, it made all my limbs shake, a spirit glided over my face, the hair of my flesh stood up. It stood still, but I could not discern its appearance. A form was before me, I heard a still, low voice. Can a mortal man be in the right before God, or a man be pure before his Maker?" (Job's friend Eliphaz in Job 4:12–17.) Those last two lines, that still, low voice, is in fact the perfect expression of the faith/guilt complex. Can a mortal man be in the right before God, or a man be pure before his Maker? But because no man can be in the right before God, or pure, a few men are called to them for correction's sake. They are called as a form of discipline, that discipline representing the way of righting what is wrong. This representation is constituted charismatically. For in their calling, they represent the right to others, as well as to themselves.

The call of Moses (in Exodus 4) is a model of the prophetic call. Much space is given to Moses' objections, and even oppositions to the call. There is always a question whether a prophet will accept the discipline of the call. Certainly that is a question in Isaiah; that is a question in Moses, and in Jeremiah, we have images of his horror and terror at being commanded. So that the commandments are in fact terrible burdens, for they themselves prevent that kind of vitality that is transgressive, magical, and, in a view opposed to the faith/guilt complex, enlivening.

As a call, the command is not so specific that it can be made analogous to a military command. The prophet, as a charismatic, has great freedom in interpreting the command, and this capacity to interpret the command heightens his own responsibility.

Yet there is often an oppositional element in the enactment of the call, an irony which indicates the hard, sharp, and direct point to the charismatic message of the canonical prophet. Amos 4:1 and 6:1 addresses the threat of deportation to a luxury-loving upper class. He addresses the threat of devastation of the land to real estate speculators, etc. This oppositional element is also a concentrated version of the faith/guilt complex, one that supports it and intensifies it, bringing the crisis that can be seen from within the faith/guilt complex to those who, in their ordinary lives, try to live outside it. Thus the constant addressing of their messages by the canonical prophets to those who are most likely to be offended by it. Nothing else so determined the credal struggle within the social structure of ancient Israel as this tension within the faith/guilt order; in justice, suffering, punishment, and disaster are the outward and visible signs of disloyalties, faithlessness to the covenant. Without this opposition of the prophetic message coming from the faith/guilt order, the social order would be a completely unchangeable horror, and without any judgment. It would, in fact, belong, so to say, to the animal kingdom, and be a world in which men remained unaware of the horror of their supremacies, of their injustices, of their ordinary lives. In its literary form, the "therefore" that frequently and characteristically connects the diatribe and the divine word, is a "therefore" of critical opposition, the one that brings the social order into its real and objective character, within the ambience of the faith/guilt order. In this way, the "therefore" is a logical connection. The prophet is a teaching charismatic but his teachings are quite different from the Socratic teachings that have affected the very idea of teaching in the Western and liberal cultures. The idea of teaching is to heighten the tension within the social order by bringing it within the context of the faith/guilt order. The two in their separation are precisely the elements of guilt that must be revealed by the charismatic teacher. This idea of teaching as itself a corrective enterprise is central to the Western tradition and to our contemporary institutions. We still see varieties of this in very confused ways precisely in those who would break the faith/guilt order for the purpose of altering the social structure. Both together—that is, the faith-teaching as an element of the faith/guilt order—can be understood not only in relation to the social structure but as traceable to the prophetic charismatic tradition.

The charismatic idea among the teaching prophets of retribution and punishment operates entirely within the faith/guilt order, and makes no sense outside it, for offense and punishment strictly correspond. Breaking the interdicts causes the evil that men set in motion to recoil on their own heads. This sense of the punishment fitting the crime, of the commensurability of offense and punishment, is part of the notion that the faith/guilt order is a fixed order, to which human life is subject. Such judgments, such assays of the retributive process of offense and punishment, in strict correspondence, are the primary form of charismatic intellectualization among the canonical prophets. There is a deeper level of the meaning of the prophetic charisma that needs to be stated here. In the beginning was the Word; the Word itself therefore is creative, and the Word is interdictory; the Word must be recited, because by the Word, and only by the Word, can the threats and perils, which everywhere beset the orders of creation and guarantee their continued existence, be guarded against. The Word, in its creativity, is also interdictory, and the charisma of the Word is in fact the charisma of truth, resistance to the disordering that men themselves, in their vitality, work. This fixed order, in the covenant, can only be supported by the order of faith and guilt, for men continue to do those things that threaten the order. The Word, therefore, is magical, in the sense that it possesses a power which extends far beyond their powers of mind itself, that is, beyond conceptual heuristic powers. These charismatic words of admonition and promise are effective in space and time.

That "the typical prophet propagates ideas for their own sake"[3] is incorrect except insofar as Weber may mean ideas integral to and undetachable from particular actions. Weber is right to differentiate prophecy from salvation, and prophets from the purveyors of salvation. The prophets strengthen the faith/guilt order within which salvation becomes possible. But they are in no sense purveyors of salvation.

One final word of warning about Weber's prophetic type. He writes, "The conflict between empirical reality and this conception of the world as a meaningful totality which is based on a religious postulate produces the strongest tensions in man's inner life, as well as in his external relationships with the world."[4] But the conflict is not between empirical reality and the conception of the world as a meaningful totality, for empirical reality constitutes, for the prophet and his credal society, the "world as a meaningful totality." Reality cannot be detached from faith; this detachment itself is understood, by the successful elites of our credal culture, as the empirical reality of faithlessness. The conflict, as Weber calls it, between empirical reality and a meaningful totality, is organized by empirical failures to adhere to the faith/guilt order itself—and, moreover, by all intellectualizing that itself depends upon a prior postulate of "conflict," in which "reality" is assigned an objectivity to which a "religious postulate" is a merely subjective reaction. Weber thus puts us near the danger zone of "religious illusion" and "empirical reality."

Credal prophecy in Israel led to a credal society, or what Weber called a confessional association.[5] What this means is a society that is specifically organized as a drama of faith and guilt, the one no less "empirical" than the other. The credal culture of the Jews survived its political society. In the great concluding sentences of Weber's "Science as a Vocation," he refers to the Jewish tragedy, of remaining for so long a credal society, and as such the greatest exponents and sufferers from the consequences of a culture Weber knows to be dying a dreadful death. But the life which is to replace it appears to him at times more dreadful. Yet, knowing no saving grace attached and integral to action, Weber is in no prophetic tradition. In the culture built upon the faith of the prophets, never dying before Weber's eyes and ours, there is never an expression of guilt, no reference to the transgressions themselves, without the empirical reality of faith. Weber is a scientist, not a psalmist; he has no right to the grimness of his vision. He's not neutral enough. His sad resoluteness opposes all prophetic hope. "Blessed is he whose transgression is forgiven, whose sin is covered" (Psalm 32:1). By "covered" I think the psalmist means compensated for, discharged. "Blessed is the man unto whom the Lord imputes not iniquity and in whose spirit is no guile" (Psalm 32:2). There is a hopelessness in Weber's science still inseparable from that science; there was a hopefulness about the virtuosi of the faith/guilt order that was inseparable from the societies in which that order was such a determining factor. In our new freedom, we are condemned to be hopeless. Faith, according to the charisma of the prophets, was constituted by obediences to certain historically given commands, those commands themselves the essential movement of faith.

In the credal culture of the Jews, the gift of obedience to renunciatory command is given, without their asking, to an entire people; they are chosen to be inward, in the variety of their individualities, and yet also as a nation, holy just in this gift. Christian writers, too, once understood the garden variety of charismata; they and their predecessors, the Hebrew writers, were far nearer understanding the actual common and shared nature of charisma than Weber, who turned it into spectacular performance by a recognized deviant, in that strange combination of romantic and rationalist predicates that characterizes Weber's thinking on the subject—as well as the popular misconceptions distinctive in our educated classes. There is more than a trace of these popular misconceptions in Freud's ingenious conception of Dostoyevsky's preoccupation with crime as an interdictory event for the uncriminal. Freud concluded that to Dostoyevsky, the criminal is "almost a Redeemer who has taken on himself the guilt which others would otherwise have to bear. One need not now commit murder, after he [i.e., the criminal] has committed murder, but one must be grateful to him, because, without him, one would oneself have to have been a murderer. That is not pure kindliness or sympathy; it is identification on the basis of a similar murderous impulse, in reality a slightly displaced narcissism."[6] Here is a parody of the clever modernist critique of Christianity with the murderer exactly in the role of Christ and Christians thus relieved of the need to be charismatic themselves. The murderer strikes for our impulses; but it is *he* who strikes.

Hans Kung, the Roman Catholic theologian, is much nearer the original meaning of charisma when, in his famous speech to the Vatican Council,[7] he denied that charisma is, in fact, extraordinary. On the contrary, Kung correctly holds that charisma is a common phenomenon.[8] Charisma is common, rather than extraordinary, only where there is a strong moral discipline, those institutional and personal obediences to renunciatory command; only then is that inwardness produced which is itself the psychological predicate of the commonality of charisma. Thus Weber's conception of charisma as an extraordinary and rare condition, and yet dependent on charisma recognition, is a kind of signaling at the theoretical level of the end of charisma as a real possibility in Western culture.

The therapeutic attack on faith and guilt is yet another signal of anticharismatic theory at its destructive work. As I have tried to point out elsewhere in this book, this peculiar kind of destructive work has long been in process in Western society. To attack guilt is to attack all those ordinary disciplines of obedience to renunciatory demands which produce not only the commonality of charisma but the basis of social order as it had been known throughout what Freud, in his own guarded subversive hope, called our "primal history." We know, if we know anything about ourselves, that all disciplines of obedience to renunciatory command will always be broken; that interdictory consciousness is inseparable from remissive unconsciousness; that there is law as well as creed; that where there is grace there must be punishment of a felt need for grace. The "gift" of grace, then, is a gift only in the sense that the "gratuitousness" of it expresses the commanding presence of authority; more precisely, of an authority figure. In our opposition to him, in his opposition to us, that figure enforces those disciplines of obedience, through guilt in relation to himself, by which societies are constituted. Out of hostility and guilt, then, that charisma is created without which societies become disorganized—that is, equally to say, amoral—and death strengthens its grip on society and its progenerative culture. It is the prophets who created the doctrine that charisma is a perfectly ordinary phenomenon, not extraordinary, that we are all, in our humanity, creatures of obedience. Reminding the high and mighty of the covenant, the prophets, being otherwise ordinary men, established the universal and common charisma of perception. From the prophets derive that credally organized inwardness characteristic of Western culture. A common culture, like a common faith, is rather like a permanent lawsuit—but the law is the moral law.

Hosea puts the matter beautifully:

> Hear the word of Yahweh, O Israelites, for Yahweh has a lawsuit against the inhabitants of the land. For there is no faithfulness or loyalty or knowledge of God in the land. They have broken out in cursing, cheat-

ing, murder, thieving and adultery, and spilt blood touches blood. (Hosea 4:1–2)

Our knowledge of transgressions, however precise, is worthless without knowledge of the law. Nowadays, we are simply too knowledgeable and yet lack a standard by which our knowledge is itself to be judged. In the prophetic meaning "to know" is a recognition of supreme authority, of the authority of inwardness, of that renunciation of instinct and of possibility that is itself counted in the Ten Commandments. Hosea's list is very much like the Ten Commandments, down to the specific words used. It is interesting that in a good deal of modern scholarship, the Hebrew verb "to know," *yada,* is understood to have ranges of meaning from "to understand" to "to sleep with a woman." But the one meaning to "to know," *yada,* that is most uniquely human is its prophetic meaning of the charisma of perception; from this perception the people of Israel fall away into disobedience.

The modernist definition of "to know" lacks entirely this meaning of the guilt of recognition. At the center of the terror that modern knowledge has let loose upon and among the knowers themselves is the political form of recognition: success. The guilt of self-recognition is precisely the one thing missing from modern knowledge. What matters is merely to be followed and not to be a follower: both power and egalitarian motifs in our culture empty charisma of its true meaning. There cannot be "great men" except in the sense of those who deliberately intend to dominate it. The canonical prophets were the original "great men" of our culture precisely because they cherished no intention to dominate it. Weber misled by omission when he understood the prophet "to mean a purely individual bearer of charisma, who by virtue of his mission proclaims a religious doctrine or divine commandment."[9] Everything depends, in our culture, on the properties of those commandments. The prophetic office was to remind those in a credal society of those essential obediences to renunciations out of which our entire culture has grown. Jewish prophecy led to the credal society that has suffered ever since for the truth of its establishment—and now not least among those Jews who see in their inheritance the most powerful of all constraints on their personal freedom.

FIVE

THE PSYCHIATRIC STUDY OF JESUS

FIRST, IT MUST BE SAID straight off that the dogma of the God-Man, Deus-Homo, is in fact a major revision of the faith/guilt order. That tension between faith and guilt in the charismatic figure of the Christ of faith is one that has had terrific destructive potential. The charisma of Jesus was, from the beginning, transgressive, or, in time, became transgressive, for it consisted of his growing conviction that he was the son of God. This occurred, of course, by divine act of adoption and indicates the kind of identification Jesus felt with the master personification of the faith/guilt order. Paul strengthened this self-deifying identity when he taught that Jesus was the son of God because a spiritual personality preexisting in heaven had become incarnate in him. This Christ spirit Paul had not yet, of course, thought of as God, but as the express image of God, and, moreover, as the archetype of mankind, the ideal spiritual man, the second man from heaven (1 Corinthians 15:47), who was destined from the beginning to appear in earthly form that he might redeem mankind, not only from sin and death, but also from the law. Here we already have, in this divine sonship, an identification beyond men, of a charismatic, a new charisma, a charisma that is really identified as that which the charismatic is given man, so that in Jesus the giver and the given are brought together.

In Hebrews (1:3), Paul calls Jesus "the very image of the substance of God, upholding all things by the word of his power." And in Colossians, Jesus is called "the first begotten of all creation, in whom and to whom all things have been created, in whom all things consist" (1:15). This identification of the charismatic with the power from which charisma is derived reaches its height in the gospel of John, in the teaching that the "logos, which in the beginning was with God, and was God, by whom all things were created, in whom was the life and the light of men" became flesh in Jesus (John 1:1). And so Christ as the son of God can no longer be considered simply a charismatic figure to whom something is given, the gift of grace; on the contrary, there is no gift of grace here. The adoption and apotheosis motif, the deification motif, completely eliminate Jesus from the category of charismatic. The third tradition, and the latest that fed into the Christ motif, was that this incarnate god or son of God, was supernaturally conceived by the Holy Ghost and born of the Virgin Mary, and so, though human, because of his mother, he is the son of God in the most complete sense of the word, because he is not really conceived sexually. This became by far the most popular tradition, and this, too, is clearly a transgressive motif in the sense that it divinizes a particular figure which was entirely against the symbolic within which virgin birth was the most obvious kind of self-deification, because here there is no father with whom to identify, and from whom one's authority emanates.

I have indicated that the son of God symbol is transgressive and against the faith/guilt order, except so far as in identifying the son with God, action against the son is itself a way of intensifying the faith/guilt order. The second element in the charisma of Christ centers on the conviction of the Christian community that Christ was manifested that he might destroy the works of the devil. In terms of the faith/guilt order, that the devil himself doesn't appear in the prophetic charisma is a projection of the guilt motif in the faith/guilt complex and thus a distancing of guilt from human beings themselves. In that sense, the charisma of Christ as the conqueror of Satan is itself most ambiguous and easily renderable in transgressive terms. Not men but the devil is responsible.

The confrontations between Christ and Satan are entirely between the incarnation of the faith/guilt syndrome, or the personification of it, on the one hand, and the personification of transgressiveness, Satan, on the other. There are three assaults by the personification of transgressiveness upon the personification of the faith/guilt syndrome, and in each case Christ comes out victorious. His weapon of victory is in fact the interdictory word. This confrontation can be traced in the narratives of the Evangelists Matthew 4:1–11 and Luke 4:1–13. Moreover, Christ as the personification of the faith/guilt order proves his superiority to, and his conquest of, the devil, the underground personification of transgressiveness, by driving out the devils from those who are possessed by transgressiveness, literally the possessed and the diseased, as we see in the narratives of Mark, 3:22 and after, and in Matthew, 12:24–29. Finally, the eschatological motif is the combination of the faith/guilt order, the time that will come when Christ, at his second coming to judge the world, will forever make an end of the power of Satan. This final victory over transgressiveness occurs in the revelation of John, and is divided into two acts. The king descends from heaven with his host of angels by the sword which, significantly enough, proceeds from his mouth. He subdues the hostile transgressive world powers that are arrayed against him. Then the personification of transgressiveness is bound and cast into the abyss of hell which is the space of transgressiveness, where he is imprisoned under lock and key and seal for a thousand years, until the end of those thousand years, Christ and the martyrs to the faith/guilt order, so to say, the fallen champions of it who have risen again, will reign. Then, after a thousand years, transgressiveness will be loosed from its confines and will come forth to deceive the nations of the earth, especially Gog and Magog, and will gather them together to war against the saints. But this transgressive army will be destroyed by the fire from heaven, that is, the space of the faith/guilt order itself, the location of it, and the personification of transgressiveness, Satan himself, will be cast into the lake of fire and brimstone, to be tormented forever (Rev. 19 et passim). Thus (and this is the important point) the myth of temptation in all its varieties is in fact the confrontation between the faith/guilt order on the one hand and the order, spatial and temporal, of transgressiveness against the faith/guilt order on the other. Parallels are to be found both in Buddhist and Persian symbolisms. It is the true structure of the historical and cultural context within which charisma develops, either in its interdictory or transgressive form, and, more precisely, in the conflict between the two forms. The tree of knowledge, if one compares, say, Jewish, Christian, and Buddhist symbolics, is that natural and supernatural organism that itself contains both forms. The significance of the tree of knowledge is that it is the organism within which both forms, the faith/guilt order and the order of transgressiveness, grow.

The pivotal figure of Jesus as a charismatic type in Western culture should be seen in terms as with the prophets of the faith of Israel, to his relation to his intensification or discharging of the faith/guilt complex, and it is to this particular problem with special reference to what may be called the psychiatric study of Jesus, that I now turn.

We may notice in Jesus the tremendous indifference to sublimation—no cultural achievements, no music, no art, or other cultural references. Rather he concentrates on this special relation, on his conquest of death and the underworld, that is, hell, as an alternative to sexuality. Jesus at once intensifies the faith/guilt complex, and offers an alternative to it in his eschatological doctrine of the conquest of death and of the underworld. The bringing of life and immortality, as in 1 Corinthians and in 2 Timothy, is in fact an alternative to ordinary sexuality. In order to understand this sublimatory effect of Jesus, in its proper and original significance, it is important to note that for the culture in which Jesus lived, death was not acceptable as a natural occurrence, but was a result of particular, if you will, interdictory and transgressive causes, that is, was related to the moral order. Death was regarded either as the judicial penalty inflicted by an offended deity, as, indeed, upon the whole race of mankind since Adam's fall, as in Romans 5:12 and thereafter, or as the work of demonic powers that had infected man with the fatal poisons of transgressivity, that is, disease and death, and that therefore brought man under the power of death, who was the ruler of the underworld and who held souls in close bondage. Sociologically, the symbolic alternatives open to Jesus as a delivery from death and disease were brought about either by a breaking of the faith/guilt order by orgiastic sexuality, which he rejected completely, or by the propitiatory offering of himself in vicarious death, identifying himself with the ultimate term of the faith/guilt order, God, and thus in his own manhood reconciling men within the faith/guilt order. This is the nature of redemption, for it is a way of alleviating the burden of the faith/guilt order, that is, the condemnation and the curse of the law. The meaning of divine grace of charisma, as stated in Romans 3:24 and thereafter, and in 2 Corinthians 19 and thereafter and in Galatians 1:3 and in Galatians 3:13, is precisely that grace or charisma is the alleviating of the faith/guilt order through this magical identification of the son with the father, that is, the perfect enactment of faith thus dissolving guilt. For it is only through the perfect enactment of faith that guilt can be dissolved within (and this is the important point) the symbolic structure of the faith/guilt order. It is in this way, then, that we can understand sociologically the cleansing power of the sacred blood of Jesus, the magical deliverance of mankind from demonic pollution which is in fact the particular expressions of guilt in sin and in death, that is, in the ultimate punishments. These are referred to in Hebrews 9:11 and thereafter and in Hebrews 10:14, 22, and 29. In his own death and resurrection, therefore, within the faith/guilt order, identifying himself as Man/God with the ultimate term of the faith/guilt order, Jesus deprives the lord of death, the devil, the instigator and the leading enactor of the events that cause guilt, he deprives the lord of death, the devil, and the satanic angels of their power over mankind. These are the references in the symbolic of the faith/guilt order in early Christianity in Hebrews 2:14, Colossians 2:15, and in Colossians 1:13 and thereafter, and in 1 John 3:8. Thus, within the very different ambience of the Christian charismatic thrust of the faith/guilt order, the resurrection of Christ, the resurrection itself is an acknowledgment of the faith/guilt order that at the same time by the propitiatory and purifying efficacy of Jesus' own death as an act of supreme faith within the faith/guilt order resolves that order, that is, resolves the guilt component within that order. The resurrection and ascension of Christ are motifs which together act as practical proofs of his charisma, that is, his victory over the punitive expressions of the faith/guilt order, death and hell, whereby Christ becomes, for those who recognize him, the prince of life, its possessor, its surety, its mediator, without having recourse to the other way of consummating or breaking or resolving the faith/guilt order, that is, the orgiastic way, the way of erotic transgressiveness, which is the alternative that is explicitly rejected in the Christian charismatic symbolic as it is in that prophetic charisma of the Jews. These references to Jesus as a prince of life, but not as the prince of sexuality, may be located in Acts 3:15, in Revelation 1:18, in St. John 9:25, in 3:13 and after, in 1 Peter 3 and 18 and Ephesians 4:8 and thereafter. The resurrection motif and the ascension motif may then be seen as the converse of the descent motif into hades which is really inseparable from the resurrection, because the descent motif into hades or into literally the underworld, into the world of criminality, of Satan, or the demons, is, in fact, the point at which Christ risks the alternative mode of breaking the faith/guilt order, that is, the orgiastic, the erotic mode, which is central to the contemporary effort to break the faith/guilt order, which is totally anti-Christian. Both the ascension and the resurrection motifs, then, combined with the descent into the underworld motif, are the complex of charismatic exaltation into heaven, in the Christian charismatic, which saves men from the realm of death, death being identified with transgressive and orgiastic and, if you will, criminal behavior. It is in this sense that Christ preached that the kingdom of heaven is within and already present, that it is always a present alternative to the death motif of the transgressive breaking of the faith/guilt order by denying both faith and guilt.

Now, the means whereby the ascended, that is, Christ, the Christ who has in fact consummated the faith/guilt order by the triumph of faith, that is, the interdicts, especially the interdict against orgiastic and aggressive or political behavior, occurs in a magical way. The imparting of life to the people of Christ, that is, to those who follow this charismatic, are, by faith in his name, which includes its open confession and invocation, this confession being at once an assertion of faith and also an assertion of that guilt which therefore consciously cancels that guilt. The references here to this element of the symbolic are in Romans 10:9 and thereafter, in John 3:15 and thereafter, in John 20:31, in John 16:23 and thereafter.

By faith, understood sociologically, I mean obedience to the interdictory commands in a particular culture; by guilt, I mean disobedience to those interdictory commands, to those commanding interdicts, that very disobedience therefore bolstering the faith/guilt order, which is the one within which charisma, the intensification and resolution of this tension of the faith/guilt complex, is generated.

Freud's doctrinal misogyny, like D. H. Lawrence's, is part of an effort to destroy the faith/guilt order. This misogynistic effort at destruction is a very complicated one, for, in the first place, it locates women as sexual objects who, by virtue of their biological constitution, are less able to generate the faith/guilt complex. Their childbearing function, their nearness to the sexual or erotic element of life, at once emancipates them from the faith/guilt complex and at the same time makes them incapable of the kind of sublimatory intensifications and resolutions of the faith/guilt complex by which cultural leadership and charisma are established. In this sense, then, women stand in this misogynistic attack on the faith/guilt order somewhat outside that order, and this is a most sinister turn in the liberationist movement, which is still now within what is now called women's lib, a built-in element of the order, despite the attack by women's liberation advocates on misogyny of such attackers against the faith/guilt order as Freud and Lawrence. This is because these women's liberationists themselves do not understand the importance, the central mentality of Western culture, as a faith/guilt order, and therefore there are conflicts with such attackers of the faith/guilt order as Norman Mailer in the contemporary culture that are totally confused.

Sociologically, baptism into the name of Christ as in Acts 2:28 is to be understood differently from the general understanding of the Christians themselves. What the washing of regeneration means is the magical transmission of the interdictory motifs of the faith. Baptism is itself a ritual enactment of the interdicts, that is, a symbolization of the interdicts, and is in this sense established as a ceremonial central to the Christian faith/guilt complex which acts both to intensify that complex and to serve as a key element of resolution.[1] The entire set of sacramental activities are themselves elements in the enactment of the faith/guilt order.[2] The sacrament of the eating and drinking of the

Lord's supper,[3] is yet another enactment of the resolutive intensification of the faith/guilt complex the two held in tension, which makes one inseparable from the other. The socio/psychological explanation of the charisma of Christ cannot be understood without seeing the sacraments as themselves institutionalizations, if you will, routinizations, in a way Weber did not understand, of the faith/guilt order which constitutes the central mentality of Christian culture. Each of these sacramental actions—baptism as the washing of regeneration, mystical purification, the participation in Christ's death and resurrection, the eating and drinking of the Lord's supper—each of these sacramental activities is itself an institutionalization, or, if you will, routinization, of the faith/guilt complex by resolving guilt and enacting the triumph of faith; that is, they are ritualistic attacks on transgressiveness. They are themselves enactments of the interdictory energies that constitute faith itself. Without them, therefore, there can be no faith, and in this sense, without the church as the body of Christ, these interdictory motifs cannot exist. The church and these enactments of the interdictory motifs are identical. The body of Christ is therefore identical with the enactment of the interdictory motifs. And, in the sense, the containment of guilt. Yet, guilt is not resolved, does not simply disappear; rather, consciousness of guilt as the reason for these enactments is in fact intensified at the same time that faith is rendered triumphant. Therefore, one can speak of guilt analogously to the way in which Freudians speak of impulses or instincts. They may be checked, but they are not liquidated, they are not destroyed by these interdictory processes any more than the instincts are liquidated or destroyed by therapeutic processes. This is more than an analogy—structurally, instinct is to the transgressive attack upon the faith/guilt order in Freudian theory, what guilt is in the interdictory symbolic of the Christians. Such a double complication of the faith/guilt order, in which the faith is triumphant over the transgressive motifs of guilt, at the same time that guilt is checked but not eradicated, is basic to charismatics of the savior type. It is not at all clear that Christ completely liquidates the guilt component in the faith/guilt complex, at least in the conceptions of the early Christians, for such a liquidation would make the various interdictory sacraments open confession and invocation, baptism, eating and drinking of the Lord's supper, unnecessary. The fact that these interdicts are present already indicates what Weber calls the routinization of charisma, but what more meaningfully, more significantly, indicates the continuing tension within the faith/guilt order, as well as the triumph of faith. Therefore, the interpretation of the saving charisma of Christ, as the total liquidation of guilt and of the possibilities of transgressive behavior, seems to me to be a mistaken reading of the charisma of Jesus. It is certainly a mistaken reading of the significance of the routinization of that charisma. If Christ is himself the liquidator of the faith/guilt complex, then that liquidation occurs through the remarkable intensification of that faith/guilt order up through the point of Christ's resurrection and triumph over death. Thus, what Weber calls the routinization of charisma in the critical case of Christianity is in fact the intensification of the interdictory motifs within the faith/guilt order which constitute the charismatic power of Christ after his death, or, more precisely, after his triumph over death.

Weber appeared not to understand this socio/psychological dynamic.

There is one element of the faith/guilt order that needs special mention here, an element of devastating cruelty, and that is the motif of the innocent sufferings of the good as a vicarious sacrifice for the benefit of those who are not good. That is, in the faith/guilt order, it is imagined that there are some, very few, who are without guilt, who nevertheless suffer, and in their sufferings, which are completely gratuitous, they compensate the commanding interdicts for the guilt of all the others. This motif first appears in the exilic prophet of Deutero-Isaiah, this is in Isaiah 43, and from the time of the Maccabees onward, this particular term in the faith/guilt order, in which the innocent sufferings of the guiltless who are thus by definition good, form a vicarious sacrifice for the guilty, occupies a prominent place in the theology of the Pharisees. This is stated in the Hellenistic fourth book of the Maccabees, put into the mouth of one of the dying heroes of Maccabeean times when, it reads: "Make my blood a sacrifice of purification, and accept my soul in place of theirs [that is, the nation's]." This conception of vicarious sacrifice is itself a particular working out of the faith/guilt order, for it assumes that the good are exemplary actors in the faith/guilt order and by their total faith and absence of guilt, yet participation in the punishments, the just compensations of the faith/guilt order, indicate the way men should rightly behave. Therefore, the suffering good are in fact authority figures in the faith/guilt order, and this reaches its climax in the figure of Jesus, but also in the figure of the suffering innocents of later times and, in fact, has its place in Albert Camus' novel *The Plague,* where again the sufferings of those who are not guilty are a sin-offering in their death, delivering others from the faith/guilt order or, at least, serving in an exemplary way to confirm the faith of those who are truly guilty. Vicarious sacrifice for the benefit of the guilty is complemented by the vicarious satisfaction of the personification or configuration of the divine justice, the interdictory term, the god-motif, so that vicarious satisfaction or punishment and pain is part of, or rather, the other part of the vicarious sacrifice of those who are guiltless in the intensification and triumph of the faith/guilt order. This way, a theodical model is established which includes the currents of pain, of suffering, and of death, which, in itself, supports the understanding of the triumph of faith in a faith/guilt order. It is only with the wish to destroy the faith/guilt order that suffering, pain, and death become insoluble obstacles to the understanding of pain, guilt, and death itself. So long as one operates within the faith/guilt symbolic, this problem is kept within adequate check. The sacred victim is sacred by virtue of his guiltlessness, but in being a victim he confirms the salvational element in the faith/guilt order. The older anthropologists, like Robertson Smith, understood this sacredness to be magical in the sense that the victim served to remove the impurity, as they understood it—the impurity which hinders communion with the divinity, that is, with the highest interdictory power. But to understand what the sacred means sociologically is to understand that the sacred as a category of interdiction is so perfect that there is no guilt. It is precisely that figure or that guiltless being, who, by virtue of guiltlessness, intensifies the process of faith/guilt. Rites of purification, on the other hand, which aim at the removal of pollution, aim at the removal of those transgressive acts or motifs which are earlier called demonic, that is, those which in fact enact the predicates of guilt and break faith. Thus, rites of purification, aimed at the removal of demonic pollution, are, sociologically, the ways in which the interdicts again function to at once express and check guilt.

The charisma of the Jewish canonical prophets completely opposes this notion of the sacrifice of the good as a way of satisfying the requirements of faith. Yet the theme appears over and over again, as I have indicated, as late as that great novel *The Plague* by Camus. Within the faith/guilt order, it is in particular the sacrifice of children as innocents that carries the thrust of this particular doctrine of the guiltless serving to absolve the guilty by virtue of their sacrifice as an exemplary expression of faith. Thus, the faith/guilt order is challenged in an immortal passage by Ivan Karamazov, in *The Brothers Karamazov.* This is again against the prophetic charisma of the canonical prophets of Israel, who treated such sacraments as child sacrifice as heathen abominations, asserting that faith in no way demanded—and in fact, interdicted—such propitiatory sacrifices, although they were clearly rooted in Semitic religion, and indeed, in other forms of the faith/guilt order. The motif of the descent into the underworld is a motif of the direct challenge of faith to the transgressive space and transgressive acts which are themselves the motifs of guilt. This descent of the figure of faith, of the interdictory figure, into the underworld voluntarily, and of his fortunate return is of course far more than Christian—it occurs in a Babylonian myth of the descent of Ishtar, for example, in order that she may restore her lover Tammuz, to life again. Ishtar descends into the land without return to fetch the water of life. The Babylonian myth of the descent into the underworld has its own interest because Ishtar gains admittance according to the ancient laws. Those ancient laws are conditions of transgressiveness, that in each of the seven gates of the underworld the realm of transgression she must pass through while shedding one of her garments, so that she might enter finally into the underworld proper quite naked, and as soon as she arrived, she would be imprisoned and inflicted with sixty diseases. Thus, the removal of the goddess of fertility, Ishtar, into the underworld, at once threatens to put an end to all propagation of human and animal life, to all procreation, and thus to bring about the extermination of all living things, as in the Demeter myth, at the same time that by the descent into the underworld the faith figure interdicts and limits that underworld, triumphs over it, and keeps it from conquering the world above, the world of life and of creation. Ishtar is rescued from the underworld by yet another interdictory figure, the hero who rescues her thus is the mediating figure between the world of life and the world of death, which is also the world of transgressiveness. This association of the underworld, the world of death, with the world of transgressiveness, is essential in all varieties of the faith/guilt order. Charisma then consists of figures of such powerful interdicts that they can, in fact, challenge the transgressions on their own grounds so to speak, and participate in that world without being a member of it, by opposing it directly. Jean-Paul Sartre's play *No Exit,* with its great line, "Hell is us," comes at the very end of the compelling power to organize social and moral life of the faith/guilt order, for in this particular Sartrean hell, which is a form of the descent myth, there is, in fact, no underworld. It is the breaking of the faith/guilt order that creates the condition in which all of us then must exist, an order in which those who commit acts that from one point of view are transgressive, cannot be viewed as transgressive, that is, create no guilt, while there is no interdictory faith with which to struggle against the guilt and transform it into faith. This is the key to the importance of the Sartre play as well as to Camus' novel *The Plague,* also the key, I might add, to understanding the present transgressive movements in the Western world that are often cultic efforts to break the faith/guilt form of both moral and social organization. This is especially true of contemporary youth movements without which I think we cannot begin to understand the inner dynamics of those movements. The raising of the dead in various myths of the mission of the great figure of faith to the underworld is the transformation of the guilty into the completely faithful, that is, into a world populated by gods or immortals. This is the true meaning of the motifs of immortality in various cultures dominated by the faith/guilt order. Conquering or slaying of dragon imagery is very much an iconographic expression of this conquest of the transgressive motifs of guilt by the figure, often the knight of faith. Gnostic myths of salvation often have this character, the disclosing through the descent into the underworld of transgression, of all secrets which are, of course, the secrets of transgressions themselves, the making known of the forms of the gods, and through this highest knowledge, which is faith, the imparting of the hidden mystery of the holy way called gnosis. In fact, the entire gnostic scheme of salvation is concentrated upon the descent into the underworld into the space of guilt or transgressiveness to deliver those imprisoned by the demonic powers that are the agents of guilt and through the knowledge of the forms of the god themselves the acquisition of that interdictory capacity which defeats and abolishes all guilt. Instead of obedience to the highest figure of faith, the gnostic depends for his deliverance upon his secret knowledge of the lowest figures of guilt. This is the basic difference between the gnostic and the Christian faith/guilt orders, and it is from the circles of syncretistic gnosticism that the motif of the descent into the underworld passed into Catholic Christianity where figures of faith and first of all the supreme figure of faith, faith himself, Jesus, contended with the malicious assaults of the demon powers who represented those transgressions that are the predicates of guilt in the faith/guilt order. The Apocryphal gospels and Acts, which were much read in the first centuries and did not achieve canonical status precisely because of their gnostic elements, nevertheless help us understand the true nature of the charisma of the early church.

The Apocryphal gospels and Acts indicate the faith/guilt order far more powerfully than those that become canonical. Thus, for example, in the gospel of Peter, the risen Christ is asked by a voice from heaven, "Hast thou preached obedience to those that sleep? Thereupon was heard the answer, Yes" (Peter 10:4). But obedience to those that sleep is, in fact, the interdicts of faith to those who are guilty, that is, in death. Thus Christ preaching to those that sleep is in fact the story of the time between his death and resurrection when he descends into hell and reveals himself to the world of the dead, the spirits, the guilty, the fallen, as their victorious lord and master. This is a myth of the total triumph of faith over the guilty. It is this total joy and pride in the victory, through all time, over transgressiveness, over the transgressiveness of the past, as well as of the present and the future, that gave the Christian organization its charisma and its charismatic superiority over other mysteries that closely resemble it. This is quite clear in the prideful words of the ancient Christian apologist Firmicus Maternus when he declared that while, in the case of the heathen deities, the faith figures, only their death is known, but the resurrection is neither prophesied beforehand nor testified by eyewitnesses, the son of God has, on the contrary, performed what he has promised, that is, he has preached obedience successfully to those that sleep. He has closed the gates of the realm of hell, and has broken the yoke of the hard law of death. In three days he has gathered together the flock of the righteous so that death shall no longer hold over them gainful sway. That their merit may not result in endless hopelessness, he has broken up the eternal prison house; its iron doors have fallen at the bidding of Christ. See how the earth trembles. This is, then, Christ waging war against the tyranny of death, which is transgressiveness, and which is expressed humanly in guilt. This war goes on for three long days until the evil forces that are death are overcome and totally defeated. It is in this sense life itself can cry out, O death, where is thy sting? War between faith and guilt is fought out in the underworld in the realm of total transgressiveness and it is there that the Christian charisma really proves itself, in this myth of the bringing of salvation to those who are in their death and defeat through death, guilty. The resurrection, then, is the exemplary event of guiltlessness and the perfect expression of faith. While death is itself the expression of guilt—the enactment of guilt—the descent into the underworld is then the triumph of faith over guilt, the final working out of the faith/guilt order. The charismatic conception of eternity, then, is a conception of guiltlessness, that is, of perfect faith, of the absence of transgression, of the abolition of any need for a theory of transgression other than faithlessness itself. The problems of concentrating the final working out of the faith/guilt order in a person, Christ, are as obvious in the vulnerability to disappointment as are the problems of the Marxist working out of the class struggle in the socialist revolution, which is the Marxist equivalent of eternity and the resolution of the Marxist equivalent to guilt and transgression, that is, class war. Albert Schweitzer, in his superb book *The Quest of the Historical Jesus,* put this vulnerability, this danger of disappointment among those who would be rid of their guilt and live in the freedom of faith, perfectly, when he writes, "In the knowledge that he is the coming son of man, Jesus lays hold of the wheel of the world to set it moving on that last revolution which is to bring all ordinary history to a close. It refuses to turn and he throws himself upon it. When it does turn and crushes him, instead of bringing him the eschatological condition, that is, the condition of perfect faithfulness and the absence of guilt, he has destroyed those conditions." Schweitzer continues, "The wheel rolls onward and the mangled body of the one immeasurably great man who was strong enough to think of himself as the spiritual ruler of mankind and to bend history to his purpose is hanging upon it, that is, the wheel, still. That is his victory and his reign."[4]

The important thing to say about the charisma of Jesus is not that he himself, in himself, has charismatic authority; that would be to render him a self-deifier. Rather, his charisma is itself a derivation from authority and, in the first place, from the authority of scripture. Thus, like other scribes, he accepts without question the authority of the law. When he was asked by the rich man, What must I do to inherit eternal life? Jesus answers, You know the commandments. And he repeated from the well-known Decalogue, Do not kill, nor commit adultery, nor steal, nor accuse falsely, nor covet, honor your father and your mother (Mark 10:17–19). Thus, the authority that Jesus offers is the authority of the faith/guilt complex, for the rich man himself already knows what he must do to inherit eternal life, that is, to be free of guilt. The rich man knows the answer to his question just as well as Jesus; he is, in fact, attempting to avoid authority. It is the task of the charismatic to remind him of the eternal presence of authority. It is in this sense that one can speak of inheriting eternal life. It is there always, in the commandments. What a strange transgressive movement our new social sciences are, with their repeated statements that we do not know what to do, and that we do not know what it is that should have authority over us. This deliberate rejection of authority is itself anti-charismatic and transgressive. It is part of the vast world movement to destroy the faith/guilt order. Rudolf Bultmann is right when he says Jesus does not attack the law, but assumes its authority and interprets it. It is in this sense, too, that the church becomes a charismatic organization. It is characteristic and definitive of the charisma of Jesus that the natural order is considered the order of transgressiveness. That order, the natural one, is characterized by the fact that the evil angels have seized control of it, so that the evil and imperfection in the present state of things are explained by a theory of transgression. Sickness and death also result from this fact, and are indeed what might be called in our language the symptoms of the natural order, which is the order of transgressiveness. At the moment when God puts an end to this interim domination, that is, to the natural order, which is the order of transgression, through the agency of Jesus as the messiah, then the perfect takes the place of the imperfect, and the good takes the place of the evil. The earth also is then transformed, as Schweitzer writes, into a splendid state, and a new fertility takes the place of the old. At the same time, death, which is itself also an expression of the natural order which is the order of transgressiveness, loses its authority. The generations that now lie in the grave rise, and, with those who survive, are assembled before the throne of God, where the evil and rejected fall into eternal torment, while the chosen enter into a state like that of the angels, that is, those whose lives are endless, that is, not controlled by the natural order, the order of transgressiveness itself. Now this total transformation also includes the established institutions which belong to the natural order and are therefore, by implication, evil. Now this transformation through the message of Jesus occurs by the obedience of men to Jesus: faith is identical with obedience. It is therefore the entire form of charisma in the case of Jesus, which is the key case, for the development of the concept is itself a charisma of obedience. This obedience is strictly opposed to every humanistic ethic and value ethic. The ethic of obedience has nothing to do with the concept of an ideal personality or with the self-realization of humanity; it is a form of action, a moment of action, an answer that men give within the faith/guilt order which transforms guilt into faith. The key point is that the commandments are kept, not only because they are commanded but because of the particular way in which freedom can be established. Freedom can be established not through some value of obedience, but through the supreme decision of man to entirely enact the triumph of faith, the interdictory modalities over guilt in what can then be called the supernatural order. If the content of the Christian charisma in its original form is obedience, then we must analyze the nature of this prototypal form of obedience. Obedience is only possible because through faith in Christ, we know what we are, that is, we know we are guilty, and obedience is therefore the struggle to resolve guilt. This obedience then exists without any secondary motive. It is a transformation of guilt into faith. It may seem a paradox, but that charisma which is obedience is a form of reward, that is, Jesus promises reward to those who are obedient without thought of reward. This is not an idealistic ethic; in fact, it is not a value order at all. This is not being of good for good's sake; the idea that every good deed is its own reward is foreign to the charisma of Jesus. Nor is the conception of obedience an ascetic one. It has nothing to do with self-annihilation as a form of behavior demanded of man in faith. Behind obedience stands the promise that is at once a demand, that is, the promise of the dissolution of the faith/guilt order.

The original meaning of obedience was translated into the far more ambiguous category of charismatic authority. The relation between authority and obedience is extraordinarily problematic. It is noteworthy that we never speak of obedience in the Weberian mode, but always of charismatic authority. Yet charismatic authority means in its prototypal historical case a certain kind of obedience. This is a kind of obedience that has nothing whatever to do with outward authority, that is, with the authority of institutions. However, it is that kind of obedience which is represented by tremendous intensification of the faith/guilt order in acts of faith, which are themselves not forms of belief, but deeds of obedience. These intensifications of the faith/guilt order in obedience are clearest in certain sayings of Jesus. I give as examples Matthew 5:21 and 22, "You have heard that it was said of men of old, do not kill. Whoever kills shall incur judgment. But I tell you, everyone who is angry with his brother shall incur heavy penalty, and who says, idiot, shall incur hell fire." And then from Matthew 6:27 and 28, "You have heard that it was said, do not commit adultery, but I tell you that every man who looks at a woman to desire her has already committed adultery with her in his heart." Or from Matthew 5:31, 32, or Luke 16:18, "Further it was said, he who sends away his wife must give her a writ of divorce, but I tell you, he who sends away his wife and marries another commits adultery, and he who marries a divorced woman commits adultery." Or from Matthew 5:33 and 37, "Also you have heard that it was said to men of old, do not swear falsely, but keep your oath to the Lord; but I tell you, do not swear at all. Your word must be yes for yes, no for no. Whoever goes beyond that is evil."

A further example of this intensification of the faith/guilt order that is the content of charismatic obedience is found in these passages from Matthew 5:38 to 48. "You have heard that it was said, eye for eye and tooth for tooth; but I tell you, do not defend yourself against injury. Whoever strikes you on the right cheek, offer him the other. Whoever goes to law with you about your cloak, give him your coat also. Whoever forces you for a mile, go two with him. You have heard that it was said, love your neighbor and hate your enemy; I tell you love your enemies and pray for your persecutors, that you may be sons of your father in heaven. For he lets his sun rise on the evil and on the good, and lets it rain on the just and on the unjust. For if you love only those who love you, what have you done? Do not the tax collectors do that, and if you greet your brothers only, what special thing do you do? Do not the gentiles also do that? You must be perfect, as your heavenly father also is perfect." In all these passages, the decisive command is the same. Weber developed his theory of charisma wholly from the charisma of Jesus. Jesus wholly separated obedience from legalism, and it is this separation in the original charisma of the mission of Jesus which is central to Weber's conception of charisma, which means that the Christian prototype needs to be examined to see what happens to it in Weber's various reworkings of it, for his own sociological purposes.

Weber's theory of charismatic authority is very Protestant, especially as it derives from Rudolf Sohm. Sohm begins with the proposition, which he takes as indisputable, that primitive Christianity was not Catholic, but that Catholicism emerged from primitive Christianity as a necessary and logical consequence. This is a clue to the Protestant pathos, that from a charismatic organization there developed a rational-legal one. It follows for Sohm that there must have been something in primitive Christianity and the charismatic organization which led to its rational-legal development, that is, to its Catholicism, and that Protestant scholarship had given no adequate answer to this question of where in primitive Christianity lay the germ from which Catholicism, the realm of law, came. Now, in this sense, Weber follows the Sohmian and radical Protestant interpretation of the ecclesia of late-nineteenth-century scholarship in which investigations of the ancient liturgy disclosed no distinct "I"; at least, no "I" distinct from the "we" of the whole community. It is in this sense that Sohm can speak and that Weber follows him, in creating the type of charismatic organization, that is, the charismatic derives his charisma in this model from the cultic congregation. The celebrant, that is, the president of the assembly and the head of the community, speaks in the name of all, for he is one with all its members, and it is in this sense that he himself is a charismatic. Now, Sohm follows the thesis that the Hellenizing of Christianity, that is, its rapid intellectualization and moralization, is a very important element in the development of its rational-legal structure, that is, its Catholicism, but that intellectualization and moralism are not identical with Catholicism itself. Moreover, in contemporary Protestantism, there has been a strong infusion of intellectualism and of moralism and of legalism. Yet, Protestantism is in this sense implicitly superior to Catholicism, but has never entirely forgotten its fundamental freedom, the principle of the religious freedom of the individual and the power of the church, and hence has never developed an infallible ecclesiastical law. The characteristic feature of Catholic organization consists in the identity which it sets up between formally binding ecclesiastical law, and the saving doctrine handed down by tradition. Nevertheless, in the primitive church, which is a charismatic organization, those who later come to constitute the officers of the rational-legal organization, the formal proponents of binding ecclesiastical law, are men of an entirely different character. The bishops were the men who possessed the principal charismatic gifts in the community. The passage in Paul that makes this point clear also ties the very Christian conception of the charismatic to the faith/guilt order. Thus in 1 Corinthians 2:14 and 15, Paul says, "But the sensual man perceiveth not these things that are of the spirit of God, for it is foolishness to him and he cannot understand, because it is spiritually examined. But the spiritual man judgeth all things and he himself is judged by no man." Now, this is what a true believer is, a true believer is a spiritual man who judges all things, and he himself is judged by no man but, of course, by the agencies of faith and guilt. Therefore, this typification or typology of the charismatic in Paul is already a tremendous intensification of the faith/guilt order, and that intensification of the faith/guilt order in the charismatic is in fact what a true believer was. A true believer was the spiritual man, who judges all things, and in that particular spiritual superiority is himself judged by no man. This is what gave the charismatic his leadership in the early church and permitted Sohm to speak of the early church as a charismatic organization, although no particular leader emerged. Charisma was not in that sense stable, but depended, as Weber himself notes, on the context of the cultic and confessional congregation. Thus, St. Cyprian puts into words a principle which is part of the tradition of the charismatic organization itself. He says, "I have made it a rule, ever since the beginning of my episcopate, to make no decision merely on the strength of my own personal opinion, without consulting you [the priests and the deacons] without the approbation of the people." In short, even though the charismatic, in his superiority, expressed that superiority in the intensification of the faith/guilt order within him, he was nevertheless a figure who was constantly supported and derived his charismatic authority from the support of the cultic congregation. This I might call the guiding principle of the sociology of the charismatic organization that is, according to Sohm, providing the model for the Weberian generalization. Moreover, if one can say that there was this idea of the bishop as a charismatic, there was also the conception in the charismatic organization of orders or degrees of the possession of charismatic gifts, and therefore of grades of spirituality. That is, there were not only different charismatic gifts which made certain people preeminent in dignity and authority, but there was also implicit a hierarchy or grades of spirituality which was then in time within the charismatic organization linked with that of grades of dignity. The bishop was then looked upon as an especially gifted person, as a head or a prince, and at the same time, as a spiritual man, someone within whom the faith/guilt order was especially intense, by virtue of his endowment with the gifts of the spirit. It was as such, by virtue of these endowments, that he was chosen, and in this way, it became his duty to lead God's people, that is, to act as the focal point and spokesman for the congregation. This decisive factor in the development of his authority as a head or a prince or a bishop was attributed, of course, to God's intervention, which means, sociologically, the intensification of the faith/guilt order. There are a great many examples of this choice of a leader by virtue of his charisma, which supports this thesis that charisma was originally some expression of the intensification of the faith/guilt order. Thus, texts like the following, from the Acts of the Council held at Carthage in the spring of 252, are a way of verifying the great number of examples of the location of the faith/guilt order. This text reads, in part: "It has pleased us, under the inspiration of the Holy Spirit, and in accordance with the *admonitions* given by the Lord, in many manifest visions," to choose so and so. This is from the writings of Cyprian, and the materials are here quoted in an excellent monograph by Adolph Harnack on Cyprian as an enthusiast, which was another version of the characteristic way in which a charismatic was chosen. The life of Cyprian was marked not only by visions but by supernatural admonitions, that is, by the intensification of the faith/guilt order. From this time forward, we find a continuous series of texts which use in regard to all the decisive acts in the organization of authority in the church the words "inspiration" and "revelation" and others of a similar type, but all of the inspirations and revelations appear to lend weight to the idea that the inspirations and revelations were of an order of intensification of what is at once faith and guilt. Thus in the charismatic organization, authority belonged to those men who were sanctified very differently, that is, they were given their authority very differently from the authority given to princes in the political and social order. Their sanctification was a kind of overshadowing by the spirit of God, this overshadowing and intensification of at once their faith and sense of guilt. The church leaders were all the more conscious of their authority in that they saw it as the vehicle of the mystery of that salvation which occurs to all men but for which they were special vehicles chosen to exemplify the particular intensification to which I refer. Thus, the exercise of their authority remained at once closely linked to a community in which the faith/guilt order and its intensification were in fact the criteria for the establishment of authority. That authority was therefore, although in one sense personal, in another sense cultic, for these charismatic figures, the original leaders of the church, became the expressive, singularly expressive, enactors of a faith/guilt order that all members of the congregation shared.

Sohm does not elaborate this idea at all in his discussion of the charismatic organization; this rather represents my own sociological and psychiatrically based interpretation of the church historical materials. The development of a charismatic organization was inseparable from the existence of a negative confessional association, not merely an association in Weber's sense, but a confessional association that was negative in the sense that it constantly expressed the specifics of a faith/guilt order. Therefore charismatic authority (and this not alone or any sense uniquely in the early church) was inseparable from the faith/guilt order, and the credal society had in fact as its structure the symbols of the faith/guilt order. This goes back as far in the literature of the faith/guilt order as the great negative confession that Wallace Budge discovers and publishes in his great volume on Egyptian culture, the Book of the Dead. This is to be found in volume 2 of Budge's Book of the Dead, from which he quotes from the papyrus of Nebseni, which is still located in the British Museum, Number 9900, Sheet 20. They indicate the way in which the symbols of life and truth are entirely interdictory. The scene is the hall of the gods, or more precisely, of the goddesses Isis and Nephthys, who symbolize right and truth, and to each of whom the deceased, the dead themselves, must address a prescribed negative statement. These negative statements are all in the form of a confession of what not to do, and are themselves the fundamental revelations, I think, of the structure of faith/guilt culture as this has come to us down to this very time, this fundamentally revolutionary time, in which the churches and all other institutionalizations, or, if you will, routinizations, of the faith/guilt order are being challenged by a tremendous effort to break the faith/guilt order itself and therefore the dynamics of charisma.

The Protestant assumption that there is something unique about the charismatic organization of the Christian church fails to take into account the appearance in other cultures of precisely the same supremacy of interdictory motifs as the symbolic of the confessional association. It is for that reason that I quote from the great negative confession of the Egyptian cultists. It must be noted here and time and again that my basic thesis is that this fundamental faith/guilt order is under a tremendous attack in our own time and for the past hundred years or so, both intellectually and for reasons of changes in the social structure, and that this makes for a type of social and cultural change and a shift in the nature of politics that is unprecedented in our culture. The attack on the faith/guilt order itself means the liquidation of charismatic authority as it was established in the faith/guilt order as a gradual emergence of a kind of charisma that is in fact the opposite of and antagonistic to the charisma that provided the model for Weberian theory. Moreover, Weber, in the deliberate neutrality of his perspective on charisma, obscures this basic issue, for he allows himself to conflate the interdictory authority of the classical charismatic type as an ideal type with the transgressive authority of the modern or political charismatic type. This is one of the essential thrusts of my own theoretical effort beyond Weber, and in correction of Weber, but of course owing a great deal to Weber's original (although I think deeply misleading) typology. Weber derived his sociological theory of charisma first of all from the case of Jesus and his early followers. He knew that this charisma opposed the political order and says as much with tremendous mastery of the dynamics of that opposition between the religious and the political. Moreover, it is important to state explicitly that

Weber thought it quite probable that just this prototype was obsolete. In

> the midst of a culture that is rationally organized for a vocational workaday life, there is hardly any room for the cultivation of a cosmic brotherliness, unless it is among strata who are economically carefree. Under the technical and social conditions of rational culture, an imitation of the life of Buddha, Jesus, or Francis seems condemned to failure for purely external reasons.[5]

What a strange, transgressive movement our new knowledge constitutes, with its pious (Protestant) or antiseptic (methodological) statements that we cannot *know* what to believe, although we can offer clarity on alternatives, etc. Again, the one and only commandment of modern culture, the foundation of all our therapeutic cults, is: *Thou shalt not believe.* This deliberate rejection of faith is, viewed historically and empirically, itself anti-charismatic and transgressive. If they are not to remain hopeless in their knowledge, then knowledgeable men need a theory of transgressions, freshly to communicate, first, for themselves, the militant truths of resistance in the endless struggle for more power.

SIX

THE CHRISTIAN MEANING OF CHARISMA

NIETZSCHE WAS SO RIGHT when he remarked that the "stories of saints are the most ambiguous literature in existence."[1] I shall begin this chapter with a rare story of a saint—rare because it is true, not at all ambiguous, and about a female saint, St. Thérèse of Lisieux. She will serve me first, as a Catholic female should, as a personification of the Christian mix of interdictory and transgressive motifs. The Christian saints are supreme examples of ambivalence made exemplary, authoritative. Her identity crisis—the time of her soul-making—is very different from that of the Jewish prophets and teaching saints. It began early in her life, when she heard a "terrifying sermon on God's hatred of the sinner."[2] Her first fixation of interest is on a triple murderer, Pranzini, when she was fifteen, three years before she entered the Carmelite order, where that extreme tension was given a certain stability; that stabilization is the function of ascetic orders, by their rigidly interdictory practices combined with the most erotically toned interest in the greatest transgressors. This criminal became, she said, "my first child." Until the day of her death, St. Thérèse never ceased to pray for Pranzini. She saw in his last-minute repentance an answer to her prayers. In contrast to the symbolic and saints of Israel, the virtuoso Christian has a sanction for testing the interdicts: the universally forgiving presence of Christ himself, the incarnation of/substitute for renunciatory demand can nullify all transgressive behavior. St. Thérèse is reported as saying on her deathbed, perhaps with Pranzini in mind: "If I had committed every possible crime, I should still have the same confidence. I should still feel that the multitude of my sins were like a drop of water in a burning furnace." This sentiment appears positively in the Christian iconography of the martyr, in which the saint is taken by society for a criminal and treated in totally transgressive ways that the church itself also adopted for its own use.

The transformation of the god-term into a remissive motif, personified and concentrated in Christ, appears to divide the faith in Jesus from the faith of Israel as a judging authority. The Jews could never accept interdicts so remissively organized that almost from the beginning Paul actually heard reports of sexual immorality, proudly done, among the Corinthians (1 Corinthians 5). To love is to choose sides, ironically, not without regret at the limit it imposes on human beings, against the presumption of moral revolutionaries and for the modesty of the obedient to revealed interdicts. In its peculiarly remissive support of the interdicts, through the freely given grace of forgiveness for transgression, Christianity had within itself the fire of revolt against culture in any form, a sentiment of respect for the great and small transgressors against the merely lawful and observant. Arguing for limit and against an openness of possibility, the Jews of law became ironists, cultivating their own saving sense of limit—or partiality and particularity. For their irony, for their truth of resistance to Christian impartiality, the Jews became the focus of transgressive behavior in Christian culture.

Christianity institutionalized the Jewish sense of limit in their religious orders, and exaggerated it, producing highly specialized renunciations of possibility at the same time that the symbolic itself appeared to undercut the interdictory form. Paul had to challenge the immediate and popular Christian interpretation of their new freedom. "I am free to do anything, you say" (1 Corinthians 12 and 10:23). "Yes, but," Paul answers, "not everything is for my good" or "good for us." Paul himself has been accused of preaching the freedom to do anything, to which he answers most literally: "God forbid." In the Pauline symbolic, the freedom to do anything composes the most complete transgressiveness; to enact such freedom is to be faithless to the God who keeps faith; faithlessness is disobedience to the master of the new covenant.

Precisely the transgressive misinterpretation of faith, in Jesus as the messiah, as a freedom to do anything, is interpreted by Paul, throughout his instructions to the faithful as opposed to "gifts of the Spirit" to which one is led under the authority of Jesus (1 Corinthians 12). Paul noted the dangers in the "language of ecstasy." Such language may be good for the speaker himself, but it is prophecy that builds up a Christian community. The prophet is worth more than the man of ecstatic speech—unless indeed he can explain its meaning and so help build up the community. Their spiritual gifts are specific forms of obedience to the discipline of faith, which are all practices of self-renunciatory demands and opposed to Dionysian feelings of freedom to do anything. Christian behavior, as Paul explained it in Romans 12, is thus inseparable from the spiritual gifts explained by Paul in 1 Corinthians 12. The Christian doctrine of charisma is more precisely understood, I think, in its particularities, the *charisms* by which each among the faithful is able to transform himself into the one thing the faithless cannot be—"a living sacrifice, dedicated and fit for his acceptance, the worship offered by mind and heart" (Romans 12:2). The classical Christian expositions of the meaning of charisma, in Romans and 1 Corinthians, demonstrate relentlessly that charisma is a particular and individual practice of faith, within and only within the cultic organization. Charismatic authority can only appear under authority, as particular practices of that authority, already organized as parts of the "body" of Christ, the church. Therefore, to Paul, it is the church, in its interdictory form, against the freedom to do anything, which is the charismatic organization. Within the church, "the gifts we possess differ as they are allotted to us by God's grace, and must be exercised accordingly: the gift of inspired utterance, for example, in proportion to a man's faith; or the gift of administration, in administration. A teacher should employ his gift in teaching, and one who has the gift of stirring speech should use it to stir his hearers . . . if you are a leader, exert yourself to lead" (Romans 12:7–8). In the Pauline doctrine of the charisms, its interdictory form is summed up in the command of "mutual love." Thus, the shalt-nots of Jewish law, "the whole law is summed up in love" (Romans 13:10). But this love is the Pauline interdictory form, under which all the charisms are particular enactments. Almost immediately after Paul has announced the fulfilling of the specific renunciatory demands of the law in love, he compounds the great shalt-nots, against adultery, killing, stealing, coveting, with further specific interdicts—

"no revelling or drunkenness, no debauchery or vice, no quarrels or jealousies" (Romans 13:14). There are varieties of practical service, under the one authority figure, by which the interdictory form is enacted so that the faithful will "behave with decency" (Romans 13:13). In the most revealing passage on the meaning of charisma as the practice of the interdictory form, Paul instructs the Corinthians that "in each of us the Spirit is manifested in one particular way, for some useful purpose. One man, through the Spirit, has the gift of wise speech, to another, the word of knowledge, by the same Spirit: To another faith, by the same Spirit; to another, the gifts of healing, by the same Spirit: to another the working of miracles: to another prophecy: to another discerning of spirits: to another divers kinds of tongues; to another the interpretation of tongues: But all these worketh that one and the selfsame Spirit, dividing to every man severally as he will" (1 Corinthians 12:7–11).

The Pauline concept of charisma was the supreme effort, now defeated, of the Western imagination to conceive the transformative plunge of theory into practice. But the deidealizing movement was antitheoretical, a tremendous effort, to move in the reverse direction, from the practical to the ideal. In a deidealized culture, soul-destroying, the Catholic concept of charisma can only mean a reidealization which, within the gospel meaning, cannot be initiated by the receiver but only by the giver of the gift. What can "grace" mean to us, who live well enough without favors from gracious authority?

In the gospel meaning, by charisma the theory of authority established itself in particular practices; by such establishments ("favors" of God, "gratuitously given grace," as Aquinas called it, in the old authoritarian language), individuals were liberated from their compulsions to disobey the interdicts themselves. Charisma is thus a particular and individual case of intervention by the ideal figure of authority, a forgiving yet demanding one.

The charisms are a gift or capacity for right action. Grace is not a substitute for right action but its basis. It is entirely a normative term, the particular expression of the interdictory form of the early Christian cultus. The receiver of this intervening ideal is related to the giver by decision of the giver, Christ, who is himself preeminently the receiver of it, on behalf of all others. In its basic form for the history of our cultures, charisma derives from the dual nature of the messiah. Christ himself is charisma incarnate, the idealizing gift of man's practical capacities. Christ is thus the prototype of all capacities at their nearest approximities to practice. The forming of authoritative practical capacities, not at odds with the ideal but its realization, involves an indebtedness to the giver, for the receiver cannot entitle himself to the gift—no more than a prophet can choose himself. It is a practical interdictory capacity given by supreme authority and, in its recognition, a pledge to practice and transmit in practice the interdictory motifs.

Charisma is the ideal in practice, and from the other end the only way in which practice can approach the ideal. Without the charisms, the gift to the soul would not correspond to anything outside, to no enactment. Charisma is thus the messianic appointment individually practiced. The term occurs seventeen times, principally in Romans and 1 Corinthians, but the key to understanding charisma is not its general meaning equivalent to grace, but in the particular charisms themselves. Only in the charisms, especially gifts or talents granted by God, through Christ, for the benefit of the credal community, is the Catholic tradition of charisma comprehensible. It is the gift of a particular type of ideal which enables its receiver to perform some office or function in the cultic organization implicitly credal in the recognition of the charisms. In the cultic organization there are the gifts which are to be employed for speech and service (1 Peter 4:10). Timothy receives charisma by the imposition of hands, a rite by which he is ordained to his office (1 Timothy 4:14; 2 Timothy 1:6). Celibacy or marriage is each the fruit of a charisma (1 Corinthians 7:7). There are several enumerations of these offices or practices of the interdictory form, each contradicting the freedom to do anything (Romans 12:6; Ephesians 4:11). A man is "justified" in his faith in Jesus by the practice of the charisms, not by "doing what the law demands" (Galatians 2:15–16). Thus the charisms become the successor to the "deeds dictated by law" (Galatians 2:15–16). Just as grace is freely given, so it is freely accepted—in wisdom, knowledge, healing, thaumaturgy, prophecy, tongues, etc.; practical evidence that the new ideal is at work inwardly and not by law. By these practices, belief is made manifest and practical. Charisma is the practice of belief, directly received.

"Then what of the law?" Paul asks. "It was added [to the free gift of grace] to make wrong-doing a legal offense" (Galatians 3:19). This legality was a preparation for the more intense practice of faith, as free men—free to "take the shape of Christ" (Galatians 4:20). In the charisms men are far more intensely guided to avoid "the kind of behavior that belongs to the lower nature: fornication, impunity and indecency; idolatry and sorcery; quarrels, a contentious temper, envy, fits of rage, selfish ambitions, dissentions, party intrigues, and jealousies; drinking bouts, orgies, and the like" (Galatians 5:20–21). If this practice is maintained, without external compulsion or fear of legal offense, then the result of such enactment of charismatic authority is "love, joy, peace, patience, kindness, goodness, fidelity, gentleness, and self-control. There is no law [that can deal] with such things as these" (Galatians 5:23). But to make this ideal character takes relentless practice, through the charisms, and, moreover, through each examining "his own conduct for himself." Paul is perfectly straightforward about the moral discipline available in the charismatic organization. In addition to constant self-examination, by which each "can measure his achievement by comparing himself [i.e., his ideal self] with himself and not with anyone else," all "brothers" in the cultic organization "endowed with the Spirit must set him [who is caught doing something wrong] right again very gently." Paul says, "Everyone has his own proper burden to bear" (Galatians 6:1–5), but it is clear that everyone in the cultic organization must bear everyone else as an example of his self-burden—gently. How it grates on the modern ear, at least of those who believe they should be free to do anything, to hear the Pauline call to the energies of guilt: "So let us never tire of doing good" (Galatians 6:7–8). But the alternative is very clear to Paul: we may tire doing evil. There is nothing indifferent. "God is not to be fooled" (Galatians 6:7–8). If we are not enacting the interdictory form, in some particular, then we will transgress those forms. In this sense, the law is better than nothing. Where there is no faith, let there be fear of punishment. In fact, Paul commands both.

Each time the word "charism" occurs in the gospels, the use is in the practical enactment of the interdictory form—against the freedom to do anything, a practical opposition to transgressive conduct. In these specific disciplines of enactment, against the transgressions that each human, in his freedom keeps free, as a possibility, are the propositions by which the cultic organization of Christ Jesus became a credal organization. The practices of service, of teaching, administration, ecstasy, and other charisms—all "must aim at one thing: to build up the church" (1 Corinthians 14:27). Paul will not be fooled. A charism is a particular service to the authority of the church, and no expression, even if not of a "lower nature" but genuinely "ecstatic," can go uninterpreted. "If there is no interpreter, the speaker had better not address the meeting at all, but speak to himself and to God" (1 Corinthians 14:28–29). God will not be fooled; he will know whether there are utterances of disorder or of peace. Domination by the interdictory form is completed in the Pauline doctrine of the charisms. The credal expressions of the interdictory form is the truth. The gospel itself is a collection of credal stories and lessons, for use in the credal organization; in all, the credal expressions are "God's way of righting wrong, a way that starts from faith and ends in faith" (Romans 1:17). Transgressiveness is a "stifling" of "the truth." Such truths as Paul preaches are against those who act on "their own depraved reason" instead of under that authority by which they would see fit "to acknowledge God." This combination, depraved reason and a lack of the charisma of perception, leads to a bartering away of the "truth of God" which is interdictory for the lie of transgressiveness. In the Pauline tradition, charismatic authority leads to practicing the rules of good conduct. To follow a false god leads to breaking "all rules of conduct," to the horror of a life full of the most terrible possibilities. To be transgressive is to be "filled with every kind of injustice, mischief, rapacity and malice." Paul thunders at the transgressors, not only in the church but outside, in prophetic rhythms of condemnation:

> Being filled with all unrighteousness, fornication, wickedness, covetousness, maliciousness; full of envy, murder, debate, deceit, malignity; whisperers,

Backbiters, haters of God, despiteful, proud, boasters, inventors of evil things, disobedient to parents,

Without understanding, covenant breakers, without natural affection, implacable, unmerciful:

Who knowing the judgment of God, that they which commit such things are worth of death, not only do the same, but have pleasure in them that do them. (Romans 1:29–32)

Paul addresses the old credal guides, the Jews:

Behold, thou art called a Jew, and restest in the law, and makest thy boast of God.

And knowest his will, and approvest the things that are more excellent, being instructed out of the law;

And art confident that thou thyself art a guide to the blind, a light of them which are in darkness,

An instructor of the foolish, a teacher of babes, which hast the form of knowledge and of the truth in the law:

Thou therefore which teachest another, teachest thou not thyself? thou that preachest a man should not steal, dost thou steal?

Thou that sayest a man should not commit adultery, dost thou commit adultery? thou that abhorrest idols, dost thou commit sacrilege?

Thou that makest thy boast of the law, through breaking the law, dishonourest thou God? (Romans 1:17–23)

The new credal guides cannot hide behind the law, but demonstrate their obedience to the truth of God charismatically. These new credal guides, "men of God," are still as other men and had better indict themselves no less than others. The Pauline doctrine of charismatic authority is very particular about even the most moralizing protesters that they, too, are among the transgressors. A credal carrier can easily protest too much. The shape Christ gave to charismatic authority makes it necessary for every interdictory figure to fear himself and his own burden of guilt at being in the wrong—and he is. The "truth of God" opposes even their attempts to lead others toward it. All guides are blind; it is an occupational disease the more professionally the occupation is practiced. Paul split up and particularized the authority of the charisms to prevent any of the blind guides from imposing their particular vision too impressively upon all those who crave guidance. It is crucial to understanding the Pauline doctrine of charismatic authority that there are many charisms. Paul exalts no personality and least of all his own. His leadership is a stunning exercise in nuances of admission that what he has recognized all others can recognize to equal effect. True, he has the gift of ecstasy and other gifts. He struggles for leadership. But he is not to be followed. His preaching is centered on one other person, and on the gift of identification with that person[3] which is to come under his merciful judgment. The responses to that judgment are in practical enactments, the charisms. Here are no leaders, only followers more or less involved in a whole range of practical and particular offices against the freedom to do what is not to be done. Among those varied offices—such as prophesying, teaching, or healing—none indicates more clearly what charismatic authority means in the classical Christian symbolic than Jesus' own gift of exorcism. For a charisma is a possession—more precisely, a particular condition of being possessed or compelled. Possession "from above" raises the possibility of being possessed "from below." As there is the interdictory gift, so is there the transgressive. In exorcism, the double issue of charismatic authority is most acutely clear.

In exorcism there is a reestablishment of the prototypal figure of authority, against the demons who are his negation. Exorcism is thus a special capacity to practice the interdictory motifs already given. In the early church, exorcism was a charism attached to no particular office.

The issue of exorcism is the casting out of authority in its transgressive form. Jesus himself is an exorcist, his gift for casting out "unclean spirits" part of his large healing gift. The exorcist charisma is a form of active opposition to the danger of moral destruction. "Do not fear those who kill the body, but cannot kill the soul. Fear him rather who is able to destroy both soul and body in hell" (Matthew 10:28). There is not only destruction but destroyers—those who are divided against themselves and wait for the unclean spirits to return to them, so that "in the end the man's plight is worse than before" (Luke 11:26). But to Jesus, the destroyers are only extreme cases of those divided against themselves. In a brilliant indictment he clarifies to one of the respectable and self-satisfied lawyers his own destructive yet disguised self-division, in which only dead prophets are honored. Thus the living prophet dares say in a tone more accusing than forgiving: "You build the tombs of the prophets whom your fathers murdered, and so testify that you approve of the deeds your fathers did; they committed the murders and you provide the tombs" (Luke 11:47). The struggle against evil demons is thus part of a larger struggle against the entire transgressive cycle. That transgressive cycle is reviewed, after the baptism of Jesus, when he led away into the wilderness of temptation. There, quite apart from the rejection of magic in the temptation of the stone, and the rejection of a magical test of God, the ultimate temptation is offered—power. For the third time, Jesus defends himself by quoting credal authority. He would not be ruler of "all the kingdoms of the world in their glory" (Matthew 4:8). He defeats temptation by the interdictory form of the word. "Then the devil left him" (Matthew 4:10). As an exorcist, Jesus' mission must be associated with his announcement that he has come not to abolish but complete the Law. Let no man set aside "even the least of the Law's demands" (Matthew 5:19). The unclean spirits are transferred to pigs, and the famous herd of them rush to their destruction (Mark 5:13) in the best way, by water. Thus the exorcist miracles of Jesus demonstrate the victory of his interdicts over all manifestations of the transgressive cycle. As exorcist, he "speaks with authority. When he gives orders, even the unclean spirits submit" (Mark 1:25). But even with Jesus, the devil of temptations only bides his time. That crucial time, the time of his testing, comes during his Passion, after he has been betrayed by a kiss. Christ conquers the final temptation, to despair at his own death; the victory of Jesus over all transgressions is a perfect inversion of the grace from below offered by "the devil" who "showed him . . . all the kingdoms of the world" (Luke 4:5). The charismatic authority given to Jesus is the exact contrary of the charismatic authority he is offered. " 'All this dominion will I give to you,' [the devil] said, 'and the glory that goes with it; for it has been put in my hands and I can give it to anyone I choose. You have only to do homage to me and it shall all be yours.' Jesus answered him, 'Scripture says, "You shall do homage to the Lord your God and worship him alone" ' " (Luke 4:6–8).

Christ's mission to the underworld confirms his charisma; his authority is identical with the acceptance of those interdicts identical with belief in their need for his existence. Christ's mere existence, without the need of the dead, their sense of guilt, is without charisma. It is this total joy and pride in the victory, through all time, over transgressiveness, over the transgressiveness of the past, as well as of the present and the future that gave the Christian organization its charisma and its superiority over competing associations and mysteries that otherwise closely resembled it.

For Christ himself descends into the underworld in obedience to the will of his father. While death is itself the expression of guilt—the final enactment of guilt, the descent into the underworld, is the counteraction of faith. "Life" is identical with faith, and faith with obedience to Christ's own call. The charismatic conception of eternity, then, is a conception of guiltlessness, that is, of perfect faith, a positive absence of transgression; Christianity begins with an anti-intellectual attitude, against all pagan puzzlements, as a cultic version of the Hebrew prophetic motif of transgression as faithlessness itself.

SEVEN

FAITH AND FANATICISM

CHARISMA IS ALWAYS A fresh objectification of the craving for authority; the covert structure of domination in every revolutionary movement is there from the beginning. In contrast, therapy releases its follower from his attachment to the prototypal authority figure. Charisma always takes the form of a new eroticism, however idealized, with the charismatic himself as the love object. Here, the nineteenth-century belief in the universality of the need for love and for a society in which the heart can not only have its reasons, but express them, is consummated by Freud in a theory which, when linked with Weber's, seems to me to be quite illuminating. Moreover, this structural difference between charisma as the reorganization of ambivalent erotic feeling, on the one hand, and therapy as the process by which a person is detached from devotion to an authority figure, seems to me to further enlighten us on the nature of the relation between what used to be called fanaticism on the one hand, and faith, on the other. The charismatic condition of personal devotion is always a condition of faith. Faith is a credal term for the particular focusing and attachment that occurs in the relation between the charismatic and his following, and may have its credal organization in institutions representing the presence or message of the charismatic. Very soon after the charismatic figure himself appears and given the reorganization of the ambivalences around him, and his message, the inner resistances are also swiftly organized and cultic or credal organizations develop swiftly to carry those new ambivalences under the flag of faith. There may be at once what used to be called a fanatical or enthusiastic following of the figure or message of the charismatic, at the same time that that figure is already being put in its place by the inner resistances expressed in the cultic or credal organization. Thus, very early, Jesus, knowing his effect on his disciples, was already laying down the characteristic inner resistances that later emerged in cultic and credal negative transferences with respect to his Jewishness and into Jew hatred as an ineliminatable feature of the charismatic organization of Christianity.

The great point of difference between the therapeutic of modernity and his earlier opposite "ideal type," the charismatic, is that, as Freud puts it in a famous passage, "The analysis requires no faith."[1] One cannot think in Weberian terms of a personal devotion that is at the same time critical and suspicious, yet that is precisely the condition of the preliminary belief and disbelief of the figure in the therapeutic relation. Therefore, the therapeutic relation is not the beginning of a new faith, but a dissolution of all faith; the revolutionary intervention of the charismatic signaled the beginning of a new faith, out of the ambivalences of the old. Thus new faith is related to old, in a tension that cannot be resolved for either side. Christianity must remain Jew-hating: Israel must remain a rejection of Jesus as the Messiah.

Faith grants a shifting in the structure and content of the ambivalences, not their dissolution; to the precedent idealizations there remain the ambivalences otherwise left behind. In the still open case history of the tension between the new faith in Jesus, as the Christ, and the old faith of Israel, it was Jesus himself who created the predicates for the subversion of the Petrine Judaizers hovering ambivalently between a condition of a renewal of the old faith and a breaking away into the new. It was left to Paul, as the successor figure, a second charismatic, to create a new cover in which the transference relation to Jesus was one that included hostility toward the Judaic idealizations preceding him. The charismatic figure may appear to contain no new formal features except in the intensity of the object choice he represents, his self-nomination, which is transgressive enough in any culture guided by previous nominations. It is in this sense that the charismatic is always a figure of disturbance.

In his "rationalizations" of self-nomination, the charismatic becomes the originator of a new edition of what used to be called "fanaticism"; those personally devoted to him were put down, as early as the Enlightenment, when the movement toward deidealization began, as "fanatics." A fanatic was that ordinary member of the culture, already peculiarly sensitive to its covert dynamics, who would emerge by the appearance of a figure specially transgressive when viewed from within the overt culture. To be fanatical meant to be possessed by a demonic figure. In a therapeutically efficient culture, there would be no room for fanaticism, and the putative followers would have overcome the pleasure principle which dominates their choice of leaders and their leaders' in relation to them. The suffering that is the predicate for a charismatic situation is therefore not material suffering as such, but the deprivation of that authority that is inseparable from the love relation. The revolutionary authority of the charismatic is not a cure when viewed from the perspective of a therapeutically sophisticated culture, but rather, another symptom of the prototypal series with the resistances reorganized to express yet different repressions.

In judging the emergence of a particular figure of fundamental change, then, the most important general question would be the condition of moral authority and its custodial institutions in that society. An analysis of a charismatic situation would begin with those transferences already effected in the culture and institutionalized in various credal and governmental organizations. It is only in the failure of those transferences that a charismatic situation obtains. Where those transferences maintain themselves, no amount of material distress becomes a predicate sufficient to produce a charismatic revolutionary. Defeat in war, or poverty, does not produce a charismatic revolutionary. Even when the prior transferences have failed, or were subverted, the charismatic must undo the transferences that still bind vast numbers of his putative discipleship. The mobilization of hostility may be correlated with particular cognate forms of distress that are not erotic in character, but "material"; yet such material distress will never produce a revolutionary movement unless the interdictory remissive structure of the society is acutely disturbed at strata that can produce fanatics adequately positioned to intervene in the larger society.

Fundamental changes of mind, true revolutionary breakthroughs, can only occur very slowly; profound changes of mind have to do with something more fundamental than a shift from one prototypal figure to another, organizing the craving for authority; the main question for empirical analysis refers to what shifts in the contents of the interdictory-remissive structure of motifs is demanded by the prototypal figure and his guiding cadres, the disciples' group penetrating various spheres of the society as a credal organization. But the main question in modernity is whether we can still refer to shifts from one prototypal figure of authority to another, or to the revolutionary transformation which occurs more significantly at the institutional rather than merely psychological level, when credal organizations build their transformative effects on the charismatic—and not necessarily the original charismatic but his primary successor. It has been often argued that not Jesus, but rather Paul, is the true founder of Christianity. The authoritative transformation of Soviet society may refer to Stalin, Lenin's true successor, and in the history of Mormon society, not to Joseph Smith, but rather to Brigham Young. We are already into the study of discipleship when we attend, as if he matters most, for the transference of charismatic authority, to the Number 2, as that figure who, in reorganizing the charismatic breakthrough, sets the structure of interdictory and remissive motifs by which the prototypal series takes effect. Number 2 becomes the key to understanding the charismatic himself; that prototypal figure remains as an ambivalent cover for a transference from old faith to new that is carried out by the Number 2. Sociologically, it is the Number 2 man who is the true charismatic. He who succeeds in becoming the first disciple, the head of the organization, becomes the one who makes over the transgressive attractiveness of the Number 1 into a model of life. Not Lenin, but Stalin—not Jesus, but Paul, become the true founding figures, the sociologically significant charismatics; the theoretical point at stake here is that everything connected with the situation of the original charismatic breakthrough represents a transference to that charismatic which proves suitable for use as resistance to him, and, moreover, to his most immediate disciple—in the Christian case, Peter, and in the communist case, Trotsky. The tension of the first period involves the originative figure in the defeat of the disciple nearest to him; the stage is then set for the sociologically and historically significant Number 2 to appear from out of obscurity. Both Peter, in the Christian case, and Trotsky, in the communist case, were too near; the truest disciple is the one most capable of defeating his master by idealizing him in the service of his own narcissism.

PART TWO

The Therapeutic Foundations of Anti-Culture

EIGHT

MAX WEBER AND THE POST-PROTESTANT ETHOS

THE FINAL STAGE IN THE HISTORICAL PROGRESS, during which Christians finally succeeded in committing identity-suicide, began in the nineteenth-century Protestant intellectual religion of criticism, successor to the religion of justification by faith alone. That religion of criticism emerges most clearly in Ludwig Feuerbach's own critical theory of authority. To Feuerbach, the divine is a willful personality—acting from pure will. Personality

> proves itself as such only by arbitrariness, personality seeks domination, is greedy for glory; it desires only to assert itself, to enforce its own authority. The highest worship of God as a *personal* being is therefore the worship of God as an absolutely unlimited, arbitrary being. Personality, as such, is indifferent to all substantial determinations which lie in the nature of things, inherent necessity, the coercion of natural qualities, appears to it a constraint.[1]

In this conception, the personal God, as the object of faith, becomes the one and only charismatic personality, both loving and arbitrary, absolutely authoritative and powerful. "God is a gracious master."[2] It is "love of God, as the predicate of a personal being," that has here the "significance of grace, favor."[3] Thus the Christian concept of charisma is:

> Grace is arbitrary love,—love which does not act from an inward necessity of the nature, but which is equally capable of *not* doing what it

does, which could, if it would, condemn its object, thus it is a groundless, unessential, arbitrary, absolutely subjective, merely personal love.[4]

Feuerbach continues:

Where love is understood in this sense, jealous watch is kept that man attribute nothing to himself as merit, that the merit may lie with the divine personality alone; there every idea of necessity is carefully dismissed, in order, through the feeling of obligation and gratitude, to be able to adore and glorify the personality exclusively. The Jews deified the pride of ancestry; the Christians, on the other hand, interpreted and transformed the Jewish aristocratic principle of hereditary nobility into the democratic principle of nobility of merit. The Jew makes salvation depend on birth, the Catholic on the merit of works, the Protestant on the merit of faith. But the idea of obligation and meritoriousness allies itself only with a deed, a work, which cannot be demanded of me, or which does not necessarily proceed from my nature. The works of the poet, of the philosopher, can be regarded in the light of merit only as considered externally. They are works of genius—inevitable products: the poet *must* bring forth poetry, the philosopher *must* philosophise. They have the highest satisfaction in the activity of creation, apart from any collateral or ulterior purpose. And it is just so with a truly noble moral action. To the man of noble feeling, the noble action is natural: he does not hesitate whether he should do it or not, he does not place it in the scales of choice; he *must* do it. Only he who so acts is a man to be confided in. Meritoriousness always involves the notion that a thing is done, so to speak, out of luxury, not out of necessity. The Christians indeed celebrated the highest act in their religion, the act of God becoming man, as a work of love. But Christian love in so far as it reposes on faith, on the idea of God as a master, a *Dominus*, has the significance of an act of grace, of a love in itself superfluous. A gracious master is one who foregoes his rights, a master who does out of graciousness what, as a master, he is not bound to do—what goes beyond the strict idea of a master. To God, as a master, it is not even a duty to do good to man; he has even the right—for he a master bound by no law—to annihilate man if he will. In fact, mercy is optional, non-

> necessary love, love in contradiction with the essence of love, love which is not an inevitable manifestation of the nature, love which the master, the subject, the person (personality is only an abstract, modern expression for sovereignty) distinguishes from himself as a predicate which he can either have or not have without ceasing to be himself. This internal contradiction necessarily manifested itself in the life, in the practice of Christianity; it gave rise to the practical separation of the subject from the predicate, of faith from love. As the love of God to man was only an act of grace, so also the love of man to man was only an act of favour or grace on the part of faith. Christian love is the graciousness of faith, as the love of God is the graciousness of personality or supremacy. . . .
>
> *Faith has within it a malignant principle.* Christian faith, and nothing else, is the ultimate ground of Christian persecution and destruction of heretics. Faith recognises man only on condition that he recognizes God, i.e., faith itself. Faith is the honour which man renders to God. And this honour is due unconditionally. To faith the basis of all duties is faith in God: faith is the absolute duty; duties to men are only derivative, subordinate. The unbeliever is thus an outlaw—a man worthy of extermination. That which denies God must be itself denied. The highest crime is the crime *laesae majestatis Dei.* To faith God is a personal being—the supremely personal, inviolable, privileged being. The acme of personality is honour; hence an injury towards the highest personality is necessarily the highest crime. The *honour* of God cannot be disavowed as an accidental, rude, anthropomorphic conception. For is not the personality, even the existence of God, a sensuous, anthropomorphic conception? Let those who renounce the honour be consistent enough to renounce the personality. From the idea of personality results the idea of honour, and from this again the idea of religious offenses.
>
> Heresy, unbelief in general—heresy is only a definite, limited unbelief—is blasphemy, and thus is the most flagitious crime. . . . For what is blasphemy? . . . Unchecked faith.[5]

It is utterly trivial and misleading to divide "religious-magical" from "political" charisma, yet not because somehow "religious" energies have "shifted" to the political sphere. When Calvin had Michael Servetus burnt at the stake, he was not acting politically. The established reference, in our cultural history, has been the early writing against heretics, to Arthur Koestler's *Darkness at Noon,* to the peculiar condition of belief and what unbelief threatens. No one saw the cross-cutting of religious and political better than Feuerbach.

But there must be a god-term, that against which the highest or religious offense can be committed. Instead of an uncompromising, living faith, can a society be constituted for long by "a sceptical, eclectic, unbelieving faith, curtailed and maimed by the power of art and science"?[6] And beyond unbelieving faith, what?

What then does Feuerbach glorify as the truly revolutionary personality, the salvational figure? He eliminates salvation by an aristocratic principle of birth, or a nobility of merit by works or faith. Again, we see the hero of sensibility or intellect emerge, the charismatic of the cultivated classes of 1841. The idea of obligation and meritoriousness allies itself only with a *deed,* a *work,* which cannot be demanded of me, or which does not necessarily proceed from my nature. The works of the poet, of the philosopher can be regarded in the light of merit only as considered externally. They are works of genius—inevitable products: the poet *must* bring forth poetry, the philosopher must philosophize. They have the highest satisfaction in the activity of creation, apart from any collateral or ulterior purpose. And it is just so with a truly noble moral action. To the man of noble feeling, the noble action is natural: he does not hesitate whether he should do it or not: he does not place it in the scale of choices; he *must* do it. "Only he who so acts is a man to be confided in."[7] Weber never explained his notion of the charismatic as determined exclusively by *inner* constraints so eloquently; he tried not to echo the nineteenth-century romance with the culture hero. Yet the culture hero, and cadres organizing that inner necessity into a creed are both there in Weber's huge conception of the charismatic. Nietzsche became his own critical hero. As a critic of all received doctrines, he has none to recommend. His free spirit is a genius who is actively anti-charismatic. Let me have no obedient, personally devoted disciples, Nietzsche says, in effect. The critical hero of Marx is the Revolution; that is criticism brought down to earth.

All criticism begins, as Marx's famous saying goes, in the criticism of religion. To criticize "religion," in our culture, is to reject both the renunciatory lifestyle and its psychological predicate of identification with an interdictory figure. In late Protestant criticism, the doctrine of charisma was first asserted against the effect of charisma itself. There can be no religion without the renunciation of instinct, but science and art are themselves ways around the renunciation of instinct, and toward the opening up of other possibilities of gratification. The liberationist ethic of the liberal nineteenth century rested upon substitution of science and art for religion.

Weber lived too late in our day to take so sanguine a position. He is himself no therapeutic of the transitional phase in the inner history of our culture. He is not one of those big children who proclaim some substitute for faith in science or art. Having no therapeutic technique to substitute for the exhausted interdicts defines, at once, Weber's relentlessly analytic language of despair, transforms despair itself into an interesting subject, full of "meanings" that shift with every exercise of that giant intellect as he moves from empirical mystery to mystery, now seeing "charisma" one way, now another, as the case seems to require, now politicized, now depoliticized—but always keeping his judgments reserved; the good sociologist, like a Christian, is no judge in the face of these mysteries. Weber raised the religion of criticism to a pitch of such refined qualifications that no judgments can be made within its own terms. The modern sociologist, under Weberian aegis, is no critical hero, although some still would like to be, even against our crying need for experts in the management of empirical-technical realities, situation-changers.

Yet who will deny that the politicizing of charisma is a human catastrophe of the same order as the politicizing of science and of art—worse, in view of the correlative exhaustion of any of the precedent traditions of charisma.

Weber implies absolute distinction between *genuine* charisma, which is not committed to any particular *political* doctrine—to any *practical* program of change and is indeed opposed to such practical programs—and institutionalizations. Charisma can be *originative* (art, religion, world-rejecting) or *politicized,* the almost immediate transformation and contradiction of *genuine* originative charisma into:

a. practical movements of change with credal character;
b. institutional disciplines, run by opportunists who make use of forces that do not owe their existence to political energy at all, originally, but to pure creative-destructive energy that attracts new members and repels old members—creative energy of the most formidable sort.

Charisma is defined, apart from specific directions of human conduct, as what is *truly revolutionary,* for Weber it is the necessarily successful imagination of a great human transformation by those obedient to the transformative quality or qualities that constitutes charisma. There follows the cashing in, more or less consciously, by those who are in position to use the new opportunities for their own interests—new or old (e.g., peasant boys become bishops; nobles become Christian, or at least their womenfolk go first).

To Weber, charisma is always, in what is significant, its transformative appeal, nonrational, even grossly emotional, with a concomitant antagonism to "intellect" and all its works and special carriers. Yet "all the great religious doctrines of Asia are creations of intellectuals."[8] And, "the Reformation [and Counter-Reformation] was led by educated men."[9] When Weber describes intellectuals offering charismatic solutions as having "undergone a process of depolitization"[10] he means intellectuals going beyond criticism, to reassertions of the interdicts, which are not rationally demonstrable. The religion of criticism stops at criticism of the interdicts. Intellectuals are "depoliticized" in a new way; prepared by such remissive activity to endless transgression, a world seen through by the revolution of a criticism proclaiming no interdicts, opened the way to purely transgressive movements. I think Nietzsche has been borne out, but in a specific way that needs specifying. The charismatic of the present, and of Nietzsche's future, is the transgressive type, for he cannot be a mere critic, a *writer* about honesty, moral courage, generosity, politeness, and intellectual integrity.

He must commit his criticism, his thoughts a life-act. Nietzsche knew the dangers, in such life-acts, if they are based on progessivist doctrines of "sovereign becoming," on the "fluidity of all . . . species," on the "lack of any cardinal distinction between man and animal."[11] Yet such total criticism, aimed at our failing guilt-faith order, is bound to reach less delicate ears, and thus itself become the guilt-faith order. Who, now, is not against "hypocrisy" and "dishonesty"? This anti-credal brilliance can easily use Christ, as Nietzsche did, against all preachers; we enlightened ones are all outspoken against them and their collective moralities. Follow no one. In the Reformation preaching, the intellectuals emerged with a fresh credal communication: follow the Book. It is impossible to consider the critical energies unleashed by the Reformation except as a book religion, one in which it became possible to follow the Word, for oneself. Luther considered it imperative to offer against the ever new authorities of the church, the old authority of the Bible; the Word needed to be translated in order to give ordinary man a proper distance from the horror of the world as it is. It has been often said the translation of the Bible into the vernacular broke the Roman church's monopoly of salvation, although that breaking of the monopoly was by no means fatal to its holders.

We must understand the sense in which that book was at once critical and infallible, for Luther is the first of the higher textual critics. He anticipates modern criticism, for that book contains everything in it that permits us to understand the horror of the empirical world and the condition of faithlessness. In this sense, he anticipates modern criticism from his preaching of the literal word. Luther wanted that book to reach the ordinary man; thus, he translates "barbarian," in 1 Corinthians 14:2, by the significant word *undeutsch.* Luther took infinite pains to note the words in everyday use, he says, in "looking into the jaw of the man in the street." He wanted to use the common German language so that ordinary men would understand him. Often he objected to particular renderings on the ground that no German talks like that. The translation of the Bible, then, by Luther, was popular, was itself a credal effort, not an effort at intellectualizing. The infallibility of the book is a straightforward effort to offer a total work of instruction on both the empirical conditions of faithlessness and its consequences with special emphasis on the horror of such a world, and on the condition of faith and particular mode of faith itself as it is offered freely to men. The infallibility of the book, then, as a substitute for the infallibility of the church, so to say, is often misunderstood by even the most educated public in the modern world, the two infallibilities are by no means the same. Luther understood that the book contained many, many incident motifs and events that were not to be followed, but were, so to say, negative instructions. With such a realistic work in hand, Luther says, any believer has better ground and authority on his side and is more to be believed than the pope or a whole council.[12]

For Luther, this book contains both tremendous descriptions of the empirical world as it is without faith, and the world as it is inwardly with faith. Without scripture, Luther says, faith soon goes.[13] The reason he didn't want complicated allegorical descriptions and expositions of scripture is, this could only obscure the meaning of faith and the faithlessness "To this wine, no water must be added," he writes, "to this sun, no lantern must be held up. You must take your stand on the plain, clear, strong word of Scripture, which will then be your support," he writes in a letter to one of his followers, Wenceslaus Link. But this plain, clear, strong word of scripture is entirely under the central mentality of Luther's reading, that lasting and guiding possession of the doctrine of justification by faith alone, and such readings can only undermine the authority of a church as a sacerdotal medium of such faith. Thus Luther writes, "In popery, we trusted in the merits of the monks and others; but now each one had to trust to and depend on himself."[14]

Although he was clever enough to give his doctrines the shield of national feelings, he was still attacking institutional authority as belonging precisely to that empirical world that is characterized by faithlessness. The infallibility of scripture, the central credal, organizing document, is only to be understood under the necessary doctrine of justification by faith alone. Once assumed, it removed the necessity for all intellectual horseplay, for all reference to allegorical, literal, moral, analogical senses. In his account of the offenders against the eighth commandment, he classifies the foolish and inane dreamers who play with such senses. The words need have no other meaning except the simplest. Of course, this removes the necessity for all acquaintance with artificial rules of exegesis or with practice in mystical speculation, but this meant that the credal elite was itself constantly threatened, and trouble immediately arose when this understanding of the infallibility of the Bible against the church was appealed to by others against the central organizing interpretation of the straightforwardness of the Bible under the reformed doctrine of charisma as justification by faith alone. Thus, the Bible was not in some stupid straightforwardness, infallible; unlike the Puritans and Ulrich Zwingli, and more like Hooker, for example, Luther did not condemn ceremonies to which people were accustomed, simply because they were not mentioned in the Bible. This was not the key. In Luther's interpretation of this credal object, if a practice were not condemned in scripture, then it might be considered profitable to the faithful. He was quite willing, for example, to tolerate the presence of the altars and the candles, but he was utterly opposed to the Mass for obvious reasons, for that gave a chance to the priesthood itself to get around the charismatic moment, the doctrine of justification by faith alone. Moreover, Luther valued music and singing as the gift of God, as he puts it in one passage.[15]

The infallibility of this document, then, its charismatic authority, came out of a reading of the Bible and a preaching of sermons from it that drove home to the hearts of the people the old message, that they were justified by faith alone. Luther himself wrote hymns which console men in the horror of life and in the condition of faith and guilt in which they needed to exist. If the scripture were so infallible, then these independent hymns would really be quite unnecessary and against the obvious interpretation of fallibility to mean exclusivity. One of the finest and simplest expressions among Luther's hymns of this triumph of the order of faith and guilt over the horror of the world as it is, comes in the hymn which runs as follows: "God's word for all their craft and force, one moment shall not linger, but spite of Hell, shall have its course, is written by His finger. And though they take our life, goods, honor, children, wife, yet is their profit small. These things shall vanish all. The city of God remaineth" (from Thomas Carlyle's translation of Luther's hymns). In fact, Harnack called the 46th Psalm the "Marseillaise" of the Reformation. Against the horror which is the faithlessness of everyday life in the world as it is, the Lutheran doctrine of charisma offered straightforwardly the faith of the 46th Psalm, which begins, "God is our shelter and our refuge, a timely help in trouble, so we are not afraid when the earth heaves." It concludes, with again this assertion that good and evil, as Schleiermacher puts it, belong to God—consciousness in the reformed doctrine of charisma, for the psalm continues:

> Come and see what the Lord has done, the devastation he has brought upon the earth from end to end of the earth. He stamps out war, he breaks the bow, he snaps the spear and burns the shield in the fire. Let be, then. Learn that I am God, high over the nations, high above the earth, the Lord of Hosts is with us, the God of Jacob, our high stronghold.

So the 46th Psalm ends, with an image of defense against the world as it really is. This defense can never become routine; in their true defense, men must remain constantly alert to significances, to those significances that teach them what the world, and they in it, is really like.

The one command of the nineteenth-century religion of criticism, to follow no one, not even oneself, has its propaedeutic in Schleiermacher's psychologizing of grace into God-consciousness. Schleiermacher writes, "We have the consciousness of sin as often as accompanying a frame of mind or approaching us in any way, a God-consciousness determines our own self-consciousness as unlust, as unpleasure, or discontent." The only way out of this self-consciousness as unlust is through faith as a conscious possession. In this sense, Schleiermacher, too, holds to the Protestant doctrine of charisma. This implies that Schleiermacher's effort to isolate God-consciousness from both knowledge and morality by placing it in a position superior to both simply subsumes knowledge and morality under that feeling of absolute and personal "dependence" that is God-consciousness. Thus Schleiermacher completely invented the Christian doctrine of personal authority for modern men by psychologizing it; Paul Tillich's doctrine of "ultimate" concern is only the latest variety of this Schleiermachian psychologizing, which, coming at the turn of the nineteenth century, made this "dependence" a screen on the independence that destroys obedience to the interdictory form. That interdictory form is most simply and clearly conveyed in the Sermon on the Mount; it is no accident that from Schleiermacher's time onward Protestant symbolists sermonized mainly from the "depths." This late Protestant sophistication radically broke with the simplicity of the Sermon on the Mount as the reformers broke with the complexity of the Roman church. Schleiermacher rejected the interdictory motif that good always yields good, bad bad. "A good tree cannot bear bad fruit, or a poor tree good fruit. And [practically] when a tree does not yield good fruit, it is cut down and burnt" (Matthew 7:18). No "God-consciousness" of evil out of good and good out of bad here. No using of necessary "enemies" to bone up a sense of "life"; no being "fruitful" by "being rich in contradictions."[16] This kind of God-consciousness, including good and evil, is the programmatic end of Christianity of Jesus. At this critical reversal, not only is the straightforward command "Do not commit adultery," and its intensification, "Do not commit adultery in your mind's eye," contradicted, but "God-consciousness" subtly introduces the likelihood that adultery may be good for you. In late Protestant "God-consciousness" it became possible to serve God and Money, and any number of other masters, by serving yourself. Schleiermacher's "God-consciousness," including good and evil, was a decisive step on the way to self-deification—orgiastic, rationalist, what have you—opposed in our tradition of personal authority.

Schleiermacher's best translation of the justification by faith alone is his famous feeling of absolute and personal dependence upon God. Thus charisma becomes a form of God-consciousness of our personal need, expressing those repressions of life in absolute dependence on God, as well as expressing the advancement of life in absolute dependence upon God. That is, both good and evil are encompassed in this God-consciousness. The first thing that the Schleiermachian doctrine attends to is the persistent and regularly renewed sense of life's obstacles. These, he says, are what we usually characterize by the term "evil." In this final reconciliation of the Protestant doctrine to the world, before its dissolution in nineteenth-century criticism, all evil becomes just as much wholly dependent upon God as that which is in opposition to it, good. Under the term "evil," Schleiermacher also includes moral evils, since where it (evil) exists, it shows itself to be an inexhaustible source of life's difficulties. The apparent oppositions come together under the doctrine of the universal dependence; the faith/guilt syndrome is thus radically psychologized. Even that which appears to a particular person to be an evil, be it his own or someone else's, or one common to many, exists as a consequence of absolute dependence and is therefore to be regarded as ordained by God. Schleiermacher thus resolves the theodical problem by saying that men wrongly represent those influences which produce permanent life repressions as if they were a separate self-contained province and thus could be isolated and eliminated; in short, that the world could exist apart from evil. On the contrary, for Schleiermacher, it is quite clear that transgressions produce good effects sometimes in individuals, and sometimes act as a great historical lever. Jesus was a Jewish transgressor and produced Christianity. Again, in the church the late Protestants again found the antithesis to the gospel. Since transgressions come to be done by reason of that capacity of man to express his inner nature outwardly, which is the source of all good, then both good and evil are expressed in this feeling of absolute dependence and in the infinitude of that upon which we feel dependent in our God-consciousness. Evil, as such, is not ordained by God, however; evil in isolation is never found and the same is true of good. Each thing or event is ordained by God, but it should be both good and evil.[17] A separate consciousness of evil in someone with faith, that is, who has undergone the charismatic transformation, is an imperfection of self-consciousness because a limitation as such cannot completely and exclusively engross a moment of experience when the moment of experience itself is rightly understood to be ordained. Activity, then in the Schleiermachian concept of charisma, is placed inside the relation of absolute dependence—i.e., of God-consciousness. Our history need no longer be naively understood as the opposition between good and evil; they are interwoven with one another and men can then be far more generous to themselves. From this generosity of judgment, good and evil in God-consciousness, Protestantism never recovered its interdictory energies; there was always something good to be said for every profane winner and an obvious evil in sacred losing. Protestantism was lost in its own product: critical intelligence.

There is a hint of the therapeutic in "God-consciousness" and especially in Schleiermacher's remarks on unpleasure. There is a hint of this determinative dissuasion in the ego system when Freud writes: "Another [regular] occasion of the release of unpleasure [as if pleasure were a stored quantum] . . . is to be found in the conflicts and dissuasions that take place in the mental apparatus while the ego is passing through its development into more highly composite organizations."[18] In brief, certain energies, or activity potentials, called "instincts" (e.g., sexual), are repressed, because they are "incompatible" with aims and demands of others, held back at "lower levels of development" and "cut off . . . from the possibility of satisfaction." When these unintegrated energies do finally struggle through to become activities (e.g., sex), either straightforwardly or obliquely, what would have been pleasurable is "felt by the ego as unpleasure." Repression (an unconscious I) turns a "possibility of pleasure into a source of unpleasure." Freud defines "all *neurotic* unpleasure" as "pleasure that cannot be felt as such."[19] The I is mistaken and destructive-disunitive. Far from offering less and less in which to "believe," Protestantism, at the end of its tether, began to offer more and more, good and evil; thus, in late Protestant culture, the condition was created for the emergence of therapeutic movements, which disbelieve in nothing and practice everything. "God-consciousness" was brought down to earth by Nietzsche as "life itself" which "evaluates through us when we establish values."[20] It is from this superior inclusiveness that Nietzsche considers that poor hick Jesus with his values all set and containing "God-consciousness"—good and evil. The last theological way station to a reality that "shows us an enchanting wealth of types," the luxuriance of a prodigal play and change of forms against which no "pitiful journeyman moralist" is longer to say "at the sight of it: 'No!' "[21] With "God-consciousness" brought into unconsciousness, which knows neither good nor evil, the interdictory form itself became not merely ridiculous but sick—moralizing became neurotic. How horrible to have all our post-Protestant immoralists, in their scientific offices, "opening wide their hearts to every kind of understanding, comprehension, approval."[22] They have the honor of setting the tone in a culture destroying itself by the less sophisticated approving of all transgressors as creative, or at least not "uptight." From protesting God-consciousness, the post-Protestant immoralizers have brought us to prodigal play, to change of forms—to being *loose, man, loose.*

It is banal and a piece of falsifying erudition to say that Weber merely "borrowed" the concept of charisma from the Lutheran church historian Rudolf Sohm[23]; the implicit polemical structure of what Weber borrowed is of utmost significance. For Sohm represented a climax of the Protestant attack on Roman Catholic institutional triumphalism, on ecclesiastical bureaucracy. Luther is the point of that attack; Sohm, through Weber, its final thrust. The Protestant interpretation was not simply that the Roman legal *organization,* its organization of authority, represented the defeat of the charismatic organization. Functionaries defeated the spiritual leaders of the Christian community. The supremacy of virtuosi of inspired worship was displaced by the supremacy of officials. That, I fear, is the vulgar version of the Protestant tradition, taught nowadays often by Jewish sociologists like myself to Protestant students now totally stripped of any knowledge of their past. I shall concentrate, in this chapter, on the Protestant doctrine of charisma and then turn to its pathetic ending, when Weber took it up.

To review the Lutheran point of attack on the Roman routinization and monopoly of the charisms, the church, not least in all its elaborate doctrines of the charisms, stood between man and God, blocking the one thing necessary to know, one's consciousness of guilt, inseparable from its *partial* resolution in faith. Luther makes *any* institution, even the Lutheran church, a most hazardous conveyance of this need. I cannot linger, in this lecture, over the Lutheran doctrine of justification by faith alone—in its implications for the problem of charisma. Here I think the Lutheran attack on structured charisma is made clearest in the passages following, from Luther's *Table Talk*, one of the great unread (and perhaps unintended) masterpieces of Western literature. One need only note one aspect of Luther's concept of faith, by way of preliminary to the piece of *Table Talk:* that *faith* is an *inward teacher.* To Luther, unlike Augustine, his real master, the nature of faith calls the church itself into question, its all too understandable tendencies to rule, and its monumental impressiveness. Karl Barth's *Church Dogmatics* is the first powerful German answer to Luther's shattering question, hidden in the doctrine of justification by faith alone, whether any man needs a church in order to discover his real need, which is for God. Luther remarked, in one of his moods of uniquely Lutheran demolition: "The knowledge of God is impressed . . . life's final breath." Moreover, this triumph of faith through the process of justification and sanctification, in the specific affirmation that follows denial and guilt, is no depressing or sad form of conduct. The world being what it is, and faith as the received, recognized suprasensible truth of opposition to it, what Christians enjoy—literally enjoy—is a very common charisma: "Christians are a blissful people . . . speak aught of it."[24]

Weber's Lutheran friend Pastor Neumann in 1903 had restated the Lutheran point of attack in a way Weber merely repeated many times, in a way that makes an established Lutheran church a rollicking Lutheran joke. Neumann restated the question of faith and the politics of any institutional life by confronting Bismarck with Tolstoy. Weber had a special feeling for both Bismarck and Tolstoy. "Either we want to rule, or we want to lovingly suffer. Either we go with Bismarck or with Tolstoy," Neumann said. "It seems to me that one has not understood Christianity in its full and weighty force unless one experiences this antagonism in his own soul short of the breaking point."[25]

Rudolf Sohm carried into his scholarly work his experience of the Lutheran antagonism, and, very Lutheran short of the breaking point, Weber's experience was far beyond the breaking point; unable to feel the need for God, he turned to the science of sociology and the reality of politics, not least in order thus to understand how our culture had developed beyond the breaking point—how, in short, the religious root of our culture had died, and not only for Weber. Sohm was still both a scholar and a man of the Lutheran faith. He found the problem of his faith in the course of his scholarship. Sohm begins with the proposition, which he takes as indisputable, that primitive Christianity was not Catholic, but that Catholicism shortly emerged from primitive Christianity as a necessary and grimly logical consequence. This is a clue to the Protestant pathos, that, from what Sohm first called a "charismatic organization," there developed a rational-legal institution. It follows for Sohm that there must have been something in primitive Christianity, in its charismatic organization, which led to its rational-legal development—i.e., to its Catholicism. Protestant scholarship had given no adequate answer to this question of where in primitive Christianity lay the germ from whence Catholicism, the mighty organization of law, came. Weber faithfully adapted and generalized Sohm's questionable theory, itself derived from Adolph Harnack, in a way Harnack expressly disapproved. It must be noted especially that Sohm could not separate his interest in the charismatics from his concept in their charismatic organization.

Sohm knew his Paul, of course. Yet, by his insistence that the charismatics, in the Word, were the church in its most general sense, that no general hierarchical church existed in these local communities of experienced charisms, he opened up precisely that distinct ego of the charismatic that was to fascinate Weber and supply him with that myth of institutional origins in which so many, in my discipline, now believe—as an article of "faith," so to say. When was "charismatic organization" defeated? What was organized? Cultic expressiveness, against which Paul hedged in his doctrine of charisms. Not enough to say that Hellenistic intellectualization and cultic moralization are the key to the development of rational-legal structure (Catholicism). Cultic moralization at the beginning: in the Pentecostal cry of Peter: Repent and believe. But the main problem is the meaning of *charismatic organization.* That which is "inner" seeks expression, has its strong infusion of intellectualism, moralism, and legalism: first appears as charisma, as structural and functional gifts. There was a certain polemical use in the theory of charismatic organization. For the Protestant professoriat of the turn of the century, its churches remained implicitly superior to the Roman, for never having quite forgotten the religious freedom of the individual from the legal authority of the church; hence, none of the reformed churches developed that weapon of authority: canon law. The characteristic feature of the Roman church, as distinct from early charismatic organization, was found by the Protestant scholars in the close weave which it introduced between formally binding ecclesiastical law, and the saving doctrine, handed down by tradition. This opened opportunities for a new type of person to assume superiority in the church: the ecclesiastical officer. Sohm can never be sure, of course, that those who later come to constitute the officers of the rational-legal organization, the formal proponents of binding ecclesiastical law, were men of an entirely different character; there may well have been "gifted" ones among them. But the charismatic *type* was defeated, *in at least his ecstatic character.* But was this the main charismatic type? No. Evidence is of many charisms. There is already a romantic individualism running through the Protestant intelligentsia expressed in the defeat of the ecstatic. This romantic pathos of late Protestantism was translated directly by Weber into a sociological pathos.

What can we say of the charismatic as a type in Protestant sentimentalism?

> But the sensual man perceiveth not these things that are of the spirit of God, for it is foolishness to him and he cannot understand, because it is spiritually examined. But the spiritual man judgeth all things and he himself is judged by no man. (1 Corinthians 2:14–15)

Institutional leadership by men of such sensitivity to a need that they know can only be met by divine favor cannot long survive. Precisely, this kind of leadership, far from the demonries of politics and the fatuities of administering this and that, granted the power of their central interest, could not long survive the survival, let alone the success, of their organization. Such leadership is bound to fail early if it exists at all, originating, and then sacrificial to, its creation. There is the late Protestant romance in a sentence. But Protestant historiography was not simple-minded. In *this* charismatic organization, a particular leader (or leaders) emerged, Sohm knew, only as parts of the cultic activity. What stability there was in these spirituals had to come not only from their gift but from its demonstrations in the context of the cultic and confessional association. Thus, in his first and model case, drawn from institutional developments of stunningly obvious importance to the history and "meaning" of our culture, Weber faced the paradox of a charismatic authority at once superior to and yet dependent upon the charismatic organization.

This connection and tension between unstructured and structured charisma supply a most complex source for Weber's ideal type.

The received idea of the officers versus the "gifted" is too simple to be derived from Weber's source in Sohm. Nor does Weber's ideal type lend itself to simplicities. Moreover, I think Weber's type is probably too complicated to sort out and defeats its own heuristic function. Sohm was far more interested in the dynamics of the Christian cult as a "charismatic organization" than he was in the charismatic as such; there is very little in his work on the charismatic. As far back as we can see, in that charismatic organization, there were ranks or degrees of being given charismatic gifts; certainly, some gifts appear more equal than others. The preaching of the Word certainly came first, although here we must understand that, in such a situation, the Word is inseparable from the propaganda of the deed. We must try to imagine something quite unlike what most of us have experienced as preaching. Not only did different charismatic gifts make certain people recognizably preeminent in dignity and authority, but in this recognition there was implicit those differences of spirituality which, within the charismatic organization, were rich in differing dignities. This was not a "democratic" or "radical" egalitarian organization. The early bishops were recognized as especially gifted persons; the head was at the same time, as a spiritual man; if this were not the case, then Sohm's thesis fails by the very lack of any concept of the transition from charismatic to rational-legal organization.

Sohm intended by a "charismatic organization" one that was at once obedient and free. It was this delicate intention Weber could not but destroy wherever he committed what Carl Friedrich called Weber's "secular and positivist" translation of the concept. The relevant sections in Sohm's work concern the original Lutheran antithesis of the church in the legal and teaching sense. It was not until Luther, Harnack tells us, that the "invisible church of faith" was sharply distinguished from the visible church of law. Yet the Roman church of law somehow emerged from the church of faith, "as a necessary and logical consequence."[26] How, in "consequence"? How did Catholicism identify the formal bindings of its law with the faith handed down in its tradition? Sohm merely carried the Reformer's revolutionary conviction, with enlightened sophistication, deep into scholarship. The object of faith can never be the organization; the true church of faith is invisible. No legally constituted church can bestow the gift of grace or even mediate it, however much men may desire such external assurances. Sohm's historical science carried forward the Lutheran attack on the pretensions of ecclesiastical organization. "Charisma" became a revolutionary weapon, prepared by Protestant intellectuals against the clerical establishment, which "annihilates the spiritual life"[27] it claims to convey. This was more than an attack on papal pretension. It was an attack on the life of organization, as such, so far as organization made any ultimate claim—any claim of faith. Weber merely extended the Protestant principle to science, but precisely for sciences that claimed to be able to *analyze* the dynamics of faith—to no decision, of course. But what is "no decision" except the permanent analytic attack on all organizations of faith? Weber's "ethical neutrality," his "objectivity," is the terminal case of the Protestant principle. Yet he was deeply aware that the case might well be terminal by a subtle inversion: the invisible body of empirical science was the precise opposite of faith. His one and only inner law is—against faith. What big scientific children, like B. F. Skinner, want, "a scientific control of human affairs," thus repeats precisely, in the Sohmian theory, the naive development of Roman church history, with behavioral "laws" where canon law once was. Weber's great warning essays on science and on politics as "vocations" come, differently from Sohm's, as a prophylactic against a takeover—but a prophylactic that is futile because the truth of resistance against such a takeover, by big science, can only come as faith, against which Weber's own neutralist, clarifying sociology is itself a powerful prophylactic.

I remind you that Sohm's thesis on the charismatic organization owed mainly to Harnack's earlier work on the double organization of the primitive church, one charismatic specific in effect, the effect of their associations and without any general organization, the other early rationalizing its cultic activities and adding others, precisely as it was fixed in locale and took on its own community responsibilities. But this dichotomy retreated before the complexity of the evidence. In all these early cultic associations of those faithful to Jesus, the charismatics, as teaching and preaching figures, did hold special rank, by the "gift" of the "Word of God"; but by the second century the basis of organization had altered by the displacement, or dying out, of the charismatics.[28] The charismatics could only operate in sovereign little associations, and this constituted the way in which the visible society of faith as a whole was regulated. There was nothing else catholic about the charismatic organizations—the whole church existed only virtually, in the powerful credal imagination of its particular cultic leaders.

Even as late as the third century, by virtue of their gifts, charismatics still emerged, within the organization, but by then, gifted thus, it became the charismatic's duty to lead God's people, that is, to act as the focal point and spokesman in the cultic association. This decisive factor in the development of his authority as a head or a prince or a bishop was attributed, of course, to God's intervention. There are examples of this choice of a leader by virtue of his gift, given by God, two centuries after this peculiar institution began to make its way to its present condition. I cite one of Harnack's texts, from the Acts of the Council held at Carthage in the spring of 252: "It has pleased us, under the inspiration of the Holy Spirit, and in accordance with the *admonitions* given by the Lord, in many manifest visions," to choose, so and so.

The life of Cyprian was marked, not only by visions, but more important, for his kind of charisma, by supernatural admonitions. The faith/guilt order had formed one of its two leading character types.

To unlock the innermost secret of morality and culture is to know, simply: what to avoid. The early Christian charismatic knew what to avoid: the world as it is, and, in particular, the world of power politics. He had his organizations of avoidance. For Weber to write, as he did, that "in its pure form charismatic authority may be said to exist only in the process of originating"[29] expresses the post-Protestant pathos, in its denial of the Protestant doctrine of charisma. Like all truly scientific conceptions, as neutralizations of the dynamics of guilt and faith, charisma is anti-charismatic, part of that very enchantment of "reason" in which he found the revolutionary force of modern culture. Weber himself knew where to draw the line between faith and science, more certainly than Emíle Durkheim or Lucien Lévy-Bruhl; he had no illusions about sociology as the successor of religion. Yet the significance of such disciplines as psychiatry, especially in its Freudian expression, and of sociology, not least in its Weberian expression, is that they have helped destroy the dynamics of charismatic renewal in Western culture. Loosed from their credal moorings, the educated classes can accept the most contrary charismatics, so long as they are "effervescent." Of course, Weber took up charisma after the force of it, as the creative impulse of our culture, had been spent. A new structure of response was then only beginning to be organized. At best, Weber's response, like Durkheim's appreciations of faith, was retrospective, if not prophylactic, as Durkheim thought science would be toward any excesses of faith. Thus, finally, Durkheim still looked forward to a rational faith, a contradiction in terms that roused Weber's grimmest sense of humor about those big children of science. Yet, by their sciences and their therapies, the educated classes, I suggest, at least so far as they are educated sociologically, are now immunized to the experience of the charismatic.

The Weberian theory of charisma constitutes a brilliant ambivalence toward the very possibility of the charismatic experience. Weber's "recognition" theory emerges as a negation, a tremendous denial of charisma and a shadowing forth of the therapeutic—at worst, in our rationalizing social order, of "charisma" squirted out of a canful of recognition-inducing techniques. By his insistence on the historical importance of charisma at the very foundations of our rationalizing institutions—and, more precisely, of our old institutions—Weber implies the historical exhaustion of charismatic authority. His concept of charisma can only achieve its own meanings in a culture cold to its own charismatic traditions and enacting their demolition. This is why it is so ambiguous to consider Hitler, for example, as a "charismatic." He is a figure of the demolition, and what follows—the leader of an anti-credal organization.

In the established sociological conception, charisma is considered in its place at the center of a burst of social and cultural "creativity," that then radiates outward, somehow, mainly through disciples and the institutionalization of their vested interests, into the social order. The more successful this radiation, the emptier its original meaning becomes at the center; finally, the old charismatic center is invested with the interests of the anti-charismatic periphery. This is the fate of charisma, its *nemesis*. The Protestant mind has cherished a historical theory of defeat of spirit by world: the logic in its own termination has appealed to the Protestant professoriat, engaged in the study of its credal institutions.

Now we see more clearly, I hope, how the Weberian theory of the institutionalization of charisma depends on the post-Protestant intellectuals' postulate of the destruction of charisma itself by its very success, by its routinization as a result of socioeconomic factors which predominantly determine the routinization of charisma. This post-Protestant moralizing is hidden behind a straightforward theory of social interests: the need of certain social strata who are somehow representative of the charismatic thrust and also privileged through existing political, social, and economic orders, to have their social and economic positions treated deferentially, even reverentially. In time, these interests, or status groups, believe it themselves. Weber's "legitimation" is very near Marxist "ideology." Thus the social order is transformed from purely factual power relations[30] into a cosmos of acquired rights, and to know that they are thus, the power-thrusters are "sanctified." These self-interests, disguised behind some sacral aura, comprise by far the "strongest motive for the conservation of the charismatic elements of an objectified nature within the structure of domination." But then the Protestant counterthrust immediately reappears in Weber's writing that "genuine charisma is absolutely opposed to this objectified form." Yet power and charisma are joined in a tense marriage, like sanctification and justification. Status interest groups of disciples can only conserve the charismatic elements by objectifying them in a structure of domination from which they themselves benefit; at the same time, genuine charisma is absolutely opposed to this objectified form. Here is the final expression of the late Protestant pathos of charismatic innovation, opposed to all institutions, and itself the catalyst of institutions. By making of charisma a pre-institutional and even anti-institutional animus, post-Protestant theorists, such as Weber, supported the rising cult of infinite personality, the creative figure, artist of the future who will have his self-portrait retouched by those who can advance themselves by carrying it before them, their shibboleth, magically alive for the simples—even the simples among their own.

But, objectively and subjectively, viewed from the perspective of origins or endings, the simples have been fooled—tremendously and necessarily fooled. The apparently inevitable transference of charisma into an organizational cult of personality appears clearly in the passage where Weber argues that it is precisely genuine charisma as "extraordinary, supernatural, divine, power, [which] transforms it, after its routinization, into a suitable source for the legitimate acquisition of sovereign power by the successors of the charismatic hero. Routinized charisma thus continues to work in favor of all those whose power and possession is guaranteed by that sovereign power, and who thus depend upon the continued existence of such power."[31] Charisma, in its cultic phase, *is* routinization; the cult of personality is a strategy of power, to make itself over into authority. The revolution becomes an opportunity, and after the success of a revolution the opportunists are those who believe in what has happened most ardently. Weber himself has subtly shifted the Protestant pathos to politics; there the charismatic himself can be the supreme opportunist. The political hero never acts in a self-renunciatory mode; on the contrary, his act is always a form of self-deification, an identity with the supreme force. Thus, the political hero is "charismatic" in our transgressive sense. Freud's work on founding fathers may be used to clarify the issue. His mythological primal father is a charismatic hero, but so is his Moses; yet the two are fundamentally opposed, and the one practicing everything but the renunciation of instinct, and the other practicing in precisely the opposite way, the great imposer, on a recalcitrant people, of renunciations. A theory which cannot account for the basic opposition between the two types is itself, I suggest, in the service of transgressive behavior, a rationalization of the ploy of power.

The Protestant pathos in Weber's theory emerges in his doctrine of the ideology of status groups, unconscious of their real aims, for which the charismatic legacy is a disguise, first of their own interests. Thus, in Weber, "charisma" is itself the opening phase of a new ideological thrust toward power or higher status of the disciples group; this phaseological meaning would hold as well, in the Weberian implication, for a revolutionary political movement, such as the Bolsheviks, as for the early Christian church. As a mystique of legitimacy, charisma becomes the Weberian analog to the Marxist dynamic of ideology in a continuing struggle for power among those social formations fortunate enough to possess this invaluable initiating mystique.

By ideologizing the "legitimizing" phase of charisma as its contradiction, Weber becomes as subversive in his theoretical effort at Marx—and, moreover, subversive without being revolutionary: the very condition of the therapeutic. Authority becomes suspect not only in its ends but in its origins. Thus, Weber's sociological theory, so far as it is influential, becomes one of the midwives attending the birth of the therapeutic.

Weber shows the effect of "legitimacy" in the revolutionary force of charisma itself in his references to the stabilizing effect of the constitutional monarch, in English politics. The dynamic of charisma is drained off by the legitimacy of the throne. That monarch formally limits the politician's quest for power because the highest position in the state is preempted once and for all. From a political point of view, this is an "essentially negative function associated with the mere existence of a king enthroned according to fixed rules."[32]

Thus, there may be a certain kind of charismatic office which limits the struggle for power. Here, as in other places, Weber uses the concept so fluently that he all but destroys it. Charisma is the quality of a new power thruster and its legitimation is a way to guard against the destabilizing effects of power thrusters. England is thus a culture in which charisma, except in service to the crown, for its protection as the highest personification of British nationhood, is depoliticized. But this should mean the reappearance of charismatic qualities among depoliticized groups of intellectuals, artists, and naïfs, rather in the matter Sohm first saw in his beloved charismatic organization. And Weber in 1910 thought he detected signs of the spirit reviving again in private little groups.[33] Anything to escape the prevailing *routinization.*

NINE

THE MEANING OF LEADERSHIP

BY LIFTING THE CONCEPT OF CHARISMA out of the symbolic of Christianity, Weber unwittingly destroyed it. He was misled into thinking that he could deepen his own understanding of empirical systems of authority by devising a purely external conception of charisma when in fact the reverse was the case: an empirical understanding of systems of authority can only develop if charisma is understood as an inward quality. The major quality of inwardness is its dominantly interdictory form—a knowing what not to do. By locating charismatic authority in the process of originating new obligations, Weber in effect romanticizes the charismatic as a figure of origins, but in a way far less profound than Freud's romance of origins. While, for Weber, charismatic authority is too "pure" to survive against the steadier pressures of historical reality, Freud saw how the defeat of the charismatic is the foundation of his real authority.

Weber simply lacked Freud's vision into the dual nature of charismatic authority. Even Jesus is not pure in the sense in which Weber uses purity implicitly. When viewed from the Jewish perspective, Jesus is a transgressive figure. Indeed, it can be argued that the charismatic attraction of Jesus was precisely that he was not only an interdictory figure, but a transgressive one. Weber is trapped between his conception of the pure form of charismatic authority as a mere methodological convenience, and his conception of charismatic authority as existing only in the process of originating, because somehow the form is basically changed in the course of time and loses its purity. This historical pathos is inextricably mixed with Weber's sense of methodological convenience in his assertion of the meaning of the pure form of charismatic authority. The historical villains of the routinization of charisma are in Weber, of course, the disciples, for they must transform the pure form of charismatic authority in order to fulfill their own status and material interests. Weber postulates "interest" as a kind of polar element, one which leads away from charismatic authority in its purity. This comes out of a profoundly Protestant suspicion of institutions, and, indeed, the whole argument on routinization is a version of the Protestant argument against the Roman church as itself somehow a contradiction of the early Christian message; as if that message in its purity permitted no church, no hierarchy. And most of all, no self-interest. The conception of the routinization of charisma is therefore Weber's sociological version of a Protestant idealism transferred to a more general historical struggle from the specific struggle between the late Protestant liberal intelligentsia and the authority of the churches out of which they came. That Weber should be unaware of the way in which he himself translated this struggle indicated the limits of sociological self-understanding; for no man had a greater opportunity to observe the origins of his own theory than Weber himself.

Weber's own notion of the transference of charismatic qualities into social organizations depends upon the developing stake of the disciples in the charismatic message. He attends far less to the creedal characteristics of social organization than to the hold of the message upon the disciples. More important, he never fixes the behavioral structure of charisma. Instead, he falls back on the notion that the charismatic foundation of this provisioning of all demands beyond the routine is entirely heterogeneous; charisma has no structure beyond its new spurious "gift of grace" and recognition.

That structure appears to have a consistent double content, interdictory and remissive. If this is the general case, then Weber is mistaken to understand the charismatic foundation of all demands organized beyond the everyday routine as heterogeneous. Nor are the leaders entirely heterogeneous. There is a logic in their emergence, especially in times of psychic, physical, economic, ethical, religious, or political distress. The distress out of which charismatics arise is better explained,

I think, not by giving up the search for some structure of charistic qualification, but by pressing the search beyond Weber. Weber's limitation in conceptualizing charisma is in part due to his insistence on using the concept in what he called a "completely value-neutral sense." Just this completely value-neutral sense blinded Weber to the structure of charisma, as interdictory, and of pseudo-charisma, as remissive. Weber's theory is anti-charismatic; it is therefore remissive in its implication. No more than a theory is, the charismatic himself is never value-neutral; on the contrary, he is always value-protagonistic. Weber's "value-neutrality" makes his vast erudition obscure more than it reveals. Thus, in his section on the sociology of charismatic authority, he discusses the capacity of the Irish culture hero Cuchulainn, or the Homeric Achilles, for heroic frenzy as a manic seizure, or of the Arabian berserk, who bites his shield like a mad dog, but Weber doesn't make anything of these extraordinary activities. Listing extraordinary activities without a conceptual structure within which to order these activities, as forms of attractive behavior, is false erudition. It is not at all clear why the behavior of an Irish culture hero or Homeric figure like Achilles, as a manic seizure, should be itself either attractive as a point of behavior, or a "gift." The "gift" upon which Weber plays is acutely ambivalent. We live in interdictory remissive structures. When a person acts in a way that breaks through that structure, transgresses it in a way that provides an example of that transgression, the "gift" is far from that of grace, but its contrary: a latent sense of infinite possibility, bred like a "contagion," as Freud put it. Because some figure is capable of significant transgressions, he becomes "extraordinary" and "mysterious" and, above all, compelling. As a transgressor, the pseudo-charismatic opens up possibility; he is a liberator from those particular limits on human action within which others have had to live. This represents the inner and sociological structure, linking the categories crime and politics with charisma. It is entirely untrue to say that the charismatic foundation for the provisioning of all demands that go beyond the everyday routine is entirely heterogeneous, that there is no explanation for it beyond the assertion of supernatural and inaccessible gifts. It is either interdictory or transgressive; either a prize or a gift. Having emptied out the theological category, not belonging himself to a credal organization, Weber had no intellectual right to speak of "gifts." Interdictory gifts are particular and specific to the credal organization as a result of the transference of the charismatic qualifications into that organization. By continuing to use the theological rubrics outside their historical and conceptual structure or context, Weber fails to see that sociological interpretation is itself evaluative, interdictory, or remissive, despite his realization that every sociology must appear within a culture. Sociology is rightly concerned with nothing more appropriate to itself than the facts of valuation, and that concern is itself valuative in effect—i.e., it must affect the interdictory remissive structure thus factually treated. By the very nature of his interpretative effort, Weber, like Freud, supported the rise of the therapeutic as a dominant type in modern society, and has, in fact, destroyed the capacity of moderns for charismatic perceptions. It follows that the concept of charisma cannot itself be used in a value-neutral sense. That is impossible to any culture in which such analytic reductions of charisma are communicated. In this light, much of what Weber accepted as charismatic—heroic frenzies, manic seizures, shamanistic ecstasies, Mormon hoaxes, all of these particular gifts—is really the opposite. They are extraordinary releases from the interdicts, the very opposite of saints, for example. For Nietzsche to say, as he did, that, under certain circumstances, saints and criminals will act in identical ways, is only to say that certain circumstances are inherently transgressive and should be avoided.

For moments, here and there in his writing, Weber's genius leads him to the notion of the charismatic as something more than the recognized one. Although he never abandoned the sociological reduction of charisma to recognition, so ruinous in modern culture; nevertheless, Weber could declare, in one of his moments of illumination, that "charisma knows only inner determination and inner restraint." But the thrust of this sentence is never carried further. Weber immediately retreated to the idea of determination by success, a telling variation on the idea of recognition. The whole problem of the inner determination of the charisma itself was left by Weber, as I noted earlier, resting on the gift of grace, a concept which comes out of another and opposing symbolic, to the use of which he is not entitled. Though he asserted that this inner determination was the dominant one, yet Weber goes on to say that the charismatic claim breaks down if the mission of the charismatic is not recognized by those to whom he feels he has been sent. Here is recognition come full circle, not as consequence but as predicate of any continued "inner determination" and "inner restraint." The circle of interpretation practically strangles the concept itself, especially when Weber goes on to claim that if the followers recognize the charismatic, then he is their "master," as Weber put it. The charismatic is master—he dominates—so long as he knows how to maintain recognition through proving himself. Yet this mastery through maintenance of recognition again escapes the problem of inner determination and of ambivalences implicit in the Weberian version of charismatic qualification.

The case of Jesus is more complex. In what sense is Jesus a master? Does he maintain recognition, or, rather, try to avoid it? In the particular charismatic qualification that Jesus sought, subtly, to transfer to his disciples, thus making them a credal organization, "the disciple is not above his master, but everyone, when he is perfected, shall be as his master" (Luke 4:40). Jesus dominated only in a very special sense. He was a master seeking to resolve his mastery, and, indeed, to make every disciple a master, once that disciple had been perfected through his obedience to the mission of Jesus.

The question of recognition is most ambiguous in the case of the charismatic of charismatics in our culture, Jesus; he did not seek to maintain recognition but, in a very important sense, to escape it. For the true charismatic, as much opposed to his followers as they to his message, " 'inner determination' must be prior to, and independent of, 'recognition.' "[1] Moses chose the Jews, not the Jews Moses. Without this initiative, charismatic authority ceases to exist. Initiative cannot be an epiphenomenon of recognition. A leader may address his mission to his followers in such a way that he finds himself subject to his followers—in the manner of an election, or deriving his right from their will. Such a leader may lead, indeed, but he is not a charismatic. The incompleteness of Weber's theory, with special reference to the transference of charismatic qualities, is not resolved by adding the additional concept of office charisma or of other external role categories. The duty of followers may be linked more accurately to the particular direction of charisma.

The structured meaning of the charismatic qualification is best understood, I suggest, if the leader is treated as an interdictory and/or remissive figure, to whom the response that is made is then a recognition in a far more precise and sociologically, spiritually, and historically determinable way. Without a theory of the inner determination and inner restraint itself, Weber is driven back regularly to only one type of leadership—power as the determination of success. Such reflective outwardness may then go so far, become so outward, so to say, that we are no longer dealing with a charismatic qualification, but with a therapeutic qualification, the therapeutic as a successor type to the charismatic.

What needs explaining is the nature of domination itself, and even the nature of the failure of domination by a charismatic. If charisma knows only inner determination and inner restraint, then its relation to success and failure is very different from what Weber's theory allows.

TEN

THE THERAPEUTIC WORLD IS WITHOUT DISCIPLINE AND WITHOUT DISCIPLES

THE NEED FOR LOVE IS A highly individual condition. Charismatics have been terrible simplifiers of that need; they satisfy it in its prototypal form, as a craving for authority, reorganizing its expression within a fresh content of ambivalences. It is only the therapist, as the anti-charismatic of our near future, who can discharge the craving for authority instead of renewing it.

As a soul-maker, by the penetrative depth of the interdicts, he represents himself as a new object of personal devotion; whatever his intention, the charismatic never discharges the craving for authority but mobilizes it anew whenever that craving is no longer gratified enough by the established institutions of an earlier charismatic thrust. This is the circle of our primal history, to be broken only when the therapeutic appears to the charismatic as an "ideal" type. Charisma, interdictory and transgressive in character, was first constituted by the reorganization and redirection of the craving for authority. The organizations of that craving have their own dynamics, however. I shall reexamine those dynamics under the twin rubrics of discipleship and discipline.

Joachim Wach elaborated on the nature of charismatic discipline in a way I have found a corrective to the Weberian emphasis on the charismatic in his revolutionary singularity. Wach writes:

> The consideration of the particular kind of *charisma*—upon which Max Weber has placed special emphasis in his religious-sociological treatise—is not decisive for us. We proceed from the experience of the respected personality; we will not only analyze it psychologically but

> understand it in its full intention by showing its meaning for the master's whole existence and the consequences of the master's life.
>
> The disciple's experience of the master is a social one [in the circle of disciples].
>
> It is in the union of friends in which the master finds the comfort and strength which allows the lonely one to experience human fellowship. The circle is the supporting and nourishing ground out of which everyone who belongs gains his strength; it is the concrete revelation of the "power" of the master, attracted by this power, moved by it, and defined through it, the disciples assemble in a circle around the master; followers and helpers assemble in ever wider circles. This is the power of which Goethe spoke, when he said that God continually remains active in higher nature in order to draw the inferior near unto himself.[1]

For the Western tradition of charisma, discipline cannot be dissociated from discipleship; but that association then contains the leader as well as his followers. In his remarks on the meaning of discipline, Weber makes discipline, in its rationally uniform expression, an irresistible power, lessening the importance of charisma. Yet, in discipleship, discipline as such is certainly not hostile to charisma. Weber is, in fact, talking about two different, even opposing, types of discipline: that of credal vanguards, on the one hand, and mass organization, on the other. Only in the latter do we find the exact executant of received orders, all personal criticisms unconditionally suspended, the toy soldier set like clockwork to his assignment. Even the discipline of devotion to a person, as such, may involve an orgiastic self-assertion, as in the cases of the mass organizational carrying out of transgressive commands that are themselves morally releasing and express the most basic hostility to culture in any form. In his neutrality, Weber could not analyze the fascinating leader or a transgressive figure, a liberator of the orgiastic and perverse from the constraints of moral order. There is a discipline of the demonic that, in its sudden appearance, whether in politics or other spheres of life, indicates failure of the interdicts.

For Weber, the decisive point about discipline is his second meaning; a force working against the charismatic relation in the discipline supplies the starch of routine; it must be "rationally calculated." Of course, "a charismatic hero may make use of discipline in the same way; indeed, he must do so if he wishes to expand his sphere of domination."[2] Both Christ and Socrates made such calculations, but Wach's point remains: that this kind of hero lives less in the "sphere of domination" than in a critical union of friendship. Without an interdictory-remissive model of heroism, Weber's "heroes" become subversively confused, for they conceal the real effects of their presence upon the conduct and character of their disciples. Transgressive leaders produce transgressive disciples; in their transgressiveness is the entire secret of their fascination, whether they be small-bore satanists, like Charles Manson, or absolute rulers of millions, like Stalin.

Discipleship may be of two types: first, a *"recognition,"* in the Weberian sense—i.e., a *reproduction* in the Freudian sense; second, a *recognition* in the Freudian sense that cuts off the prototypal authority figure series and is, therefore, therapeutic rather than charismatic—a relation in which the master prepares the disciple to be as his own master. The second type recognizes a "countertransference" that Freud himself feared to admit, and one for which Weber lacked a psychology; there is a dependence of master on disciples, a narcissistic love responding to love; thus it is in his group of disciples that the charismatic experiences those fellowships from which he draws the self-confidence to continue in his lonely course. Such a figure is acutely lonely and yet sustained within that loneliness by the support of those with whom he shares his new sense of superior obedience and to whom he espouses fresh communications of the interdictory form. In contrast, the "fascinating leader," as transgressive, has a far more direct power, for he encourages the releases of transgressiveness among his disciples. Discipleship in anti-credal groups is inherently unstable. The master eats up his disciples, and encourages them to eat each other up. This is the nature of direct power, and characterizes transgressive leadership.

Not enough is explained even by thrusting beyond the Weberian ambiguities of "charismatic recognition" to Freudian analyses of followers or disciples, with transferences of cravings for authority intact—indeed intensified. For there to be true charismatic recognition, there must be a charisma of perception. Such charisms of perception are the practice of fresh interdictory contents, communicated by the idealizing figure of authority. Only with the charism of perception, upon which the true charismatic must depend, does the charismatic relation become a stable point of departure, in a new moral direction. Yet, from the standpoint of the established but failing structure of authority, the true charismatic must appear Janus-faced; his fresh communication of the interdictory form may, in its contents, appear transgressive, as Jesus appeared to the Pharisees. In the context of the established credal organizations, the charismatic does face both ways, and draws his first disciples from the membership of that credal organization. The tension between the charismatic and his disciples is inseparable not only from their interdependence in the newly created interpretative group, but also in their common derivation from the older group. Often, the true charismatic must communicate by indirections subtle enough to hold his followers who, like himself, cannot make a total break from the prior interdictory-remissive contents.

But there is a basic difference between the true charismatic, as a soul-maker, freshly communicating the interdictory forms, and the false charismatic who is transgressive with reference to the interdictory forms in any content. The true charismatic proposes a relation in which the disciple is being prepared himself to become a master with reference to yet another disciple; thus a structure of charismatic authority is implicit in the original relation, so far as the nascent credal organization itself is to establish itself beyond the immediate relations of the true charismatic.

In therapeutic recognitions, however, similar in other respects to the liberations of disciples by the master, there is one fundamental difference: no interdictory forms are communicated. There may be a tactic of renunciatory commands which informs a therapeutic relation, but the object in the truly therapeutic process is a breaking of the prototypal form of authority, which is constituted by personal devotion. The truly therapeutic relation conduces to no faith, and certainly not in therapy itself. Freud shared the endlessly critical energies of the deidealizers who have dominated our thought and changed our sense of direction.

All faith, in the therapeutic view, is a particular fanaticism. To Freud, as our greatest theorists of the therapeutic, "the *furor sanandi* is no more use to human society than any other kind of fanaticism."[3] Every fresh communication of the interdictory form implies a moralizing attitude, and just that attitude implies everything to which therapy is opposed. In this precise sense, the true therapeutic is a transgressive figure, and yet communicates no particular transgressive practice. What joins the therapeutic and transgressive figures is, rather, that both oppose the intensification of interdictory forms, which is characteristic of the true charismatic. But this is to say, too, that the transgressive figure may be a false charismatic, while the therapeutic can only be anti-charismatic. As the prototype of the therapeutic, the therapist takes onto his role the emotion transferred from the original problematic figure, the authority figure, in order to destroy that authority figure, which is not at all what the transgressive figure does, in his "charisma." Transference, in the Freudian sense, enforces the transformation of the fixed emotion that has itself become problematic, especially because that fixed emotion attracts to itself credal motifs of renunciatory obedience, thus weakening the credal motif by entanglement with repressions in the Freudian sense. In a culture dominated by strong credal organization, it is the interdictory motifs that attract the repressions to themselves. This difference in direction makes all the difference: between a neurotic in a failing moral order and faithful membership in a successful one. In a failing moral order, the therapist himself becomes a figure in relation to whom a recognition resolving the failed authority figures can take place. The patient-follower projects onto the therapeutic figure, as distinct from the charismatic, qualities that belong to himself, not to the therapist. A therapeutic effect depends upon the recognition of the therapist by the patient as a cipher of old authority figures and their role in unconscious constellations of repression and interdictory motifs. Therapeutic recognitions resolve the transference. The patient becomes aware he has made the therapist an authoritative actor in the drama of his unconscious decisions about what is to be done or not done.

Political theater is a middle ground between charismatic and therapeutic recognition. Great politicians become actors who are intent on not resolving the transference relation: by the art of authoritative gestures, they induce the master in relation to disciples who are never to become masters themselves. Napoleon's pose, of hand tucked inside his waistcoat, was suggested to him by the actor Talma. Bertolt Brecht, in his play on Hitler, the *Resistable Rise of Arturo Ui,* has a poor, defeated hack of an actor teach Hitler how to strut about, how to fold his arms, how to appear utterly self-confident. The mantle of Caesar, and other less traditionalist arts of disguise, are most ambiguously related to charismatic and therapeutic recognitions; the rise of the mass media has brought these arts nearer the therapeutic mode, I think, inducing decision without personal devotion or its subsequent working out in credal convictions. *Jesus Christ Superstar* can only exist as a special theatrical irrationalization within a structure of rationalization. All leaders become theatrical figures, star personalities, with emblems of therapeutic recognition, to encourage action no less decisive for being without conviction, without credal meaning. A mixture of transgressive and therapeutic parodies of personal devotion, without intensifications of the interdictory form, now dominate both our cultural and political life. Religion and politics merge in mass theater. The mask is the face; it need not be taken off for there is nothing behind it—a sucking vacuum, that voracious emptiness that characterizes the power politician. Charisma becomes the art of masking effects, to destroy the charisms of perception; as all true discipleship becomes impossible, under these theatrical conditions, so all charismatic authority becomes false, which is the same as to say transgressive—against the interdictory form rather than an intensification of it. The gimmick itself becomes a masking affect, hiding the absence of genuinely personal authority in the older sense, an absent superiority. So, in our theatrical age, with everyone encouraged to act out, the interdicts themselves are treated as indecipherable old scenarios. The film, with its constantly changing perspectives, its very short clips, is the greatest technical device in aid of a therapy of recognitions, freeing decision and action from any depth of conviction. The positivist hope for new public ceremonials, of a reasonable faith, become the irrationalizing theatricals of anti-credal order. With the coming of the camera, both intimacy and monumental distance can become almost instantly sequential. The disciples of charisma become the technicians of therapy, specialists in changing perspectives; the carrier class of the culture of the therapeutic becomes these specialists in quick change; the decorum and deportment slowly built upon charismatic authority by credal elites gives way to the therapies of effervescence produced to create action all the more responsive for being without any of the old weights of conviction. The leader himself becomes weightless, a flickering shifting image. There is nothing of the old monumentality about him in this new epoch of recognitions. His portrait need not be painted; his status is as ephemeral as the memories of him. The old portraits carried tremendous significance as a summing up of social status and careers, a handing down of features to one's descendants, a monument of oneself to later ages. Modern portraiture was itself linked to the rise of credal societies in northern Europe; it may be interpreted as another mode of legitimation of established authority, but descent. Where no imagery is especially compelling, where the "charismatic" message itself carries no interdictory weight, then the medium itself becomes supremely important. In this special sense, Marshall McLuhan's doctrine is correct; his intuition is of a cultureless society, seen as a communications network in which what is communicated has no claim to endure and set the direction of our conduct. That the medium has become the message is itself a corruption of that Catholic tradition to which McLuhan belongs, in which a certain credal organization becomes the exclusive medium of the transformative message. The charisma of perception, in the main traditions of Western culture, constitutes acceptance of renunciatory discipline. The interdictory figure is swiftly involved, by his recognition, in the enactments of something other than self-will. That figure may be transgressive in relation to the culture through which he has broken, but transgressive only in this special sense: to mobilize fresh energies of obedience to renunciatory commands. To recognize the charismatic is to accept a militant truth, opposing things as they are, incarnate or taught by the charismatic. That truth resisted the constantly shifting self-affirmations of everyday life. "The world affirms itself automatically," Schweitzer writes, in his very personal conclusion to *The Quest of the Historical Jesus:* "the modern spirit cannot but affirm it. But why on that account abolish the conflict between modern life, with the world-affirming spirit which inspires it as a whole, and the world-negating spirit of Jesus?"[4] This is a superb statement of the received traditions of charisma from which our culture derived its energies. But the modern spirit is a clever spirit. It is learning how to make personal rejections of the world part of an endless affirmation of itself; loose to all symbolics, including the world-rejections preached in the sayings of Jesus, the therapeutic is developing techniques of recognition that make for a rapid turnover in the inventory of world-rejections. The Weber category of "recognition" needs to be so transfigured that, by that category, we know whether we are in the presence of a charismatic energy or yet another world-affirming therapy, with a dash of rejection, if good for nothing else than for old times' sake. Weber transformed "recognition" from a special kind of response to charisma, in our history, into the merely sociological force of worldly success; as a sociologist, he had no choice in this matter of recognitions, no matter than in the heterogeneity of the quality of charisma itself, viewed cross-culturally. Charisms of perception can never be reduced to their sociological explanation; no more can they be induced sociologically. They can only be induced by credal organizations, drilling the interdicts as in character.

Repression will then follow creed. Freud made the understandable error, in a time when all creeds were in death throes, of thinking that creeds followed repressions—that only happens to neurotics, who have some after-effects of creeds to contend with. The rationale of all soul-making procedures is to make the interdicts and remissions so correct that they become unconscious: "So that a complete automation of instinct is achieved—the precondition of any kind of mastery, any kind of perfection in the art and master, any kind of perfection in the art of living. . . . To that end the law must be made unconscious; this is the purpose of every *holy lie.*"[5]

Like unconscious processes themselves, credal organizations—interdictory elites—need time in which to work. Their work can only be done slowly, so that there is a gradual restriction of ugliness of manner, an almost imperceptible closing down of transgressive possibility, complete with rookeries for them.

Coming before his credal organization, the true charismatic can never make a profession of it, nor can his "recognition" record the varieties of possible successes, unless he and his people are "wandering," at loose ends, with nothing to do except get a fresh grip on themselves. A true charismatic, were he able actually to appear among us busy, distracted people, would have to deny our recognition of him. What else could he do, nowadays, except deny himself? Never fear. In the world as it is now, only transgressive or therapeutic figures can appear. In a deidealized culture, "the advancement of culture values . . . seems to become a senseless hustle in the service of worthless, moreover, self-contradictory, and mutually antagonistic ends."[6] The accepted "meaninglessness" of the hustle is exactly what the technicians of recognition, successors to the guiding cadres of our old credal organizations, can count upon. The carriers of our emergent cultureless society are calculators of ends now acceptable only in their ephemerality, their intrinsic worthlessness, their mutual antagonism.

True charismatics have been notable calculators of the transformative emotions they arouse among their immediate followers; read, for example, the *Crito,* in which one of Socrates' more ardent followers so far forgets the nature of his discipleship as to try to persuade Socrates to escape from prison, and so act against the central meaning of his gift. As the one man of understanding, Socrates knows better than to play the political game, with all its trickery, of which the prison break and life in exile are classical examples. Weber's assimilation of the meaning of discipline into military organization derives from his scientifically trained incapacity to accept purposes of the interdictory figure, the true charismatic, as the one man of transformative understanding, in the history of our culture: the chief purpose of the charismatic, in the truth of his message and example, has been to liberate his disciples from the outwardness of obedience and shackle them precisely to the truth of his message, as he himself has been shackled to it. In his teaching, therefore, the true charismatic becomes no greater than his disciples—and his disciples are such on their way to self-mastery. The special kind of obedience excited by a charismatic is both subjective and objective: to the person of the charismatic, and, at the same time, to those interdicts by which the charismatic submits himself to condemnatory judgment superior to himself. Discipleship is thus supremely objective in character; it is a devotion shared with the charismatic. The true charismatic is himself a disciple.

Weber split off discipline from discipleship and thus turned the charismatic discipline into its opposite, as devotion exclusively to the personality of the charismatic. But cults of personality are not charismatic organizations, not in our tradition, either that of the Christian or faith of Israel. Reducing charisma too often, as he did, to cults (originating in self-advertisements) of personality, Weber takes too little into account the devotion of the interdictory figure to his disciples. Take away this mutuality, and there is one fewer vital and enduring difference between Christ and Kurtz; every follower becomes a fool, in patches. Loved and unloving, in his chief sociological significance, radically politicized by Weber, the charismatic merges into Freud's prototype of a love object—a mere folly of overesteem—and worse: a narcissistic and very big baby, a bawling danger to all his indulgent craven parental followers, a voracious mouth of a person. Among all Weber's heterogeneous and contradictory authority figures, under the concept charismatic, the chief one is politicized and thus made over into a destroyer rather than savior.

But the interdictory figure is himself a disciple of the one necessary truth that he shares with his disciples. This liberating dynamic of submission—of the leader himself to the interdicts—makes of him the original and author of his disciples; Weber's mysterious "inner determinations" and "inner constraints" of the charismatic, as the father of a reborn cultural authority, are constituted by his own exemplary submissions to the old interdicts, which it is the unavoidable purpose of the charismatic to reinterpret and thus make strangely new. Without the discipleship of the true charismatic, there arises a fatal question about the truth of his charisma: self-deification merges with the sheer fascination of power. Thus the charismatic of our tradition is changed into his opposite, the man of power, an innovative figure of a "society" which confuses criminality with creativity. Weber in theory regularly permits this conceptual changeover, although it may be hidden behind the awesome never-ending waves of post-Protestant Germanic erudition, drawing the poor student swimmer, himself traditionless and directionless, in a vast "heterogeneity" of charisma. Weber's "heterogeneity" reduces to the leading character of a social order, viewed from a nonexistent vantage point outside that order, by scholars (and culture consumers) who live their lives on the fringes of violent disorder. Nothing remains to the leading personality except its expressive functions, the modern cult of voraciousness and vomit. "Heterogeneity" is the modernist voraciousness intellectualized, its ultimate refinement, harmless only as it remains buried in a historical sociology so erudite that it remains all but indigestible to the modernist reader, who is completely beyond all continuities of learnedness. Weber's learnedness serves to protect most of his young readers from the total subversiveness of his theory of culture. His theory of culture is so subversive that the question arises whether modern "society" exists, except as more or less "legitimated" winners and reciprocally ideologized losers in the interminable struggle for power—from which "religion" has been the ever-recurrent, ever-failing escape. How fond Weber is of putting every one of his key concepts inside quotation marks. It is the way of "Science," applied to the history of "Society," after all. But the effect on less inspired minds, without "Science" as their vocation and mighty fortress, of the "heterogeneity" of charismatic authority, as an empirical generalization, must be to decrease the resistance of militant ideals, truth, to the fascination of any transgressive figure. Thus does the rationalization of scholarship itself contribute to the prevalent hostility of the educated (*not* the uneducated) to culture in any form. It may have been better, for our inherited culture, had Weber never published. Not his relentless analytic power has been absorbed into the terrible excitements of order-hopping, with all the dead gods risen as god-terms, and Western society infected by fee-collecting swarms of academy-debased "prophets," every one of them hawking a therapy that, in their aggregate, leaves nothing in which we need disbelieve. Thus does the world-historical process of rationalization, of which Weber was a critical genius, lead, as he feared, to its own irrationalizations. "Heterogeneity" of "charismatic authority" is one conceptualized symptom of the triumph of the therapeutic. Our first task, as scholars and teachers, is to disbelieve in our own rationalized symptoms. Of course, Weber knew that much; will we, who could ourselves modestly among his successors, ever again know more? Weber thought that the acquisition of that superior knowledge, of a compelling and necessary trained incapacity that we, as scholars and teachers, were obliged both to acquire and to practice in our unique, constantly threatened institution: the university.

I cannot disagree. In fact, my practice of my agreements is my professional obligation. Yet there are masters and masters, disciples and disciples. The university should contain only one highly specialized form of that relation. Other institutional forms have existed (and continue to be reinvented) that are analogous to, but radically different from, the relation of master and disciple (if any such may be said still to persist) in the university. In those other institutional forms, too, personal devotion can acquire an objective character where the task of the master can also be to encourage a cognate masterliness to his disciples. On the other hand, such discipline can become the technique of dazzled obedience to commands, supported by the magic of proofs of power—or, as Weber calls it, in his dazzling neutralist, unassailable style: "rationally intended success."

But the devotion of discipleship, of master and disciple, cannot, by its own logic, evolve into the mass discipline commanded by a transgressive figure. In mass discipline, according to Weberian theory, there is no discipleship; inwardness of obedience is not the military form of discipline. An officer is not a master. Therapeutic discipline is yet another form, nearer the charismatic relation of master-disciple, and yet subtly opposed to that relation. For a disciple to become "as his master" is successively to receive that same gift of inward obedience enjoyed by the master. But in therapy, inward obedience is the problematic beginning, not the salvational end; the form of discipleship reinterpreted as fixation in the prototypal series of problematic relations to authority figures. To become free of the primary figure of the interdict, the father figure, is to end the series of inward obediences. Such inwardnesses stipulate Freud's grim psychohistorical conceptualization of the "neurotic": those no longer protected from the instinctual (intrapsychic) and the "transgressive" (interpersonal) thrust of desire after desire, isolates in their failing idealizations. The neurotic is "abnormal" in his inability to become thruster, or whose thrusts, ever "successful" in appearance, remain unrealistic (i.e., still inwardly obedient). A successfully discharged patient emerges with a certain immunity to discipleship. Nor, if he moves from the role of patient to that of therapist, does he, as therapist, become a "master," successfully to be freed from all old masters and to crave no new ones. The final purpose of all truly modern critical therapies, not only the psychoanalytic, is the abolition of the dependent and idealizing condition from which either the interdictory or transgressive authority develops. Like the neurotic in search of authority, the true therapeutic may engage in order-hopping, from one authority relation to another, complete each with its "godhead"; but the resemblance is deceiving. Such therapeutic movement does not repeat the old search; rather, it is a parody. All orders are there to be used, way stations on the road to nowhere, ways to keep going. What looks like the marvelous modern plentitude of orders, among which one can "choose," and make a "commitment," constitute our shopping center of therapies, in which no choice is sacred or final. A "therapeutic community" is a contradiction in terms. No therapy can admit the sacred, which is always and everywhere interdictory in form. No community can exist without the sacred; thus, too, we can dispose of that most naïve of early modern fancies, the "scientific community." No genuine science can include the sacred; the best a science can do is to be interested in the nature of the sacred, interpret it according to its own godheads and orders of conduct, analyze the consequences for conduct of memberships in its orders. The fact remains: in a true science, there can be nothing sacred. A scientist must live alone. A "scientific community" is a communication system of loners. The institutionalization of creative loneliness is a precious invention of modernity and under the most terrible threat to its precarious existence by youthful therapeutics, who, in their excited order-hopping, discover one "salvational" truth after another and threaten the one order from which they might analyze and clarify their order-hopping: that pursuit of science as a vocation which is the supreme (and only) justification for the existence of the university as a type of institution unique in its necessary autonomy from the demands of all the risen "gods" and their therapeutic "orders."

Once upon a time there were true and not therapeutic orders. The classical form of interdictory authority is credal and neither scientific nor therapeutic. The personal itself merges into the credal. Therapeutic freedom is constituted by the anti-credal resolution of the transference relation of authority. Thus, therapeutic organizations cut across all earlier credal lines—for example, all the divisions established at the time of the French Revolution between political "left" and "right." Such political (and social) divisions are now obsolete. Neither our political nor our social institutions have yet understood or admitted the anti-credal animus that dominates our common life; but that domination is more and more evident, as there is less and less "repressiveness" from which to dissent. In the emergent historical case, "dissent" itself, like "conformity," become interchangeable contents in the movement of (and for) life. A "conservative" may even put out more flags, but his patriotism is no less for himself than the "radical" who puts out only the black flag—or none. All creeds are now understood, however opposed to each other; they are ideologies—yours, mine, "the Establishment's," "the Movement's"; but never for itself. Rewrite the old credal sentence: "If I am not for myself . . ."

A very different "charisma" from the credal type originates in the discipline of war, among heroes, among warrior-leaders, and among ordinary restless moderns mindful of being for themselves whenever they go for anything. Even to the consciousness of his followers, this fighting type is a transgressive figure; his special virtues as a man-killer, from which his dominance derives, is hedged in with rituals of safeguards against his special character. The transgressiveness of the original man of power, his idea-typical business as a killer, must at least be poised, in its meaning, against the opposing interdictory figure—man-saver, messenger of life (as in the personal stories and state politics of the Old Testament) as the continuing form of condemnatory judgment, when seen from a superior height, as from the vale, at the same time.

In all cultures before our own, life-and-death combats are a transgressive motif, and to be hedged around with interdictory rituals. These ritual preparations and aftermaths have all but disappeared. A horrific fact stares at us: we can prepare neither for death nor for life-and-death combat. Under an avoidance of all judgments that carry interdictory significance, our moral passions are being flattened. Unprepared for him, by the very nature of our knowledge, we cannot raise, against our own "impulses" and their peculiarly modern engines of expression, that interdictory figure or one man of understanding who can transform our knowledge into the right conduct of life and a serene acceptance of death. The more we know, the more we fear everything that we cannot control and the more we hate everything that inhibits our endless movement.

Of course, analogies can be easily made between interdictory and transgressive disciplines. It is easy to see analogies between, for example, the spiritual exercises of Ignatius of Loyola, and the use of emotional means for mobilizing morale by military leadership. Yet the *Spiritual Exercises* aim to mobilize fresh renunciations of "instinct," or possibility, while the means used by military leadership are, in fact, the "instinctual" means: gratification in whatever particular, the promise of booty, women, etc. Military morale-building must be more directly representative of instinctual drives. Freud was unaware of his own analogy, in his letter to Albert Einstein, between the "warring state" and his conception of the unconscious; but his intuition was correct. Warring states are instinctually expressive; even modern electronically mediated aggressiveness is transgressive; therefore—the effect is known, beforehand, to be mightily destructive. Magical death-dealings, raised to a precise technology, like their institutional predecessor, holy wars, are supremely transgressive occasions, covered by interdictory shibboleths, slogans, and the abstract language of "body counts." Even the new model army of contemporary Israel, Moses much altered as Moshe Dayan, cannot always be expected to resist the terrific opening up of human possibility that is war. No side can be spiritual victor in a war; it is the most transgressive of all human events and yet one that no large-scale credal organization has been able to renounce when the death-dealing is in defense of its own interdicts. In this special sense, a period of war, in the degree of its violence, is a predicate of transgressive action and interdictory reaction. The canonical prophets represent precisely such reactions. Violence is the enactment of hostility to culture in any form. The task of culture is to contain violence in modes that will not subvert the most significant interdictory motifs: the general mode of containment is that in which an aggressive act becomes transgressive. Such general modes are necessary, in all societies, because acts of violence open up, rather than close down, sheer possibility; they are "instinctual" enactments. War is a collective transgressive act, with those who specialize, more or less exclusively, in the competent performance of that act. Compensatorily, such transgressive professionals may develop codes of "honor," interdictory contents applying to their specialized activity. But, despite such codes, warfare as such is culturally subversive, and its discipline transgressive. However interdictory the discipline of professional fighters may be, the ultimate activity of the military is man-killing; and such activity, the more it occupies a society, the weaker its interdictory forms, although that general weakening may be delayed or even reversed for a time by the reactionary charismatics, intervening on behalf of the godheads and their revealed interdicts. "Permanent revolution," like permanent war, must shake the interdictory structure and intensify individual transgressiveness in any society. Individuals go all out for themselves, as Mother Courage knows, when the conditions permit—even mother against son becomes possible.

But such catholicity of action can be more refined, less crude; it can appear as a cultural "ideal," a pursuit of wholeness, balance, the best of everything. Matthew Arnold's call for the best of everything, a many-sided (Hellenic *and* Hebraic, modern *and* traditionalist) "perfection" among the cultivated classes was itself an example of how subversive the most refined self-cultivation can be; the unconditional becomes conditional, all faiths become interesting—even significant. None are to be rejected. How does one reject the sea? Arnold, Strauss, and other religionists of culture argued their case against the supremacy of the interdictory forms in their own inherited culture before the modern period of mass discipline which began only with the defeat, among the cultivated classes, of that long yet unstable supremacy. With the victory of evolutionist assumptions, cumulatively transgressive in effect, all interdicts in quotes, our culture entered its present period of "principled" violence. Credal constraints are displaced by hypotheses about our psychophysical apparatus adjustable to their demands of the "outer world." But what is the "outer world"? It is instinct parading as reality, even as reason. In this period of endless adjustments, even man-killing, one of the two supremely transgressive acts becomes reasonable—and certainly rationalizable.

Weber was caught in this age of rationalization. To write, as he did, that "the discipline of the army gives birth to all discipline,"[7] is to dismiss the opposing connection, between discipline and discipleship. Rationalized transgressiveness becomes the primal form of social action. Man-killing, one of the two supremely transgressive fantasies, becomes enactable; "culture" thus destroys itself; the interdictory form of which culture is a substatiation in special contents of what is not done, and done, becomes the focus of critical attention by the most cultivation. The religion of culture merges with the religion of criticism. In this merged, early-modern religiosity—in the great epoch of Arnold and Nietzsche—both discipline and discipleship lose their connection to the renunciatory demands that are the organizing elements of culture. The content of transgressive discipline in mass organizations is finally a consistently rationalized, methodically trained, and exact execution of received orders. At the end of the religion of criticism, all critical capacity is unconditionally suspended; the actor is unswervingly set for carrying out commands—precisely because he is a mere actor, playing his role, not a creator of resistances with his own truth to set against the tempting assaults of experience. Superego and instinct reunite. The perfectly disciplined one will do whatever he is commanded to do. He feels no guilt. He is not immoral. On the contrary, because there is no one to transgress, he has acted in a way that satisfies his conscience. Many a modern "criminal" needs no therapy; he is a therapeutic already. The modern criminal is the real forerunner of our ideal type; politicized and publicized, he becomes the anti-credal incarnation of the charismatic—"called from below." The devil becomes our one living godhead, and he has many principles, by which everything can be rationalized.

Not only the discipline of the army, but also that of the factory, is transgressive. Rationalized man-killing is complemented by rationalized soul-taking in labor—what Marx calls "self-alienation." Weber verges very near this insight when he writes that

> The individual is shorn of his natural rhythm, as determined by the structure of his organism; his psycho-physical apparatus is attuned to a new rhythm through a methodical specialization of separately functioning muscles and an optimum economy of force is established corresponding to the conditions of work.

Self-alienation may be a much more precise term than "discipline." Weber rightly observes that "this universal phenomenon [of rationalization] increasingly restricts the importance of charisma and of individually differentiated conduct."[8] Disciplinary routines herald the movement toward machine men. To speak of devotion in its purposefulness, and according to its normal content as being of an "objective character," is to understand a man truly self-alienated, in a condition in which he cannot be himself, but some thing, directed from outside; there is nothing inside except the social organization "personified."

Yet even in that great didactic legend of a nothing personified, the golem is dangerously capable of acquiring precisely that creativity which, in the Jewish myth, made his creation the ultimate challenge of transgressive humanity against divine authority. "The real and not merely symbolic creation of a golem," by men in their knowledge, "would bring with it the 'death of God'!"[9] To create perfectly obedient creatures takes the created creature outside the interdictory form; to be willing to do whatever one is commanded implies an attempt to escape all command and attempt everything possible. Only monsters and geniuses, in life or art, live outside interdictory form. Gershom

Scholem quotes a great passage from a Kabbalistic text on the creative knowledge of man. "Truly, one would study these things only in order to know the power and omnipotence of their Creator of this world, but not in order really to practice them."[10] In certain forms of the golem legend, that thing is animated magically by "means of the names of God." By the twelfth century, at the latest, Scholem writes, the legend of that trespass upon God's creative power, by imitating it magically, as did the magicians of Egypt, who were thought to make creatures, was transformed, by a ritual *representing* an act of creation, into a mystical experience—to demonstrate the "power of the holy Name" and to accept the danger of our own powers of creation to ourselves and to the creator. Scholem concludes that the danger is not that the golem, become autonomous, will develop overwhelming power; it lies in the tension which the creative process arouses in the creator himself. Finally the golem ritual was transformed in the popular Jewish mind into the "making of an automaton,"[11] a demonic servant, without a soul. But this servant's discipline, according to the central attitude of Jewish culture, is the source of a terrible reversal. Once aroused and set in motion by the name of God, in faith,

> this guiltless creature can break loose from the credal inhibition inscribed on his forehead and then the servant becomes a Tellurian force . . . it rises up in blind and destructive fury. This earth magic awakens chaotic forces. The story of Adam is reversed. Whereas Adam began as a gigantic cosmic golem and was reduced to the normal size of a man [and given a soul] this golem seems to strive, in response to the Tellurian force that governs him, to regain the original stature of Adam.[12]

It is through our relentless mystique of change, making all interdicts swiftly changeable, that humans are in danger of puffing up their scientific knowledge to a stature that can only come at the end of a culture, not at its beginning. Durkheim's remarks on "the spirit of Discipline,"[13] however cautious, propose a typically critical relation to the interdictory form which can destroy it.

> If discipline is a means through which man realizes his nature [writes Durkheim], it must change as that nature changes through time. To the extent of historical progress and as a result of civilization, human nature becomes stronger and more vigorous with greater need of expression.[14]

We have progressed so far with our new earth magics that not only the content but the form of discipline changes "the way it is and should be inculcated."[15] Where sacred prohibitions were, there rational explanations will be—to children first of all and in our schools. "Society is continually evolving; morality itself must be sufficiently flexible to change gradually as proves necessary." This evolving condition "requires that morality *not* be internalized in such a way as to be beyond criticism or reflection, the agents par excellence of all change."[16] *Not* to internalize the renunciatory demands is to render them less and less demanding (until, in Durkheim's contrary hope, a new charismatic situation develops). But this is a perfect prescription for order-hopping, and for the endless consumption of god-terms. Durkheim failed to grasp that the critical capacities themselves were derived from those idealized authority figures without whom internalization does not occur. The interdicts must remain beyond criticism if criticism is to retain its moralizing form; otherwise, criticism itself transforms all its predicates, the godheads, into god-terms—and, in consequence, criticism itself becomes no better than what is criticized.

It is under this modern attack on the interdicts, as themselves the chief objects of criticism subverting the interdictory form as the very basis of all critical reflection, that the "charismatic" reappears as the herald of a new discipline. The ambiguities of the evolutionist position have never been more clearly exposed than in Durkheim's reflection on Christ and Socrates. "We have contended," Durkheim remarks, "that the erratic, the undisciplined, are

> morally incomplete. Do they not, nevertheless, play a morally useful part in society? Was not Christ such a deviant, as well as Socrates, and is it not thus with all the historical figures whose names we associated

> with all the great moral revolutions through which humanity has passed? Had their feelings of respect for the moral rules characteristic to their day been too lively, they would not have undertaken to alter them. To dare to shake off the yoke of traditional discipline, one should not feel authority too strongly. Nothing could be clearer.[17]

How stupid of Durkheim; how liberal. Both Christ and Socrates felt authority more strongly, not less; they intensified as they criticized the received renunciatory demands. Durkheim misstated the modern problem of authority in a typically modernist way.

> Doubtless, with some of the great moral innovators [he continues] the legitimate need for change has degenerated into something like anarchy. Because the rules prevailing in their time offended them deeply, their sense of the devil led them to blame not this or that particular and transient form of moral discipline, but the principle itself of all discipline. But it is precisely this that always vitiated their efforts. It is this that rendered so many revolutions fruitless not yielding results corresponding to the effort expended. At the point when one is rising against the rules, their necessity must be felt more keenly than ever. It is just at the moment that one challenges them that he should always bear in mind that he cannot dispense with rules. Thus the exception that seemed to contradict the principle serves only to confirm it.[18]

Durkheim's moral revolutionary thus emerges as our classical charismatic, the creative deviant who establishes new interdicts; he is the first traditionalist drawing a new enclosing circle of authority within which we can then make our interpretations free of the "yoke of traditional discipline." But, in his "scientific rationale" for discipline, Durkheim has not resolved the modern problem; rather, he merely dodges it by making a characteristically enlightened critique of the relation between the refined pursuit of pleasure as the remissive (and only) form of culture—for Durkheim offers no *active* alternative.

> In order to get through life, we have to accept many things without contriving a scientific rationale for them. If we insist on a reason for every-

> thing, all our capacities for reasoning and responding are scarcely enough for the perpetual Why? This is what characterizes those abnormal subjects whom the doctors call *doubteurs.* What we are saying about intellectual activity holds equally for aesthetic behavior. A nation insensitive to the joys of art is a nation of barbarians. On the other hand, when art comes to play an excessive part in the life of a people, subordinating in the same measure the serious things of life, then its days are numbered.

Like Weber and Freud, Durkheim opposes the various cults of experience. All three understood the hostility to culture in any form explicit in the critical movements against critical idealizations of restraint, and an effort to

> . . . provide us with a sense of the fullness of life. From such reasoning derives the veneration that so many 19th century writers accorded the notion of the infinite. Here we have the lofty sentiment, par excellence, since by means of it man elevates himself beyond all the limits imposed by nature and liberates himself, as least ideally, from all restrictions that might diminish him.[19]

None of the great critical theorists of the nineteenth and twentieth centuries could do more than generalize vaguely about the necessity to "specify fair limits of conduct that must not be transgressed."[20] But, as scientists rather than prophets, even the greatest critical theorists could generate interdictory energy against transgression. On the contrary, precisely their critical theories have contributed to that "malady of infiniteness" from which Durkheim concluded "we suffer in our day." For Durkheim, "the function of morality was to prevent the individual from encroaching on forbidden territory."[21] But, under a scientific or therapeutic rationale, there can be no forbidden territory. Even in Durkheim's generalization that a "moral system . . . is shaken" when it fails "to respond to . . . new conditions of human life,"[22] we get an echo of a position he is at pains to condemn—in which "it is life itself that makes its own laws; there can be nothing above and beyond it."[23] Again to subject the experience of life to law, so to inculcate the feeling of moral limit, law would have to codify and render variable a comprehensive interdictory symbolic; this means taking off the neutralizing quotes around "transgressions" so that punishment could again give its irreplaceable meaning to criminality. Modern criminality, like the revolutionary act against the state, has taken on transgressive authority—the modern champions of "life" renovate the "infinite" in the persons of those who act out their indisciplines. Our historical period has gone beyond "the malady of infinite aspiration" to the healthiness of universal theater, with each man encouraged to behave in a way that will demonstrate his freedom from any particular interdictory motif; either by hopping from one order to another or by rejecting all. Our most advanced social science and jurisprudence demonstrate ways to achieve this new freedom of life from law—and all orders except that of transgressive authority, which must end in grandiose bouts of violence, individual and collective.

How is a true and stable order to be recognized? First, by the reaction to offenses against it: interdictory authority can be compensated for transgressive behavior only by the creative act of severe punishment. Humans will know fear; much depends upon which fear they know best. The best knowledge is best conveyed in the preventive disciplines of inward obedience, under which social organizations, no less than individuals, are subject to condemnatory judgments and their punitive consequences. Law is a codification of necessary denials. Law loses to the experiences of life, criminality gains a peculiar prestige, wherever the transgressive sense, generated in the denials, has been sapped by the kind of "rational" criticism that itself admits the legitimacy of no denials and looks vaguely forward to a "natural man" who will emerge at the end of our cultural history—a "man" so "natural" that he will need no culture. The "natural man" at the end of history is the nineteenth-century genius stripped of his special gift, every man his own genius. This is the rationale of "doing your own thing."

In that form of law deriving from the authority of charisma, a society will not tolerate a retaliation that is less grave than the injury done. A disproportion between injury and retaliation may compound crime with injustice. For justice is a retaliation proportionate to the injury.

Thus, for a death—death; the only exceptions should be exceptional indeed. A culture survives on transgressive threats against it. In its organization of justice, culture copes with transgressive acts with equivalent retaliations. The progressive failure of modern law to maintain retaliatory principles is tantamount to the judicial support of transgressive action. The modernist lawyers work against law, and against all orders of authority: that is their perverse "vocation." But this only indicates the disproportionate influence of the law, as a profession, in a situation which must reach into the courts: the lawyers merely share in that widespread loss of a sense of evil which reflects the loss of interdictory authority, the absence of any secure feeling that something may not be done; that some act constitutes, in any but the "legal" sense, an offense; that, by the contagion of opening possibility, a transgressive act threatens the group and, thus defined as crime, must be rooted out. Without credal prohibitions, deep inside its necessary, modern casuistries, our laws cannot help us govern ourselves. The legal establishment of an offense as criminal must be in relation to the authority of charisma, expressing the inwardness of men. But a particularly decisive professional cadre is in a position to strike down widely desired punishments. Even where and when the rank-and-file of a culture feel that lawful retaliation against a transgressive act is necessary and right; and, moreover, want to ventilate their own transgressive impulses against those who have expressed them, a strategically placed elite can successfully support the transgressive movement, against the ordinary law-abiders. So, without "consent," punishment gives way to rehabilitation; rehabilitation gives way to decriminalization. The lawyers themselves advocate decriminalization, as a strategy against the revealed impotence of law, as if "public opinion" will not support severe punishment. The case is, rather, that the progressive lawyers are powerful figures among those educated, professional classes who have rejected a culture founded upon internalizations of critical authority figures. "Decriminalization" of the law becomes a logical expression of that celebration of possibility by which law, made outward as mere legality, becomes itself an instrument of permanent revolution against culture in any form. Thus, the enlightened solution for a rising rate of crime becomes a redefinition of crime. Indeed, transgressive criticism has its own "life" logic: the new evils to be rooted out from our midst are the forms of renunciation themselves. The interdictory motifs, in every specific, become, according to the transgressive logic of an endless criticism of all inwardness, not the language of our salvation—or, at least our willingness to abide by the laws—but the language that causes evil. The problem of evil is thus to be solved by breaking the repressive tyranny of good. There is a sense in which the progressive lawyers' ardor to "decriminalize" the law is supported by "educated" opinion; for the educated themselves hold the law in contempt, as a matter of high principle. The richly educated are our new spirituals, to whom everything should be possible. The guiding "principle" of their education has been the therapeutic dissolution of inwardness—of that graveness of character upon which depends the very existence of all law and every true order.

The majesty of law is thus thrown down by a breaking of the systematic relation between law and normative order. Weber, for one, makes the cardinal error of opposing charisma and lawful order because he failed to understand that interdictory motifs characterize both—and both precisely in their relation to each other, Weber's symptomatic analysis rightly culminates in his theory of modern domination through bureaucratic rather than credal organization as the historical successor to charismatic authority.

The famous "impartiality" of a bureaucratic order is easily coupled with a culture in which the basic particularity of true humanity, its partialness, gives way to a recognition of self as acting out changeable parts and partialities. The primary history of culture as a symbolic of moral discipline is ending in a symbolic of therapy, in which each recognizes himself in all his parts and gives no special authority to any. Marx called this nightmare vision "species-man"—a man without ideals that confine him to one interest or group over another. Against this vision of "man" liberated from all disciplines of credal partiality and group particularity—against the instinctual call from nothing to be everything, which means to experience everything and thus become demons—our truths of resistance to that can only be mustered from those gradations of charisma that take their beginnings in the intransigent particularity of the Jews. It is from the Jews, and from the history of their intransigence, that we can continue to unlearn the lies of a demonic universalism; alas, that Jews have been in the forefront of almost every movement away from their own truth of resistance to the call, from nothing, to be everything.

ELEVEN

ORDERS OF AMBIVALENCE

I MUST TURN NOW TO SOME EFFORT to solve the mystery of institution-building of the charismatic inwardness. Neither Weber nor his followers solved this mystery. There are hints here and there, as I have tried to indicate above, hints that consist largely of special references to the distress of the followers, but what is necessary is a conception that bridges that gap between—and indeed, the opposition between—charisma and institution; between character and social order. No such bridge was built by Weber and no such bridge is presented even in blueprint by his followers. So my task in this chapter is to present a schematic building of the bridge between charisma and institution.

Now, the fundamental proposition with which I begin is that institutions are the form taken by morality. The charismatic is the historic response to the failure of such an established form. The charismatic response is by reorganizing or, more precisely, by providing a focus for the reorganization of ambivalences in working form. This focus of reorganization has a very specific tendency—the charismatic reorganization of ambivalences is toward the reestablishment of interdictory contents to supersede failed interdictory contents. By contrast, the therapeutic represents a historic response to the cumulative failure of the charismatic to reorganize those ambivalences in working form and in particular to reorganize the interdictory contents. The therapeutic thus represents a break with all reestablishments of interdictory contents and therefore an attempted break with institutions as themselves moral forms. The therapeutic is engaged in an unprecedented effort to resolve the ambivalences themselves. It is in fact a freeing of the ambivalences. In this sense, therapeutic institutions would have to be considered under the paradox of their anti-institutional character. Therapeutic movements in modern Western societies help us understand what T. S. Eliot was groping for when he made his baffled, and yet profound, remark, in "Notes Towards a Definition of Culture," that "we have to consider whether the modern world is hostile not merely to any particular antiquated form of culture, but to culture in any form." Eliot makes an equally baffled remark in the same essay. "So far," he writes, "have we proceeded already in the direction of a cultureless society that the foregoing considerations may seem to most readers in these times to be of only trifling importance." But how shall we understand a cultureless society? How is a cultureless society possible? What are its institutions? They are precisely these institutions which would not put morality into a form. The whole tendency of therapeutic movements is thus anti-cultural. In a third remark, again largely of bafflement, Eliot suggests the possibility that "the highest achievement of a culture may mark the end of that culture." Now here, I don't think Eliot is appealing to some Spenglerian analogy with the organic life-cycle. What he refers to is the highest achievement of modern culture and that highest achievement is precisely its critical and analytic thrust into the interdictory contents themselves. Thus, the highest achievement of modern culture may mark the end of that culture precisely because it breaks with institutions as morality put into a form.

But the purpose of this section is not to try to find answers that T. S. Eliot did not find for himself. I am interested, rather, in solving the problem of bridging the conceptual gap between charisma and institutions somehow deriving from the charismatic thrust, and charismatic innovation. My first resolutive hypothesis is that the charismatic serves to induce and stabilize ambivalences. Those ambivalences have been brought to the surface by the failure of the established symbolic; they usually consist of emotions of love and hate, the inducement of the ambivalences itself exists in a way that further stabilizes them, and this induction and stabilizing of the ambivalences is characterized by the deep installation of new interdictory motifs. As soon as these new interdictory motifs are introduced, then the institutions are already on their way to creation, for, in the name of the charismatic message, the institutions become the organizing forms of the ambivalences based on the supremacy of the new interdictory motifs. In its origins, these new interdictory motifs are broadcast by the charismatic, who, by his sheer presence, by his kinesthetic effect, induces a new order of ambivalence. Indeed, ambivalence is not only at the very center of his appeal, but, more precisely, the stabilization of that ambivalence is also at the center of his appeal. The charismatic stands for a particular resolution of the distressing instability of the ambivalences, for the suppression of one side or the other. The therapeutic resolves the ambivalences differently—he stands for the expression of both sides, for a ventilating of the ambivalences. Both charismatic and therapeutic thus engage in a kind of resolution of the distressing ambivalences, but the important thing here is that the conceptual bridge between the charismatic quality and its institutionalization may be specified by this reorganization of the ambivalences in the charismatic by the installment of new interdictory motifs at a deep level of character structure of both subject to the charismatic message, and among the therapeutics by an effort toward the resolution of the distressing ambivalences through a dissolution of the interdictory motifs themselves. This leads back to a deeper understanding of the inner quality of charisma as a way of resolving ambivalences otherwise grown intolerable in their intensity. Institutionalization may be considered the formal resolution of these ambivalences—their stable administration in relatively stable systems of love and hate. The Christian church is the model institution of such a stabilization of ambivalences, with a new distribution of interdictory remissive motifs; the Communist Party, under the Marxist motifs, is another example, and Maoism, where the Communist Party in this sense treats the bourgeois and the Jew as remissive figures and proposes new interdicts. This is quite clear in the Maoist version of the party symbolic, with its distribution of interdictory remissive motifs that center on the remissive figure of the American and his "running dogs."

The therapeutic does not stabilize the ambivalences by reestablishing interdictory motifs of a deep level; rather the therapeutic expresses the transgressive side of the intensified ambivalences and raises the transgressions themselves to a principle of action. Successful institutionalization means the stabilizing of ambivalences, ambivalences grown so intense that they cause distress, as Weber says. The church represents such a stabilizing of ambivalences with no interdictory motifs deeply installed, but including the inversion of the status of Christ's own people as a remissive focal point for the stabilizing of ambivalent feelings. Anti-Semitism is thus a part of the Christian institutional structure, and the charismatic thrust is carried in precisely the movement from Jesus himself to the church of both the interdictory motifs and the new remissive motifs, with special reference to the Jews and to, first of all, Jesus' relation to the Jews, and, second, the relation of the gentiles to the Jews. The institutional meaning of the charismatic is in the form and content of the ambivalences constituted by particular interdictory and remissive contents, as these are communicated successfully by the charismatic to his first circle of followers.

TWELVE

THE MYSTIQUE OF THE BREAK

DOSTOYEVSKY'S FIGURE OF AUTHORITY SAT SILENT, in his prison cell, while his tolerant and wise successor did all the talking. The Grand Inquisitor embodies the historicist pathos at its best. Jesus had had his say. "Genuine" charisma occurs, after all, only as a brief outburst, yet fundamental as a stimulus for institutions that would then take on the responsibilities of methodically reorienting conduct. Institutions may be "burnt-out shells" of the emotional charge generated during a charismatic moment in history, but the shell is a very different one because of the original creative flame. All this seems right enough, within the Protestant pathos of Weberian theory: a short, hot burst of transformative personality and a long cooling of that personality in its various institutional molds, for the care of the weaker spirits who come after the great one. For Sohm, this long cooling began, in the Christian case (the one and only case, for a good Christian such as Sohm) *after* the period of the "charismatic organization"; for Harnack, the cooling begins *during* the period of the charismatic organization. Weber follows the Harnackian irony rather than Sohm's theological romance, which was a scholar's version of Reformation primitivism, a final academic idealization of the first organization of any profound change and its institutionalization, not its originality but repetitiousness. Then, after the knowing recognition of the repetitive character of authority, there is the possibility, raised by the logic of Freudian theory, of a genuine break: from the authority of charisma, with its covert dependence upon historical precedent, to the freedom of therapy, which has no historical precedent. Therapy is the "charismatic" originality by which modern men can break with the past. But if this break is to occur, then the mystique of the break in the Christian tradition, at the end of which came Weber and all nineteenth-century liberal scholarship, needs analysis in the theoretical forms already established here.

The Protestant inheritors of the Christian interdictory symbolic psychologized it relentlessly; this is most evident in Schleiermacher's god-term, the "Infinite," which reflects the consciousness of modernist man breaking away from all interdicts. Weber, at the end of the Protestant era, need no longer psychologize; rather, he can *assume* its effect upon his readers, and as a scientist, systematically ignore the difference between remissive and interdictory motifs in all symbolics of authority. What Weber did was essentially to neutralize the traditional Christian theory of justification, by grace of which members of this credal order were freed from the world penalties of their transgressive sense, and so kept orderly, by transforming that ancient Augustinian theory into a sociological theory of "basic *legitimations* of domination."[1] Here, in the Weberian translation of justification into legitimation, is the basic step beyond the Protestant pathos, and its implicit psychologizing of authority into the transparent world of the therapeutic, in which "legitimacy" itself becomes legitimation and can be managed (for others, as well as for oneself). There were other intellectualizing movements toward a resolution of authority, however, more naive than the sociological.

A genius for dismantling the justificatory dynamic in all structures of authority has also surfaced, in a way which Weber could also take for granted, in evolutionist social theory: by way of the distinction between magical techniques and religious ethics. In Frazer, pig taboos, for example, are not distinguished from the structure of luck concepts which are in fact remissive motifs. Steiner points out that "thousands of Jews who have had to choose between death and a meal of pork have chosen to die; nevertheless, the notion that mentioning the animal's name would impair their success in a gainful occupation is quite alien to them."[2] The fact is that there is no remissive motif accompanying the interdictory one, which is entirely associated with the so-called pig taboo in the faith of Israel. Positive and negative magic—the negative being ritual avoidance behavior or taboo—is not equivalent to remissive and interdictory motifs. In fact, the very liberal distinction favored in nineteenth-century scholarship, between positive and negative magic, merely obscures and contextual structure of interdictory and remissive motifs. One fine British anthropological critic of the evolutionist arrogance put it in its proper place in his essay "Is Taboo a Negative Magic?"[3] There R. R. Marett says that "magic," as Frazer uses the concept, is "not a savage concept or institution at all but merely a counter for the use of the psychology that seeks to explain the primitive mind, not from within but from without."[4] For the liberal evolutionists, magic became a pejorative counter-concept, from which the superiority of the advanced cultures over the primitive, the entire interdictory motif structure of primitive culture could be dismissed with a wave of the scientific wand. Marett clinches the case beautifully against the evolutionists: "As well say that taboo is 'superstition' as that it is 'magic' in Dr. Frazer's sense of the word. We ask to understand it and we are merely bidden to despise it."[5]

Further, the notion that a "taboo" is a kind of vitality which leads straight to the notion of charisma as a kind of vitality is thoroughly destroyed by the orthodox Jewish scholar Steiner. He writes:

> The assumption that taboo-breaking may release either good or bad power—to put it in a slightly more adult form of speech, destructive or protective power—is a flight of the imagination. Those tabooed things which have "the power to cure no less than to kill" are not typical, they are rare. To say that the use of a tabooed thing for protection or cure means the release of good magic or mana through the breaking of the taboo is nonsense. The taboo is not broken! *The beneficial power of the tabooed object is secured through special ritual behavior which is in every case protective.*[6]

Blinded by its rationalist optimism to the interdictory structure of all working symbolics, nineteenth-century social theory assimilated the interdicts themselves, as Weber does, too, implicitly, to an acceptance, as "original" and "creative," of a transgressive action. The man of "genius" became a charismatic and, for those privileged to study from hypothetical vantage points above the eternal wars of culture, charisma developed a "heterogeneity" that could be positively criminal. Even in Weber, for all his knowledge of the fact that no social scientist can jump out of his cultural condition, modern sociology has been constituted largely by an implicit attack on all interdictory symbolics. Moreover, in Weber, the special theory of *modern* society is that all interdictory symbolics are being "rationalized" away. Yet he knew, in the double thrust of that knowledge, that there can be no interdictory symbolic without an order of transgression. "Charisma" could occur in modern as in traditionalist culture.

Lévy-Bruhl writes:

> To us a transgression signifies the violation of a rule, the infringement of a material or a moral law. The terms "crime" and "punishment," like the term "transgression," run the risk of misleading us. To us a transgression signifies the violation of a rule, the infringement of a material or a moral law. To primitives, it is an abnormality, something unusual and unheard of—a sinister omen, the manifestation of a malign and unseen power. So, too, when we are told that sorcerers, incestuous persons, violators of certain taboos, etc., are "punished" with death or some other penalty, we see in this (and it is thus that most observers have understood it) the "chastisement" of their crime. We are introducing here the concepts that are current among us; our point of view is juridical and ethical; that of the primitives is above all mystic.[7]

It is hard to know what Lévy-Bruhl meant by "mystic," for, indeed, it appears to be opposed to the "rational," as punishments among "primitive" peoples are opposed to the "rational" concept of punishment.

But there is no rational punishment. As soon as one asks for a rational punishment, one is already subverting "punishment." In this misconception of punishment, not only has the theory of transgression been more or less abandoned, but, more important, the transgressor has been transformed into a charismatic authority. This is the implicit tendentiousness behind the Weberian assumption that a charismatic is he who makes a break through the established order.[8] It is in this romantic individualist sense that Weber understands the prophet, as a leader making personal some antagonistic and particular struggle between contending social strats and interests. A time of acute social struggle is a time of many transgressors; in such a time the feeling of danger is heightened, even unbearable. Thus that transgressiveness that is popularized in the modern social order as freedom and creativity, generating the energy for a break through the social order, is in fact itself the course of the popularity of the term "charisma"—completely reversing its meaning in the inherited structure of our culture, as the reassertion of authority "from above." The modernist assertion of "charisma" from below is not of authority but of the destruction of authority. The term "charisma" has become literally meaningless, for it covers an endless assertiveness against authority as such—i.e., against culture in any form. This raises the problem of conceptualizing the modern militant, as against the premodern fanatic, which we shall do in another place.

In this place, it is more appropriate to ask yet again: What is a transgression? Steiner defines transgression brilliantly as "the passing from inside—outside the individual's rights or competence."[9] Transgression can be understood more sharply as the failure to observe an interdict. I do not mean to intellectualize the phenomenon of transgression; the failure to observe an interdict is the failure to act in terms of an interdict. The liberal evolutionist discovery of "taboo" was in effect an assault on interdicts as "mere superstitions." This assault was carried on a crest of rationalist optimism that old patterns or interdictory contents could be taken for granted and left unprotected, as forms emptied precisely of their oppressive and "savage" interdictory contents. The transgressive and destructive rationalist dichotomy and intellectualist dichotomy between magical and religious ethics is the one from which the concepts of progress and evolutionism, the general evolutionist theory and that variety of it that includes, at its twin climax, Freud's theory of neurosis and Weber's theory of world disenchantment. By the time of Freud and Weber, however, there remained no arrogance of superiority by the "secular" theorists at the abdication of the "religious." The mystique of the break had taken on a grim apprehensive air, a realization that the opposing of the ethical to the interdictory, which was assimilated to magical ambivalences, was itself profoundly destructive. Both Weber and Freud saw that the movements of the nineteenth and early twentieth centuries led nowhere; but theirs was not prophecy—rather only knowing apprehension. In the old order of culture, where the godheads had not yet been intellectualized into god-terms, prophecy arose to defend precisely the old order, to recall its historic meaningfulness; prophecy was a foretelling of a return, however primitive, of authority; interdicts already established but threatened were supported by "prophecy." The prophetic "future" was not a future in our sense of "future" at all. Freed from the binding membership in an order, within the power of his science, Weber could only prophesy a world without prophets—or, even worse, when viewed from within the old culture, of false prophets. These new prophets of the end of prophecy, of a past beyond recall, themselves become leading agents of a unique breakthrough; not to a "higher" order, but to a rationalized and systematized meta-order, an order competing against all religious ethics, which in turn would allow all manner of order-hopping, for the rationalist order implied no specific ethic. When all ethics can compete, and none win or lose, then disorder becomes institutionalized, with the erotic as the functional equivalent of a religious ethics in a rationalized world—a permanent remissive modality in a new and unique culture: one without eternal and superior interdicts. It is in this foreseeable condition that all prophecy becomes false, for none becomes alone necessary and therefore true. It is in this foreseeable condition that "charisma" has become a popular scientistic rhetoric of the mystique of the "break" which itself breaks the essential interpretative, and ordering, link between meaning and authority. Through such mystiques of the break, the new prophet of meaninglessness, whether in science or art (e.g., Dada), becomes that strangest of prototypes: the permanent revolutionary, the one who will not leave his presence behind to oppress his posterity.

In this hidden context, within which both Weber and Freud need to be put in order to be understood, all prophecy becomes a "break with the established order,"[10] rather than the break that compels a return of the old order reinterpreted. Weber was the last and most brilliant flower of this irony, which can only encourage all those who are not active analysts of the false prophets to follow them.

The origin of this irony is certainly in the Protestant pathos: in its hatred of priestly culture and its ecclesiastical organization; this hatred was "sublimated," so to say, into scholarship by the Protestant intellectuals, as charismatics of the armchair, critics of the priestly organization, revolutionaries of the act of research, making their monographs into life-acts. Nietzsche was the sublime representative of the late Protestant hatred of the church and its "civilization."

The mystique of the break has spread widely and has taken on the most "reasonable" rhetorical form. No mystagogue was more reasonable than Alfred North Whitehead, for example, when he wrote, in his little book on symbolism, that progress in society is always of the prototype of the break and, in fact, any genuine progress all but destroys the society in which it occurs. Whitehead's passage reads as follows:

> It is the first step in sociological wisdom to recognize that the major advances in civilization are processes which all but wreck the societies in which they occur: like unto an arrow in the hands of a child, the art of free society consists first in the maintenance of the symbolic code, and secondly, in the fearlessness of revision to secure that the code serves those purposes which satisfy an *enlightened reason.* Those societies which cannot combine reverence to their symbols with freedom of revision must ultimately decay either from anarchy or from the slow atrophy of a life stifled by useless shadows.[11]

Notice the mystique of the break in Whitehead. If that mystique is politicized, it leads straight to a rationalization of those monopolizations of office, by one party or movement, which can serve "major advances in civilization," or the "urgent needs of Society," or "the People." The "maintenance" of the *new* symbolic code, the mystique of the break itself, justifies any exploitation of the dominated on their own behalf by those with the science of Advance at their fingertips—and with the foreknowledge that you cannot make omelettes without breaking eggs (or Serres vases) or, in Whitehead's pallid English, "all but wreck the societies in which they occur." I can see no "reason" why Whitehead's dictum should not serve to justify the liquidation of the Jews or of all literate Poles, or an abolition of all university courses that do not respond to the urgent "needs" of Society, state, city, or particular ideological group. But the art of a *free* society consists, first, in the maintenance of its symbolic as a hedge against the mystique of the break which Whitehead here proposes. In a free society, all monopolizations of office must be under the most severe interdict. The state, and its professionals, aided by their scientists, of whatever persuasion, cannot be allowed to be the agency of "major advances in civilization." A variety of institutions must be protected against the politicizing of such advances, so that they may advance—or retreat—in their own, perhaps indirect and circuitous, ways; or not at all. Above all, that unique chatter of "enlightened reason" must protect itself from those "major advances in civilization" by recognizing precisely that such advances are often politicized and can wreck the university as a unique civilizing institution. The "enlightened reason" of the university, and its students, must recognize the wrecking dangers of political passions if they are built into its internal order. But this is certainly—especially in its appeal to enlightened reason—a secular version of the mystique of the break, which is to be found more systematically elaborated in Weber. From the terrible failure of such first-rate evolutionist theorists as Whitehead and Weber to realize that the art of free society must consist, first and last, in the continuous redevelopment of a symbolic code which is primarily interdictory in character derives that evolutionist mystique of the break which is itself the successor to the Protestant mystique Reformation. A free society cannot exist with a symbolic that is not primarily interdictory. This is what the critical and liberal evolutionists of the late nineteenth and early twentieth centuries had forgotten, with the forgetting of their own (religious) past in order to live more exclusively in time passing. How can there be a vital theory of transgressions without an understanding of the fundamentally interdictory character of the symbolic code that must not only be maintained, but continuously reinterpreted? But note: the revisions that occur within the symbolic can only satisfy "enlightened reason" when they are within the hermeneutic circle by which the order of human action is itself limited. That is what both Isaiah and Plato realized: that they were links in an interpretative chain. It is not until practically our own time that these links have been broken, our cultural life destroyed in the name of what has proved to be a deadly new bioethic, by some of the best minds in our culture—including such disparate names as Weber, Whitehead, Frazer, Freud, and Georges Sorel.

Yet Freud understood, more deeply than any other breaker of the chain of interdictory interpretations, that any such break could prove fatal to our culture. He knew that all interpretations are necessarily revisionist rather than revolutionary, that they must be severely limited and cannot be combined with unlimited criticism of the symbolic. Reverence is the symbolic itself: of such a deeply interdictory character as to limit the freedom of revision. Whitehead appears to have missed all those points. Weber understood—and Freud even more deeply, with an intuition that came out of his long wrestle with the meaning of Moses and with indeed the meaning of the faith of Israel, the chosenness of Israel.

Freud sees the correct meaning of charisma and prophecy in his description of Moses as an interdictory figure, asserting an interdictory symbolic. Even so, Freud's ambivalences toward the meaning of his own psychological Jewishness were so powerful that he stands as the culminating figure of what he, in his nineteenth-century critical rationalism, called the "taboos"; those "taboos" emerge from their quaint ethnological usages of the nineteenth century into our century as the irrational units at the dynamic nucleus of individual and group "neuroses."

Freud's dependence upon Robertson Smith and on James Frazer was far from accidental; he completed their historic mission of intellectualizing hostility to their own repressive culture. I must briefly expose the hidden dynamics of that hostility which was intellectualized first as "comparative religion" and last as "therapy."

The Protestant mystique of the revivifying break through the failing interdictory-remissive order expressed itself, at its reforming extreme, as a yearning for an eternally self-renewing charismatic order of life which needs no administrative and disciplinary agencies—i.e., no interdictory institutions. The Protestant pathos opposed the state's aspiration to become a church and the aspiration of the Roman church to become a state. This double opposition led to a paradoxical self-destruction. The Protestant mystique led to a cultural condition in which there were no churches assertive enough to contain and limit the state's aspiration; the mystique degenerated into that therapeutic individualism called "religious experience" that William James tried so desperately to understand, in his Gifford Lectures, before the time of the therapeutic had quite come. The one institution that remained intact, almost to our own time, to oppose the ultimate consequences of the original Protestant mystique of the break, through constantly "newly" founded institutions, through the varieties of religious experiences to the politicized therapeutic individualisms now sweeping the Western educated classes, was that unique invention of the West, the university. Nowadays, it is the university, that last institution surviving in some significant way as a temple of the intellect, still in the reinterpretative service of the necessarily interdictory order of culture, that is under the most furious attack for not being a therapeutic and/or revolutionary institution; small wonder, the university, as a temple of intellect, is the one place in which the forging of further links in the chain of interpretations can take place. The modernist revolution is therapeutic and modernist therapy is endlessly revolutionary: both aim to spring the individual outside the confines of all hermeneutic circles and their institutional expressions. The university, not the state or any church, is the last bastion in defense of culture.

Freud's genius enables us to refine the mystique of the break into a dynamic theory of its contradiction, for the breakthrough is sealed and the process of its interdictory institutionalization begun, in the defeat of the charismatic himself. Thus the old mystique of the break is transformed by a psychohistorical theory of the conservative working out of the transgressive sense. Even as the charismatic organization preserving and elaborating that transgressive sense (i.e., in Freudian theory, the nearly Mosaic cadres) preserves the memory of the interdictory figure—who has been rejected, denied, even murdered by the transgressive masses and *their* leading cadres—his particular symbolic, with its interdictory animus, gathers strength in the face of the suffering intensified by a common life outside the sacred interdicts. As the horrors of freedom become more oppressive, the charismatic organization (which may have to bide its time for generations) succeeds, in part, in imposing its interdictory discipline upon those many who remain recalcitrant to it. That is the formal inner structure of Jewish history and character: it constitutes the return of the repressed Mosaic interdicts, preserved after his murder, by those of his disciples who founded the Mosaic cadre. The character of the Jew, as a psychohistorical type, was formed by its dependence upon the delayed promulgation and practice of the original repressive idealization of the character of Moses in the form and contents of his "law." Thus, by a further development of Freudian theory, the mystique of the break shows its right and proper conservative aspect—and so cancels out the mystique itself. Every true charismatic break is in fact a double break: the second break is the true *charismatic and organizational* one, in which the interdictory figure is imposed as a constraining symbolic, upon the larger recalcitrant group which has broken with the original figure in his own time and presence. *Charisma* thus represents, in its pure form, a *return* of the interdictory symbolic, never its dissolution. The modern mystagogues of the break, therefore—the R. D. Laings, Wilhelm Reichs, Kurtzes et al.—represent not charisma but its transgression, not the return of repressive authority but the orgiastic and murderous revolt against all authority, against both its personal and institutional form. These revolutionaries are false charismatics. They have a certain authority—the authority of what-is-not, of death, of destruction, even as they preach "Life." One sign of the exhaustion of culture, in any form, is the rapid multiplication of these false charismatics and of their order-hopping "followers," most particularly in the educated classes.

The earliest sociological clue to false charisma is its association with magic. Weber makes this association both primitive and, as primitive binding, in his conceptualization of a magical act as one that distinguishes between the greater or lesser ordinariness of whatever phenomenon is in question.[12] For Weber, this criterion of extradordinariness is at the center of both acts, magical and charismatic. Charisma is a mystery in the same sense that magic is mysterious; "mystery" is sociologically understood under the categories "*ordinary*" and "*extraordinary.*" But, after sociology lays hold of it, charisma becomes the last mystery. It is a name repeating the "breakthrough" mystique itself, but without authority—more precisely, against authority in any right and proper sense. What "authority" "charisma" acquires is entirely transgressive and anti-cultural. It is what-is-not, the authority of death, of violence. Now we can better understand why Weber, without himself quite knowing why, treats charismatic authority as a mainly political rubric. He thus expressed his intuition into the transgressiveness of all modern charisma, emerging as it does out of a rationalizing world. Add to "mana," "orenda," or the Persian *maga,* a modern term from which all the magic of modern charisma derives, the organization of violence in the modern state around the personality of one transgressive figure. Weber did not live to see his inchoate vision fleshed out in apparitions of Stalin and Hitler. No matter: it is they who have held, in themselves, those "extraordinary powers" to which Weber referred the ancient gift.

Magic and charisma are so close in Weber's discussion of charisma that the former must always be seen as the predicate of the latter. The modern charismatic is a magician of power, himself struggling for power—and for nothing except more power, which is the capacity to deal death to others. Thus does our ancient, moralizing charisma become superseded and evolve into something that contradicts its older meaning. Thus charisma becomes the conceptualization of an endless "breakthrough," a dynamism that is transgressive without the classic interdictory peripety.

Weber distinguishes between charisma of two types—the first is a "gift that inheres in an object or person simply by virtue of natural endowment."[13] By "natural endowment," Weber may have intended sheer vitality, which is disturbing in any culture. Such primal vitality Weber calls *"primary charisma,"* and asserts that it cannot be acquired by any means. The other type of charisma, Weber writes, may "be produced artificially in an object or person through some extraordinary means."[14] One thing is clear: "natural endowment" must itself be extraordinary for the many do not have it—nor even the few; it used to be reserved for some rare individual. What is so disturbing about modernity is the impulse in it to democratize the occurrence of primal vitality, which is repressed and/or sublimated by culture in any form: Weber's theory of the "magical" origins of charisma is one type of this disturbing bioethical thrust against all culture. Both primary and what may be called, by implication, secondary charisma emerge now under the culturally subversive category of the *"extraordinary,"* which is the category of the magical. Weber goes so far as to assume that charisma of the second type—the type with which he is primarily concerned—can be developed "only in people or objects in which the germ already existed, but would have remained dormant unless evoked by some ascetic or other regimen."[15] At once, Weber implies a tension within charismatic authority, between its primary and secondary properties, its transgressive germ and interdictory elaboration. For it is by virtue of some interdictory discipline, as the extraordinary means by which charisma is produced artificially, that charismatic authority can exist. Weber fails to recognize the significance of his own assertion that the extraordinary means by which charisma is generated must be of a disciplinary order; there can be no charismatic order without an original discipline. Nor is there any implication in which he can understand the difference between primary charisma as a natural endowment and which may have no implication of order through self-discipline and that charisma historically more significant, secondary charisma, which is in fact dependent precisely upon disciplines—which must have interdictory properties. Skating over the surface of his own conceptualizations, Weber regularly avoided those implications which would destroy his theory of the original heterogeneity of charismatic authority.

How is it that a sociologist of Weber's subtlety and penetration did not see the implications of his own key conceptualization, the "artificial production" of charisma through "extraordinary means" generated by an "ascetic or other regimen"? Secondary charisma must be dependent upon the effective working of the interdicts, without which there is no discipline. I suspect that Weber's insight at this point was blocked by the hidden and uncontrolled tendency of his sociological theory of charisma; the mystique of the break is perfectly clear in the evolutionist assumptions that dominate Weber's theory. These evolutionist assumptions have long encouraged a certain trajectory of movement—from simplicity to complexity, from individual to organization, from mysterious force to rational system, from magic to religious ethic. But even more economical than any of these historical trajectories is the mystique of the break itself, which, in Weber, following his Protestant predecessors, takes on the peculiar tension of a theory of charisma in which the *primary* (magical) germ remains ever present to explode the *secondary* (institutional) husk. Yet the Weberian theory of charismatic authority derives from the (Sohmian) Protestant doctrine of *charismatic organization,* not from *charismatic impulse;* from *cult,* and only indirectly from the transformative character that becomes the object of the cult. Sohm's charismatics of the primitive church can be seen as magical characters, their organization doomed to defeat them, as Harnack thought, by a more and more elaborate institutional disciplining of their gifts—as Paul already implies in 1 Corinthians. Weber takes over this Protestant pathos in all its tension: his charismatics are loci of creative instability, around which the primary transgressive and secondary interdictory properties of all authority—past, passing, and to come—are reordered. The evolutionist trajectory may then be further complicated by the Freudian model of guilt-victory; it is only in the wake of his defeat that a true charismatic, through the organization of his fresh defenses of the received culture, can triumph. The idealizations of the charismatic thus remain "original," carried as they are by a vanguard or by disciples (i.e., a moralizing elite), which cherish and maintain the interdictory motifs personified in an ideal figure or lawgiver until such time as they are strong enough to reimpose leadership upon a recalcitrant but putative followership in distress for lack of precisely such restrictive guidance.

There are implicit links between Weberian sociology and the Nietzschean vision. Nietzsche, too, operates according to a mystique of the break. His charismatic is in fact Superman, the psychological man of the future, who also does evoke some ascetic discipline or regimen but evokes it to break that repressive interdictory symbolic which has in fact returned from defeat by heroic anti-priests in order to dominate society primal time after time. Nietzsche, Weber, Freud: all were prophets, in their own reluctant and apprehensive ways, of a breakthrough to end the repressive cycle of breakthroughs, an endlessly critical breakthrough that will resolve that craving for authority figures themselves which first plants the germ, the "natural endowment" of undisciplined vitality by which alone the authority of old disciplines can be broken. Once the mystique of the break becomes endlessly critical, as it does in Nietzsche, the way is prepared, not only for Weber and Freud, but for a wholly new anti-authority figure, the therapeutic, with his interminable criticisms of all deeply installed disciplines. Then, and only then—after Nietzsche, Weber, and Freud—are the theoretical predicates established for the displacement of authority by therapy as the form of action. Weber sensed the tension of transgressive and interdictory authority; yet he nods to the supremacy of the interdictory form, to grace given from above, by an authority superior to the figure of authority himself.

Thus

> Even at the earliest stage of religious evolution, there are already present *in nuce* all forms of the doctrine of religious grace, from that of the *gratia infusa,* to the most rigorous tenet of salvation by good works.[16]

How this sentence follows from the earlier is not at all clear. The connection is not made, as is so often the case in Weber, but the clue is in the assumption of evolutionary stages in religion; *in nuce* there is present all the varieties of interdictory content; "religious grace" would appear best interpreted, I think, as authority from above. All charisma in its "religious" form is interdictory. There is the stunning and regular implication that all charisma in its "political" form is transgressive.

That implicit tension, both within the Weberian conceptualization of charisma and between its two spheres, the religious and political, is summarily stated in *Politics as a Vocation:*

> There is the authority of the extraordinary and personal *gift of grace* [charisma], the absolutely personal devotion and personal confidence in revelation, heroism, or other qualities of individual leadership. This is "charismatic" domination as exercised by the prophet or—in the field of politics—by the elected war lord, the plebiscitarian ruler, the great demagogue, or the political party leader.[17]

That charisma means at once authority from above and from below makes a significant change in the Weberian assumption of original "heterogeneity"; that "heterogeneity" is now seen to mask a tension Weber himself could not face; he was an anti-charismatic theorist, no less than his greatest anti-charismatic predecessor, Nietzsche, or his great anti-charismatic contemporary, Freud. In the Weberian meaning of political charisma, as "grace" from below, Weber's own theory becomes therapeutic, a way beyond the tension implicit in all structures of authority, from their very beginnings to their ends. What is important in Weber's description of the relation between charisma and grace is that he associates all forms of *religious grace* with the presence of some interdictory discipline or "other regimen," as he puts it.

We see now, too, what charisma, as the concept of religious grace, has meant in Western culture. In that culture, authority right, or justified, is the gift of an authority superior to the receiver of the gift; in that very concept of a *gift*, authority always finds its own right and necessary limit. Only so can a figure of authority perform salutary acts. Thus, in all forms of the doctrine of religious grace, authority is self-interdictory; in all forms of the concept of charisma politicized, authority may imply a "discipline," but it is no longer self-interdictory. Service to the political "cause" of the charismatic, by that figure, serves to cloak service to his authority. Weber shared the privileged knowledge of the early Christians, that the political work is "governed by demons."[18] *Charisma,* in the Weberian usage, thus disguises a tension of which he was aware, and about which he could not but despair; the two main revolutionary forces in the world appeared to him never less equal and never more irreconcilable. Although he saw it coming, Weber did not live quite long enough to see with what base abjectness Nietzsche's disgusting priests, custodians of the interdicts, who were Weber's religious professionals, would themselves adopt the second meaning of charisma and become not only small-bore prophets of orgiastic behavior, but go even further and transform themselves into rhetoricians of therapy. Thus, after Weber's time, in therapy, the "magical" element, to which he refers relentlessly, has been rationalized. Of course, therapeutic rationalizations of orgy have their priestly precedents.

> To this day, no decision of church councils differentiating the worship of God from the adoration of the icons of saints and defining the icons as mere instruments of devotion, has succeeded in deterring a south European peasant from spitting on the statue of a saint when he holds it responsible for the favor he sought did not materialize, even though the customary procedures were performed.[19]

Quite unself-consciously, Weber pursues a line of attack that implies the present movement beyond all priestly interdicts to the priest as therapist, with the role of peasant played by id.

We shall have to learn to read backward, from the modern mystique of the critical breakthrough that announces the end of our civilization to the mystique, shared by Weber, of all innovative breakthroughs. Note that, for Weber, the entire dynamic of abstraction—that fateful dynamic that has finally led us to this end point in the history of civilization—does not begin under the aegis of any particular economic condition, but occurs in a variety of particular transgressive and interdictory motifs, such as the belief in spirit; but, in most advanced societies, that spirit belief is linked more closely to a transgressive rather than an interdictory figure—or, to a figure made interdictory by his successors, and his original magical (i.e., transgressive) powers suppressed. Even as late as Dostoyevsky, the Jesus figure and his opposing successor, the Inquisitor, are far more ambiguous, in their meaning, than Dostoyevsky consciously intended. Jesus appears as a magical presence, quite outside the law; by his very presence, he practices the oldest vocation, to which the second oldest is intimately related. The magical personality is "naturally" or "supernaturally" endowed with charisma as transgressiveness. In this sense, Weber implies that civilization begins with a transgressive figure of authority and his defeat—at least, his defeat in that magic aspect—by his chosen successors, who transform his magic into method. It is the charismatic who makes the break between one form of consciousness and that form involved in the process of abstraction itself. But the process of abstraction is also a process of moralization, however qualified and compromised. It is not the charismatic who binds his followers together in mutual constraint, but they themselves, under the justification of his name. Sanctification always follows justification; method succeeds magic; interdicts surmount their transgressive predicates.

It follows, in Weber's implicit logic, that the primordial form of communal association is itself an institutionalization of the subjective condition of the charismatic, his ecstasy. The institutional form in which charismatic ecstasy occurs is the collective orgy. It is orgy, as the original institution that parallels that character of the transgressive figure, as the predicative conditions against which the charisma induced by "artificial means" develops, as if by reaction.

Yet to assume orgy as the primordial institution is already to assume something not only occasional, as Weber says; in its being occasional, orgy must represent a break from another form, which must be interdictory. All logics of transgression argue against the primacy of transgressive behavior; primary charisma is to secondary as "impulse" (in John Dewey's devastating critique of Freud) is to habit. The conception of orgy as the primordial form of communal association cannot be separated from the assumption of interdictory forms that obtain between transgressive occasions. The returns of the repressed interdicts thus become charismatic; grace always returns from above. In expressing the two elements, the magical character of the charismatic with the emphasis on the beginnings of the process of abstraction and the institutional form of the orgy, Weber pressed in a special way only one mystique of the break—and that mystique opposed the established, failing one. His mystique of the transgressive (political) break itself depends on unspoken and unexamined assumptions of other and prior forms which are important precisely because they are so neglected in the Weberian conceptual structure. Weber dismisses these interdictory forms (or rather, encapsulates these interdictory forms in failed "religious rejections of the world" as it is, and diminishes them) in his casual and dismissive reference to the "routine demands of living." Because of the routine demands of living, the layman may experience ecstasy only occasionally, as intoxication, Weber tells us; the basic religious thrust is described as having "orgiastic purposes." Weber is caught in his own interpretative circle. Religion and religious communal forms are associated with the mystique of the transgressive break, and with the reaction against that break. But this links the rise of religions too closely with transgressive motifs, which seems to reverse the entire thrust of his own theory of religion as organized, essentially (i.e., originally) against orgy. How Nietzschean to make the original communal experience the orgy, and the original artifacts of culture alcohol, tobacco, or similar narcotics, and music. Weber presses the Nietzschean polemic against priesthood into the service of a sociological theory of religions as primarily transgressive and only secondarily interdictory, following the division between "primary charisma" and secondary. But this leaves the creative organization of culture to secondary charisma.

A good Weberian could argue that the present transgressive forms in modern culture, again of orgy and narcotics, of the dance, of rock music, are a rising of the old gods, a reassertion of the basic transgressive thrust of communal association, while the interdictory thrust has been weakened by its association with the "routine demands of living." The interdicts have grown banal, while the transgressions seem "novel" and "natural." The interdictory demands, grown routine, are less and less deeply installed; rationalization of them makes depth unnecessary. Thus the historic success of specific interdictory contents appears to lead to their failure. When the time-weakened interdicts fail, old transgressions reappear. Orgy can have many new names. This is a key point in understanding the mystifiers of the break. We are now witnessing, and some of us are participating in, a rising of the oldest gods, and some of us are precisely, in our most progressive sciences and therapeutic arts, engaged in one or another effort to practice the oldest of all vocations: that of the professional necromancer. The present upsurge in the interest in and practice of magic represents the return of the most archaic form of self-expression and, in its orgiastic aspects, of communal transgressiveness; in sex and violence, the erotic and the political, fascination and power, converge. We feel and see the effects of those convergences, but understand them so poorly that many of the most "radical" among the most "educated" preach, again, some orgiastic message of going back, for the sake of going forward, to the most primitive forms, forms that permit the breaking of the stultifying routine of the demands of contemporary life.

The contemporary unconscious polemical thrust of Weber's symbolic is never far from the surface of his style and thought. It is astonishing when, on close examination, one finds Weber associating the rise of religions with the conditions or orgies, yet that is in fact the case, and the link figure is in fact the magician's charismatic experience. Charisma is thus, in its most primordial form and content, transgressive in character and purpose. The transgressive character and purpose of charisma, entirely politicized, is the point at which all understanding of the Weberian mystique of the break, as the expression of the more general modern transgressive mystique, must focus.

A key sentence in understanding the Weberian mystique of breakthrough comes immediately after a rather futile discussion of the variety of meanings attached to the conception of soul and spirit in primitive religions, and also the importance of personality. Weber writes: "What is primarily distinctive in this whole development is not in personality or super-personality of the supernatural powers, but the fact that *new experiences* now play a role in life."[20] Here is the mystique of the break without qualification: "new experiences" are the cultural property of transgressive symbolism. The very newness of what is experienced, and the role they "now play," carries a transgressive meaning. Interdicts are never new. Now I am prepared to indicate the true significance of the first time Weber refers to interdicts: when he is describing, in a rather perfunctory way, funerary prescriptions, with special reference to the hands-off attitude toward the property of the dead lest the survivors rouse the envy of the dead. Weber writes that one of the interdictions during the mourning period is related to the occupancy of a benefice or inheritance. The implication here, and more generally, is that the interdicts are themselves functions of this process of moralizing abstraction by which things take on meanings of threat and benefit of danger and favor that they do not have in the so-called natural world. The interdicts are treated as secondary and protective expressions of that process of abstraction set against the "new experience" itself. Moralization is thus linked to a secondary charisma; authority is reactionary. All forms of moralization are in this sense secondary rather than primary. Yet culture begins with an interdictory germ hidden in the magical mind, in imagining that "behind real things and events there is something else, distinctive and spiritual, of which real events are only the symptoms, or indeed the symbols."[21] This passage has a further pathos; it is the charismatic task of science to penetrate this magical art which is mediated through the new experience, and see that there may be nothing behind real things and events which are distinctive and spiritual, which are symptoms, or indeed symbols, that is not itself, in its significance, a figment of the reasoning imagination. At the end of our cultural epoch, the charismatic experience, rendered scientific, defines itself.

Weber goes on to say that under this assumption that behind real things there is something else distinctive and spiritual: humans felt they had to make "an effort" to influence, not the concrete things, but the spiritual powers that express themselves through concrete things. This was done through actions that addressed themselves, through things, to spirit or soul; this address was made by artifacts of meaning, i.e., symbols. Naturalism was thus swept way by a flood of "symbolic actions."[22] Such symbolic actions reached their highest point in our culture in the creations of those artifices of eternity we call poetry and prophecy, to which sciences and therapies, with their short intense lives, are our successor artifices. As scientists, as therapeutics, we know no eternities—and scarcely any meanings authoritative enough in their duration to be called "true." But it is the task of our anti-charismatic sciences to break with the old searches for meaning and not allow the new science to be swept away by a flood of "symbolic actions." This is the clear import of Weber's own science and of the peculiar "neutrality" which he claims for that science precisely in the study of culture, within which no human can be neutral. So the epochal reign of the necromancers, the priests, and their successors, the scholar-scientists, may end. For

> The occurrence of this displacement of naturalism depends upon the success with which the professional masters of the symbolism use their status of power within the community to impart vigor and intellectual elaboration to their beliefs.[23]

This displacement, of naturalism by symbolism, leads to the establishment of a master class of symbolists. But we are at the end of the era of interdictory symbolization. The mission of scientists and the therapists excludes the creation of "new values" and even the idea that science or therapy can, or ought to, provide them. Under Weber's terms, a scientist may be the analyst of all symbolisms and their social structures but the prophet of none. If priests are the first intellectualizers of meaning, organizers of authority, then perhaps we sociologists may be, rightly considered, the last intellectuals, organizers of meaninglessness, way-makers for our immediate successor-type, the therapist. What sadness there is in Weber's sociology, with its central dependence upon the analysis of meanings; that analysis of meanings is patently dependent on a dissolution of those meanings through the analysis itself. By "meaning," in its original necromantic sense, Weber can only mean "beliefs." Like every therapeutic discipline of social science, sociology stands beyond "belief," as a continuing analysis of "belief" dissolving "belief." Weber's interpretative sociology is powerful in the precise and special sense of its ultimate meaninglessness.

We can now see more clearly what is wrong with Weber's conception of objectivity, for objectivity in culture is the truth of resistance—what Kierkegaard called *subjectivity.* Every cultural truth must be a truth of resistance, bracing the practitioner even against his meaningless science; for that science cannot organize his life and direct his conduct except as a scientist—and then only in a special way and within a special kind of institution reserved to that activity. With what arrogant, swift dismissiveness our student militants of the social sciences now dismiss the scientist and his institution. His special calling—which is disloyal to all positions, to all points of view, to all political passions—within the temple of intellect is scarcely understood; he is rejected as a mere specialist, when, in fact, he is doing the most difficult thing in the world—following truth, a slave to its every twist and turn, expressing himself entirely in this quest for it. It is the highly specialized objectivity of the scientist, then, that is the condition of his risky business: an endless expressional creation, the "acute constructional." Into the objectivity is poured the subjectivity of the scholar. It is only by the blinkered intensity of his devotion to the "acute constructional" that a scholar can resist the assault of experience, politicized and moralized for him—before him. Weberian "objectivity" is entirely misconceived by its student denigrators. His "objectivity" is a tremendous passion, related to a strong character—one so strong that it can bear the burden of acting within the limits imposed by every acute constructional.

In the character of the scientist, Weber signifies an ineffaceable mark, a graveness, as Kierkegaard called it, which is entirely against the contemporary conception of personality as endless expressional creation precisely without understanding. In the modern world, only the scientist achieves a new truth of resistance to the strain of observation and to the assault of experience: the "acute constructional" gives the dedicated scientist the only way in which a character can remain both stable and fresh and retain a freshness to communicate. In this sense, objectivity of the scholar or scientist is anything but neutral and passive. It opposes success with understanding, will with intellect, doctrine with the analysis of doctrine. But this understanding is only possible, as a discipline, to those happy or unhappy few who are called to it; the vast majority of others can only inquire after and return to their old gods—or subject to quite another kind of endless expressional quest: in sex, in politics, finally in any and all therapies.

Our culture is dying mainly because the objectivity it requires is destroyed by constructions of endless expressional quests that have nothing true and resistant about them. The "acute constructional" is the most demanding of all experiences. Far from new, such an experience, of the feeling intellect, can only take place as our interpretative link, in a chain of interpretations, continuing from time past into time passing and to come. Then the mindful human can and will mean something—and, moreover, learn obedience to that meaning. All meaning is under authority. No grace lives except that it decides and enables us to know that decision. That known decisiveness implicates no success, or any recognition of its superior claim by others; it is made for personal use that may yield no public profit. In Weber, the scientist, too, is called; his character is graven and his intellect so passionate that it resists every sacrifice of itself. This is the latest truth of resistance, which is no neurosis or specialized bêtise, but a "vocation" beyond the comprehension of any person who does not have it. Such a vocation, to clarity, gives a freshness to appearances, a tragic distance between self and its engagements. Those engagements—to fight, always in an erotic fever—are, as Henry James knew, vulgar and empty enough. Maisie, somehow, is gifted with a certain inner distance from her necessary erotic engagements, yet without deception. For her concealments are not deceptions. Her self-concealments save her in the midst of her total dependence. That total dependence is erotic and yet in the midst of the erotic circles of ill will in which Maisie lives, she somehow knows enough to know the truth of resistance; she does understand what she cannot say. Compare this moral sense with that of so many militants, on behalf of practically everything, who have acquired the horrifying habit of saying what they do not understand. Thus the new cant of "truth," "honesty," "change." Weber helps us understand how this new cant arises, out of a too deliberate, too direct quest for "meanings." Then more and more things and events are encouraged to

> assume significances other than the real potencies that actually or presumably are inhered [inherent?] in them, and efforts [are] made to achieve real effects by means of various symbolically significant actions.[24]

The endless expressional quest develops its acute constructionals on the cheap. Analysis becomes formula-thinking; complex and delicate threads of thought become incantatory slogans, quick to take over minds prepared only in the receptivities of distress and impatience. This becomes a "charismatic" situation. The intellect sacrifices itself, progressively, to the demands of action. Marx is succeeded by Lenin; Lenin is succeeded by Stalin. The struggle for power takes over both ends of the charismatic connection, between authority and meaning. Authority becomes "legitimated" power—but power, nevertheless. The charisma of intellect is sacrificed on the altar of power and its movement.

But charismatic authority means something quite different when it is not thus politicized. Weber tried to grasp this other meaning, in its special authority. He writes:

> The first and fundamental effect of religious views upon the conduct of life and therefore upon economic activity, was generally stereotyping. The alteration of any practice which is somehow executed under the protection of supernatural forces may affect the interests of spirits and gods. To the natural uncertainties and resistances of every innovator, religion thus adds powerful impediments of its own. The sacred is the uniquely unalterable.[25]

Here is the crux of the anti-political meaning of charisma: the interdicts must be uniquely unalterable—i.e., sacred. Political charisma is patently anti-interdictory, a form of desacralization—in short, transgressive, which is so utterly opposed to the "uniquely unalterable" that transgressives treat their acts, rightly, as the ultimate alternative to the sacred. In a culture without sacramental action, indeed, transgressive motifs have displaced interdictory as the most demanding. We scarcely remember what the sacred is—and are horrified by what we have forgotten. Anything that is uniquely unalterable horrifies us even to imagine, because we are living, acting transgressions. We are the horror. To us, nothing is sacred—not even the feeling intellect. Thus, we are living witnesses to the collapse of the last sacred institution of Western culture, the university, that temple of intellect of which Weber was the last truly great and knowing high priest. Now, the youth of the university, its novitiates, are dancing their final war dance against the uniquely unalterable, the vocation of intellect itself, ordered in its special institution, the university. The students caper around the sacred, in its last phase, producing their heroic little frenzies, mimetically anticipating their victory, the death of the sacred, by calls for ever new "values" and "criticism," produced on order by the university, for immediate political use. When the temple of intellect is destroyed, or converted to use for political change or as a therapy center, then truly nothing will be sacred; everything will be alterable. Luckily, for me, I shall not live to see exactly how a cultureless society works. It will be the horror personified in numerous Kurtzes; I see them, in their adolescent years, all around me now, thinking they are bringing a higher civilization to us white brutes.

How can we be saved from these dancers? Perhaps the sacred is also the uniquely enduring. The connection between authority and meaning may again be reformed, its unique unalterability may yet dawn on the dancers themselves, especially after they are assaulted by the creatures they must let loose to rule over a world in which nothing is sacred.

The "uniquely unalterable" cannot come to us as a man, however; it must come to us as a God, who is "forever identical with himself, and possesses all individual things, controls them, or somehow incorporates them all within himself."[26] When God reappears, then cult will follow. In earlier crises, as Weber writes, the gods were frequently constituted as an "unordered miscellany of accidental entities"; then they could be "held together fortuitously by the cult."[27] In such a happy time, cults could actually precede their gods, because the world was not yet "disenchanted" (another use of desacralized). Since nothing—or almost nothing—remains of the sacred, not even intellect, cult can no longer precede God. Nor can we pray for a return of the old gods. They have all risen, for therapeutic purposes, to occupy the time of increasing numbers of order-hoppers. We cannot pray, for prayer was a magical coercion of the gods and a god is defined in turn as the monopolist of the disposition of this capacity to magically coerce others. Charisma, in its mediating capacity, was misconstrued as a magical talent, a way of coercing some superior power and therefore the nearest thing available to man to that superior power. Such acute misconstructionals fed straight into the doctrine that knowledge was power; prayer was succeeded by scientific technique, unfailing instrumental routine. The treatment of prayer as a magical coercion of the gods is the true beginning of scientific technology, which knows no inner constraints. Intellect becomes sheer instrumentality.

At least in prayer, as in the interdictory disciplines that produce charisma in an object or person, a superior power is itself recognized. Prayer, as Friedrich Heiler points out, was at once the provenance and givenness of the grace of God. The existence of a uniquely unalterable being, in the interdictory form, is basic to the meaning of prayer; stripped of its magical coercive power, prayer can only inquire. Prayer can never rightly require; it only responds to requirements. Thus, although it appears paradoxical, we could only pray to what is uniquely unalterable in its superior and interdictory capacity, to which the prayer must always respond confessionally, as if guilty of the death of the sacred, by some doing of what-is-not.

As charisma represents Weber's special objectification of the mystique of the break, so, for all the religious, prayer is the central phenomenon of religion pointing to the existence of an interdictory demand to which men relate themselves in the very activity of prayer. What Weber sees as institutional dynamics ordering the nature of prayer, as for example to ancestral gods, what he calls "sacral motivations"[28] are another form of the interdictory process without which no culture can exist. For example, dangers to blood relatives would be intensified if someone from outside the blood relation, for example, the stranger, were to offer sacrifices to the ancestors of the clan; the sacrifices would lack authorization and might bring down the revenge of the ancestors. Sacral motivations are themselves a psychological predicate for the interdictory process.

> The decisive consideration was and remains: who is deemed to exert the stronger influence on the individual in his everyday life? The theo-

> retically supreme god or the lower spirits and demons? If the spirits, then the religion of everyday life is decisively determined by them, regardless of the official god concepts of the ostensibly rationalized religion.[29]

The decisive consideration is whether the theoretically supreme God can be altered by the lower spirits and demons. This is the implication of Weber's own dichotomy and this alone leads to the consideration of most primitive dualism as decisive for the future of culture. The theoretically supreme God is interdictory in character, while the lower spirits and demons are transgressive.

The sacred being uniquely unalterable, however, it is from the lower spirits and demons that an innovative cultural thrust should occur. That this is not the case in, for example, the culture of ancient Israel does not deter Weber in his hidden Nietzschean polemic against the sacred.

In the tradition of the mystique of the breakthrough, Weber proposes, against the charismatic and his historical enactor, the prophet, that whipping boy of all progressivist theory, Nietzsche's favorite villain turned into culture custodian, the priest. Just as it is upon the interdictory sacerdotal figures of divinity that rational economic practice and the secure regulated hegemony of sacred norms in the community depend, so the priests are, in Weber's theory, "the primary protagonists and representatives of these sacred norms."[30] Priests are opposed to charismatics, one innovative and protecting the sacred norms, the other attacking them. It is a convention of both rationalist and romantic polemics, and Weber uses the convention for all it is worth, supported, as he thought, by the "higher criticism." This enlightened and scholarly detestation of priesthood is perfectly standard and not at all unusual to Weber. The work of the Nicene Creed, writes Harnack,[31] was a victory of priesthood over Christian popular faith. How standard was the hatred of priesthood to the scholarly mystagogues of the break. The contrast that Weber regularly sets up is between priesthood and varieties of priesthood—"Striving for a firm regulation and control of life"[32]—and those individuals (and their schools), classes, and movements whose appropriate reaction to the supernatural powers or to life itself is the plunging into the "disorderly irrationality" of "faith and adventuresomeness." We are warned by Weber that "we shall find this same contrast significant in many other contexts." This "disorderly irrationality" of fate and adventuresomeness, Weber calls "charisma." On the other hand, *secondary* charisma is established precisely by an ordering of irrationality precisely in those asceticisms and abnegations that appear characteristic of a striving for a firm regulation and control of life. The contradiction, one of many, is never resolved in the Weberian canons. "Charisma" achieves its present sinister aspect in a passage the inner meaning of which I doubt Weber himself grasped. He writes:

> Whoever possesses the requisite charisma for employing the proper means [for coercing the spirits into the service of man] is stronger even than the god, whom he can compel to do his will. In these cases, religious behavior is not worship of the god but rather coercion of the god; and invocation is not prayer, but rather the exercise of magical formulae. Such is one ineradicable basis of popular religion, particularly in India. Indeed, such coercive religion is universally diffused, and even the Catholic priest continues to practice something of this magical power in executing the miracle of the mass and in exercising the power of the keys. By and large, this is the original, though not exclusive origin of the orgiastic and mimetic components of the religious cult—especially of song, dance, drama and the typical fixed formulae of prayer.[33]

Here is charisma revealed in its transgressive modern meaning, not only in its political property as a thrust for power, but also as a therapeutic capacity to coerce all others into the service of oneself by the singular assertion that there is absolutely no connection, except magical (read therapeutic, or erotic), between meaning and authority. Nothing is uniquely unalterable. Everything can be used to alter things as they are and need to be. Thus, song, dance, and drama become new instruments in the struggle for power. Even self-sacrifice would thus become a magical (or therapeutic) instrumentality in the service of coercive power. In a world without meaningful authority, all "acts" are coercive. The gods, Weber tells us, also need the soma juice of the sorcerer-priests, the substance which engenders their ecstasy and enables them to perform their deeds. This is the ancient notion, he continues, of the Aryans as to why it is possible to coerce the gods by sacrifice. It may even be held that a pact can be concluded with the gods which imposes obligations on both parties. This was the fateful concept of the Israelites, in particular. Weber continues to hold to the very complex notion of charisma as, at once, the subjective condition of fundamental change (his mystique of the break) and of a fresh access of power. Change and a fresh access of power: a partnership of concepts full of sinister promise for our nearing future, in a cultureless society.

PART THREE

The Triumph of the Therapeutic over the Charismatic

THIRTEEN

EVIL ANGELS HAVE ALL BUT SEIZED CONTROL OF THE WORLD

ORGANIZED BELIEF PROTECTS AGAINST transgressiveness no more than organized intellect. On the contrary, in that struggle of powers, the interdicts are the more easily broken, not least by those who possess office charisma. Anyone knowledgeable enough about himself as an organization man knows that evil angels have all but seized control of the world; everything is explained by my deeply felt theory of transgressions except the way out. In politics, organizations of the faithful can transform them into evil angels, both when they recognize and refuse to recognize the special sphere that is the political. For Weber, political religions are special structures of legitimate violence; those legitimations may be significantly supported, or even integrated, into a faith, as in the Hindu order of life.[1]

In a curious way, Weber, in *Politics as a Vocation*, repeats the renunciatory motif of the Christian rhetoric: that, inwardly, a politician must take power as if he took it not, maintain an inner distance, avoid "vain self-reflection in the feeling of power." The alternative is that "sudden inner collapse" of the "mere 'power politician,' " when we can "see what inner weakness and impotence hides behind" all the "ardently promoted cult . . . to glorify him."[2] But how can the striving for power by a political leader, and the renunciatory demands of an interdictory figure, first against his own strivings for power, come together? The notion of 'political religions' derives from the Catholic doctrine of structural charisma, from which Weber derived his concept of office charisma. This theory belongs to the analysis of how charismatic authority is transformed into organizational controls of the sacramental form.

The abbot who presided over the extermination of the city of Béziers during the Albigensian Crusades, chanting "Kill them all, God will know his own," is alone sufficient to point the problem of structural charisma. But this is to dignify the problem, raise it too high, as Dostoyevsky did, with his agonized old Inquisitor. The real problem of structural charisma is in the daily life of those subjected to its authority, beneath the stakes of politics where only persons are at stake. The Middle Ages were the great period of structural charisma in the history of our culture. Something of the terror of that period can be gauged from certain extracts from *The Medieval Manichee* by Steven Runciman:

> In 1157 Bishop Samson of Reims complained that manicheeism was being disseminated throughout his diocese by itinerant weavers who condemned marriage and encouraged sexual promiscuity. The presence of these "poblicani" was discovered by the refusal of a girl to submit to the attentions of a young cleric. Such chastity was considered ominous, and the girl, when questioned, admitted that she believed virginity to be obligatory, and called in her friends to support her, thus revealing a whole nest of heresy.

Sometime earlier, a certain Pons had appeared at Périgueux with a following which claimed to live as the disciples had done:

> They were ascetic in their habits, wholly vegetarian, almost teetotal, and owning no money. . . . They rejected not only the cross, but also almsgiving, and they disapproved of private property. . . . They were believed to indulge in magic. Indeed, it was impossible to keep them in prison as the Devil always released them.
>
> In 1167, a group of heretics was rounded up in Burgundy and tried at Vezelay. These were convicted, in spite of their refusal to talk, of denying all the sacraments, and in particular the value of baptism, the eucharist, the sign of the cross, holy water, oblations, marriage, the priesthood and monastic life. The ordeal by water was applied to them. One was scourged and set free, and seven were burnt.

Runciman captures nicely the psychology of those made subtle by their exercise of office charisma. A girl refuses the advances of a functionary dedicated to a celibate life. The bishop identifies her instantly with a sect that encourages promiscuity. Some vegetarians are mysteriously freed from prison, like St. Peter: it is assumed to be magic and the world of the devil. A group of people are discovered minding their own business. It is clear that they do not conform. They refuse to recognize the court or give evidence. They are convicted of a list of denials, in which there is no distinction between important doctrine (the Eucharist) and form, custom, and superstition. They are subjected to the pagan irrationality of the Ordeal, and either flogged or burnt according to its decree.

It was during the testing period of structural charisma that the medieval "manichees" denied the redemption of this world, for which they could see little evidence. They felt within themselves capacities of life, freedom, and happiness which the world systematically denied. They identified the repressed part of themselves with the divine, and the whole structure of repression as devilish. It was an attempt to solve the problem of evil which the medieval church had patently failed to solve. It implied the denial not only of injustice and oppression, but of the human race itself. Its logic was race suicide, so that the sparks of imprisoned life could be permanently freed in the divine. New imprisonments begin with the reconciliation of freedom and obedience in charismatic organization, however wisely the first leader may warn about the snares of that reconciliation. Jesus' warning about the significance of a certain pious mother asking a favor of rank or honor for her two sons is a model of prescience about the fate of structural charisma. "You know that in the world, rulers lord it over their subjects, and their great men make them feel the weight of authority; but it shall not be so with you. Among you, whoever wants to be great must be your servant, and whoever wants to be first must be the willing slave of all—like the Son of Man." Continuing to refer to himself in the third person, as if at a certain distance, the first leader gave a warning about the tragedy of leadership everywhere observable: "He did not come to be served, but to serve." Thus the model of greatness in that particular organization was set: no one was to lord it. But how not? Jesus himself was an imperious ruler. Something more was involved in his leadership: not merely "to serve" but also to "give up his life as a ransom for many"

(Matthew 20:25–28). The Passion of Jesus opposes the more familiar passions. The Christian faith tried to reorganize passion in a most interesting way. Passion is "doing something else (y) when something (x) is done to you." Passion, Collingwood continues, "is the power of the not-self, reflection on passion is the discovery of that power." It is "the essence of Christianity," concludes Collingwood,

> (as savages beat the gods who fail to answer their prayers) so Christians should vent their wrath and . . . with God's own approval, upon God's own wounded head.
>
> When we show in our churches the likeness of our God scourged with rods and crowned with thorns and suffering the death of a criminal, and in the central rite of our worship commemorate, as some of us say, or as other say actually repeat that doing to death, we prove to the world that we hold God responsible for whatever evil there may be in the world; and think we cannot serve him better than by wreaking on him our inevitable wrath.[3]

Unless it is a passion to end all other passions, all freedom to be passionate will end in the most terrible transgressions. In the passion play that is the faith of Christ, each must know, in himself, what he wants to do against that authority who has made him what he is. Luckily, in the Christian symbolic, the job has been done for him, the angry passion completed of doing that Y for the X done to you. Yet the way this second job has been done, by the doer himself giving up his life *as a ransom for many,* takes all in this peculiar order of action beyond fear and beyond anger—to guilt. We did it; we played god to God himself. And the one who has lorded it over us has invited us to defeat him, arranged the entire passionate episode. This episode, the Passion, met our need to do something else when something is done to you. The exchange of passion, doing for having been done to, is what politics is all about. It is one small step to the complete and cold intelligence of political warfare: to be the first actor in the exchange of passions, to become the X who does unto others before any Y is done to him. Link politics with faith and the greatest transgressions become justified. Divorce politics from faith and the greatest transgressions become as nothing. We are beyond the point where it helps to know, outside a common and knowing acceptance of the interdicts, a credal culture, that the repressions of our passions are unconscious denials of what it wanted. That kind of knowledge proposes no interdicts but only makes us more sophisticated about our transgressiveness, under either reign—of pleasure or reality principle.

In the Catholic tradition of charisma, a dominant structure must be sophisticated enough to allow the interdicts to freshly communicate themselves; this is "nonstructural" charisma—the first version within our radically politicized concept of charisma, of a loyal opposition.

But the Catholic tradition of charisma is also nonstructural. Nonstructural charisma is a term which describes the activity of the free and autonomous Spirit operating through other than structured channels. In every age, the Spirit raises up saints, founders of orders or movement, members of both hierarchy and laity who speak to their age by virtue of a divine mandate personally received through revelations or vision and effectively legitimized through miracles and works of wonder. For Catholics still aware of the richness of their tradition in this matter, the results of nonstructured charisms may be seen in the martyrdom of Christians in personal dedication to the service of the church in the missionizing activity of its members, and in its social reform movements.

The antagonism between structural and nonstructural charisma grew in importance as the church grew toward the societies it evangelized, and those societies found the church a force contending with its other forces—and cooperating with them. Yet the intellectuals of the Roman tradition could never admit what the Protestant asserted: that the charism of office translated easily—and the more easily the higher up one looked—into office charisma. In the Catholic tradition, the tension between structural and nonstructural charisma serves to discriminate between genuine and pseudo-charisma (at least outright deception). The distinction, however, did not prevent the hierarchy from assuming characteristics of authority special to structural charisma. Under that structural charisma, all imitation would have to come from above. Even so, the hierarchy must be especially wary of judging the truth of the charism. The Catholic solution was prudential: a judgment ought not to be made hastily—seeing it where it is not—not bureaucratically—demanding excessive proof so as to stifle the Spirit. The case of Francis of Assisi (twenty-eight in 1210) and Innocent IV is perfect to illustrate "nonstructural" charisma, renewal approved and petitioned, as Francis petitioned Innocent. What success followed. In ten years' time, five thousand Franciscan mendicants assembled at Assisi to celebrate the first chapter of their order. The Catholic symbolists are now busily incorporating new gifts as fast as they can find them. This tolerance of the grand old world party for new gifts, this prudent interest in using them, is the sign of an organization intent chiefly on its survival. Not only is there a foreseeable end of mandatory celibacy for the Roman clergy, but I see nothing to prevent official welcome to the new gift of promiscuity. Survival is best achieved by anti-credal organizations in which the interdicts are constantly subject to critical rejection. The Protestant churches are already anti-credal, their clergy wedded to every "new gift" that comes along and willing to try out all the old ones, anything to keep the flock together. It is quite unclear what "new gift" would replace the old one of celibacy as a device of separation by which the sign of a transference of office charisma to a credal guide has been so long guarded by the Roman church. The "new gifts" are being handed down, like marching orders anyway, from the credal guides to the laity—for celibacy, against the old liturgy. I am glad for every little tactical error made by this incredibly prudent, self-serving old organization.

At least, a little removed from the transgressiveness of the "world," even under such scandalously abused charisms as celibacy, a Christian who had received the thrust of interdictory authority could maintain a decently harmless conduct of life, long after the prototypical disappointment, the eschatological failure.

FOURTEEN

WHEN THERAPY REPLACES CHARISMA

IN ORDER TO GROW MORE PRECISE in our efforts to save ourselves from our own uniquely powerful hostility to culture in any form, we need a theory of *transgressions,* outside quotation marks. Being righteously scientific, Lévy-Bruhl put his theory inside quotation marks. Even so, he intuited the transgressive, in all its plasticity, well enough.

> The main characteristic of . . . "transgressions," the quality that makes them so immensely moving and terrifying to the primitive, is that they "bewitch," i.e., they bring disaster. Directly this menace (of disaster) vanishes, the emotion subsides, and the act that aroused it becomes a matter of indifference. The greater incest always arouses horror, because there is no known method of "neutralizing" the evil influence it exercises. But, provided that the necessary precautions have been taken, the lesser incest will be tolerated; since it no longer entails disaster, it ceases to be even shocking.[1]

Most ardent emotions, in "primitive" societies, Lévy-Bruhl supposed, were horror, surprise, terror, a wish to escape the disaster that must follow an intrusion by the extraordinary. "Primitives" endure one little crisis after another. Far from peace, the primitive mind is at war with itself; transgressions are the frequent intervention, in one degree of intensity or another, of monstrous exceptions to the rule of his life as it must be. The "culture" of the "primitive" is lines of defense against these interventions.[2]

Lévy-Bruhl had no idea what to do with the recondite fact that some orders of sorcerers, in pursuit of their vocation, commit incest; after all, in Lévy-Bruhl's reading of the comparative literature, "incest" was the worst "evil." Before the double mystery, of the fact and its denial, Lévy-Bruhl stops theorizing about "transgressions." The word is securely locked away in quotation marks; a resolutely rational, tolerationist custodian of facts and their contradictions knows the "value" of quotation marks for getting beyond moral reality. But Lévy-Bruhl does venture the opinion that there may be two types of "transgressions," discriminable according to the degree in which they are socially acceptable; we shall review, briefly, examples of these two types.

In the Trobriands, as in Lévy-Bruhl's dear Paris, adultery is not really horrifying and portends no disaster. The "transgression" may be built right into the social order, without any urgency about chastisements. I would prefer to call these mild and acceptable "transgressions" remissive motifs, for they may actually support the established order or moral demands. No social formation is less subversive than our suburban wife-husband swappers; often they trouble to get divorces, and carefully guard their property from the ambiguities of their sexuality. We know these "mild and acceptable transgressions." They are committed by well-known bores and endured by well-known doormats. Freud can still refer to girls "wise" enough to prefer marrying experienced husbands, although themselves resolutely virginal. The "double standard" may be considered a remissive motif in late Victorian culture. One can think of remissive motifs in contemporary society. Folk wisdom still describes them rightly as those exceptions that prove the rule. The arranging of book reviews, for example; it is not done and yet done. The peddling of bibliographies; the puffing of trivial research into "highly original" contributions to "knowledge." Every little world has its examples; we academics have had ours. Some of the examples are brand-new: the raging anti-establishment teacher. That brand-new example, in his self-publicity, belongs as much to the world of public relations—advertising—as to the academy. The Raging Revolutionary is most successfully remissive, although there continue to be efforts, even by statute, to strengthen the interdict on certain kinds of stunting on campus; even so, what reputable university can afford to be without its Raging Revolutionaries, to balance the other Professors of Marketing?

The revolutionary gimmick is to expand these remissions into transgressive behavior, until they take on their own imperative quality; then the thing not to do becomes the thing to do. But then, in the classical model of change, the thing to do spun off its own interdicts. We are after bigger game: an order that is no order; "Transgressions" that do not become interdictory; a criminal Christ who becomes no god; thefts for which there are no punishments; injustice for which there are no justices; "greatest of crimes" made routine tough luck; the "victim" blamed; the "criminal" praised for his brave response to intolerable provocations by the System and its personifications. Let us put an end to what is "unheard of," to everything extraordinary, uncanny; to the breaking into the "natural" order of a "malign" force. "Evil" is an establishment enchantment. Nothing is, by nature or superior decision, "abominable." With such revolutionary gimmicks, we can protect ourselves indefinitely from all "abominations"—by continuing the "deabominizing" movement. Our primitive sense of caution, our suspicion of all experiments, is like virginity—something a remote ancestor may once have practiced, for a lack of a didactic rapist.

It was Freud who announced a theory of "guilt" which deepened the critical attack on "transgression." In that theory, the gravity of the interdicts themselves gave weight to the transgressions. Nothing is really "contrary to nature." Human nature includes, in developmental stages that are not eliminable, all our "transgressions," thus all our "transgressions" are "natural." It is the unconscious character of the interdicts, as well as the conscious holding of interdicts too severe for the catholicity of our "natures" that make us ill—with those failed pleasures Freud called "neuroses" and even "psychoses."

Weber took yet another strain of critical theory on this matter. He gave a hint of interdictory and remissive institutions precisely where Lévy-Bruhl did not: "Apropos of the ritual crimes of the leopard-ment . . . that these sorcerers practiced incest, for the strengthening of their magical powers, no doubt." Weber would have seen immediately that these public performances, these "sabbats" of incest, were "on the rites of membership of the society" of these sorcerers[3]; Weber would have known that this was one of those regimens by which the authority of these "charismatics," in his theory of the utterly heterogenous "meaning" of "charisma," is acquired, renewed, or proved. Lévy-Bruhl found it merely "curious to note that in this respect as in many others, the *vihibi* [leopard-men] seem to enjoy transgressing the laws of their tribe."[4] Weber not only translated the ancient theory, implicit and explicit, of "transgressions" into the "neutral" category of the "extraordinary," but he merged the transgressive with its opposite, "grace," in its received, acknowledged, and enacted meaning in or culture. "*Charisma*" thus began its comical modern rise to fame and fortune, such a patched heterogeneity that it can now, with a legitimacy equal to any other, mean "celebrity." In its sociological heterogeneity, "charisma" may refer to both the most "graceful" and "transgressive" states—and perhaps refer to both together. Moreover, where it appeared, "charisma" could have the power not only of something to be dreaded, but something to be welcomed. Nowadays, I think, charisma portends a certain kind of "disaster": the magic of power, a positive absence of interdicts. In our own deceased culture of authority, disasters were prophesied mainly in support of interdictory motifs. But the Arab berserker; the blond beast of Byzantium; the great criminal; the chief-king who is engaged in the biggest business, man-killing; the power politician who is the man-killers' typologically degenerate descendant—these are, to a modern man, charismatics. There is something extraordinary about them, entailing anything but reliefs from distress, unless relief from distress can be a catharsis of destruction. It does no conceptual or empirical good to split off charisma in the "magico-religious ambiance" from charisma in the modern world as a form of political leadership.

I speculate that Weber's concept of charisma has grown, both in the esteem of scholars and the chat of the generality, not least because the concept contains within itself not only the motif of "personal devotion" to one who will relieve this or that distress, or all; more important to the modernized concept is its strong, if hidden, transgressive element. Like our dear primitives, fear of the transgressive character brings forward the compliant recognition, of nonresistance, to the extraordinary quality of power itself. The magic of power remains the most powerful magic of all.

Even a rationalist like Lévy-Bruhl, looking at the supernatural in the mind of the primitives, though more sympathetically than a rationalist of Frazer's arrogance, could see that there was something here more than "gross superstition." He saw that, for the primitives at least, there was a power that was positively occult in its transgressiveness; more precisely, it was the transgressiveness of the extraordinary, of what is not done, that constituted, to the primitive mind, a power scarcely resistible and therefore in need of the most extraordinary defenses. Thus magic can be either transgressive or interdictory.

What does the return of "magic" portend in our culture? It is part of a revival of religion? Such a question, of revival, or of survival, makes little sense unless we have a theory within which we can describe, and perhaps fight, what is being revived. I suspect the present revival of "magic" is predominantly transgressive, that it is one minor, but sociologically and morally significant, aspect of the most fundamental revolutionary attack our culture has ever had to undergo: against both guilt and faith—against culture itself. In the dulling of the transgressive sense, or in the deliberate contravening of that sense by acts that may be called either revolutionary or criminal, there is the paradigm of hostility to culture in any form—not a new morality but an ever-new amorality.

A "scientific" theory of "transgressions" can only be put in sociological quotation marks, where all related words—"sin," "evil," "vice," "perversion," "crime," etc., are equally neutralized. But this is to divide up the spheres of the world and set them to fight a smart draw with each other. More important, from a place on the ramparts of a culture it is to identify the normal with the actual, and hollow out all the foundations of authority upon which culture stands. Without God, there can be no sin. Without a metaphysics, there can be no evil, for evil refers, whether deprivative or positive, to a condition of being. Without an ethic, there can be no "vice," for vice belongs to actions and characters which ought to be regulated in some regimen, but are not. Like "perversion," "vice" is a moral term; it is moral evil interpreted as an offense against the ideal or law given in the "nature" of man; both are the fix in which one finds himself, "fixated," as Freud would say, in one of his many moralizing passages, by a departure from "nature."[5] As a legal term, "crime" denotes the violation of the law which a society or state has framed for its own preservation and the protection of its members. Put all those terms of transgression in quotation marks and culture itself must be in hazard. The quotation marks, in their neutrality, are marks of hostility to culture. For, in culture, without quotation marks there are nuances of all these terms, and institutions enacting those nuances in their connection. There are no cultures without a more or less developed and complex transgressive sense. "Evil" maybe a metaphysical term. It may denote some condition, circumstance, or act that somehow interferes with complete perfection or happiness of being. But in the psyches of ordinary members inside a culture—or, more precisely, the culture safely inside them—the terms force a certain alliance, often very close. Perversion, too, is a kind of incompleteness and participates in the meaning of evil. A sin is a criminal act, a breaking of the law of God. It involves, like vice, being in an incomplete state of nature. Crime carries, with sin, intimations of revolt and wrong, culpability and penalty.

What "sin" did, before its sense was dissolved by rational criticism, was to strengthen the truths of resistance to otherwise less resistible transgressions; sin enlarges the truths of resistances and supplies a certain unity to the style of our rejections.

Science itself is transgressive. Not wishing to offend the method of science, and himself considering the faith of Israel and cult of Jesus "also superstitions, indicative of prelogical and mystical mentality,"[6] Lévy-Bruhl, yet another of those academic Jewish revolutionaries, mild and philosophical, put the general sociological category, "transgressions," in quotation marks. He was a mild transgressive, against whom no penalties should be exacted, a student of culture whose study, although a form of attack on the defenses that are culture, need not be censored. There are far worse studies, that mask hostility to culture in any form, that we might consider censoring.

Uncensored, even celebrated as "creative," our inherited culture is plagued by swarms of tiny charismatics, all parading their public transgressions as the private equals of any interdict. The transgressive figures now muster into anti-credal organizations—Gay Liberation Fronts, what you will—proclaiming the equality of all behavior; in its pedagogic form, these proclamations imply the superiority of transgressive behavior. Criminality, personal and political, is charismatic; what else can possibly be? In our established and failing culture, the transgressions must carry a special attraction. These semiprofessional transgressive figures are the entirely "new prophets" now rising, charismatics of a sort. Weber's concept of charisma, outside the god-terms to which that charisma once belonged, remains one acute expression of the main problem of our culture. There is nothing new in our so-called crisis except the unique peculiar resolutions of it now taking power over the problem itself. The new man, in a culture constituted by permanent therapies, is learning to go naked, his eternally restless mind encouraged to play, fast and loose, with all creeds so that the culture of the masses, like those of the upper classes, can be construed as anti-creeds. Sin was, in its positive expression, the triumph of self-respect over the form of respect superior to self; such self-respects are now organized, in America, in a thousand therapies against our saving sense of guilt. The psychological term for sin is guilt. Without a certain kind of authority, from which "charisma" originally derived, in its various reproductions of authority personified, guilt can only go into its purdah of quotation marks, as the "sense of guilt."

The critical advantage, in any culture, must always belong to the critics of that culture. Transgression is the critical principle of every order, seen from membership inside that order. Those who would break with the transgressive sense can always point to those in the charismatically founded establishments who are themselves transgressive—and yet without penalty; on the contrary, with reward. Our inherited culture is more attacked, and less comprehended, by its official defenders, than by its most ardent critics and therapeutic actors. There is no particular recency in what too many are pleased to call the "crisis" of our culture, society, or self. Rather, the rhetoric of "crisis" has become part of the therapeutic routine of the emergent culture.

A revolutionary condition obtains most acutely when and where guiding cadres routinely adopt transgressive symbolics, even as "Sciences," or as "long overdue reforms," in law and custom. In our particular cultural situation, consent and obedience within the social order are severely challenged—from the top down, not from the bottom up. We have more to fear from the revolutionary rich, in all their public cults of the pleasure principle, than from the realistic poor. A theory of culture that will serve, truthfully, in its defense, is a dead theory of a dying culture; the theory cannot live without its culture, nor the culture without its theory. The first task of any critical theory—critical of what has been our critical theory—is to remove all quotation marks from around itself. Then, and only then, can the interdicts give men back their saving distances from each other. Then the arts of self-concealment will flourish and we will cease to be transparent frauds. Then, at the level of character structure, the structure of culture will repeat itself in repressive-impulsive patterns, while the key to social structure will be, as it should, the distribution of privileges and deprivations, including discriminating access to material good as well as esteemed activities. No one will have everything; everyone will have something, very much their own.

The better to confute the symbolics of culture and every established social order, modern transgressive theorists have turned to a symbolic of "creative" catastrophe, an opening up of sheer possibility, the cultivation of transgressive activity as a personal and political therapy of reversal, in which *all* that is now last shall be first. The historic mission of the modern transgressive activist-theorists, post-Marxist if not always anti-Marxist, is to make the catastrophe of the failing symbolic creative.

Why must the new creation begin in catastrophe? The revolutionary symbolics of creation through catastrophe are implicit admissions that the defenses constituting our culture are still so deep that they can only be penetrated by extraordinarily disruptive enactments. "Charisma" has returned to us only one rhetorical cover for the cultivation of whatever is disruptive. The one atonement for the interminable tactics of disruption, by platoons of "creative" self-respecters, remains a credal culture, one that will close off more than a few possibilities of action, one in which "meaning" is not there for the money we "will be paid to create" it, with no seventh day, during which we can rest from our task of meaning creation.

The modernist quest for "meaning" is one animator of the therapeutic, as an ideal figure of hostility to culture in any form. He constitutes the most powerful denial that an action must mean just this, and not that; as an "ideal" type, the therapeutic is the perfect anti-credal personality, the supreme prophylactic against any denial to man that everything is possible and nothing is true. Until practically our own stage of cultural development, an anti-credal culture has seemed a contradiction in terms; the horror of it is not yet fully perceived. Learned men discourse on Nazi "doctrine," as if it were yet another creed rather than the experience of assault. We must bear with the confusing fact that the intellectually, socially, and politically established classes have become completely identified with their own anti-credal positions, and yet without enacting those positions. But just behind the "free spirits" are the liberated thugs. Behind the flower children of Haight-Ashbury were the cycle gangs. The revolutionary rich, and their undisciplined children, genteel, still inhibited, unbelievers, cannot grasp the demonic energies released by their own exemplary preaching of every conceivable freedom.

Two anti-creeds compete for mastery over our peculiar mastery of life: Science and Politics. These two show signs of forging an alliance that will make all earlier demonries of domination look as trivial as a Skinnerian reward apparatus; nor is any truth of resistance possible, from Science itself, in that alliance. On opposing sides politically, modern Science and Politics are on the same side culturally. All main contending movements are transgressive. After Dr. Alfred Kinsey and the Pill, "Make love, not war" is not an interdictory slogan; it is a particular version of infinite aspiration and can therefore be easily reversed. All the putative guiding cadres in our culture, including the old pastoral organizations, are dominated by their consciousness of the quotation marks around their transgressive sense of this or that action. Nothing now is too dangerous; even our imagination of disaster is part of the game of seeing how much further we can go, in a particular direction, before we learn how to outwit the disaster itself.

The interdictory and remissive motifs that specify a culture have been animated, until modernity, by "supernatural" dangers and punishments, by a self-defensive social order that acquired a constraining interpretation precisely in its self-defensiveness. Each such social order had its specialists in defense, "priesthoods," they are generally called, institutionalized as "churches." Durkheim, like many of the best minds of his time, considered that the interdictory-remissive order could be best continued by a development in which the schoolteacher replaced the priest, as the chief cultural functionary, and school replaced church, as chief cultural institution. Magical interdicts were to have their equivalents in rational explanations. Matriculation would replace baptism. This was the best sociological theory, and *defense,* of culture in the late nineteenth and early twentieth centuries. It is still widely held, and I cannot say that it has been proved wrong. Indeed, coming out of the orthodox faith of Israel, as Durkheim did, the school and teaching in it was the likeliest place for me to go. But the school is not a church, although for a time, in America, under the influence of John Dewey, it was looked upon as that place from which "creative innovation" was bound to come; school was imagined as a charismatic organization, so to speak. Many still imagine it so: our first and last best hope against the crumbling of all hope. But professors are not prophets and they have ceased even to be priests in the temple of the intellect. Rather, they are entrepreneurs, engaged in fast turnover of all truths of resistance, their business the putting of everything, including possibly that most malignant power of the invisible world, "death" itself, in quotes. If our newest business, the knowledge industry, can put death between quotation marks—and with "sin" and all its cognates already in quotes—then surely men will be gods, each and every one. Leaps from necessity to freedom will be perfectly ordinary accomplishments and the new man can be reborn as often as he likes. At last, there will be a permanent escape from the cages built to the design of credal organizations.

Then, and only then, when therapy replaces charisma, is our society in a uniquely "revolutionary" condition, a "revolution" to end all revolutions in the established but failing sense of that concept. Knowledge, not poverty, is the key to the release of those activities we may call, with some hope of foreseeing a gathering reality, "revolutionary." Creative catastrophes, massive therapies of violence, are only one among many techniques available, a technique not excluding the others, to the new man of my heuristic vision. "Freedom" itself was once, in our culture, intensely ordered. It was a term with theological, psychological, and legal resonances specific to obediences felt and enacted within the "moral demand system," a phrase I suggest as perhaps slightly more explanatory than the better and older world "culture." In the upper classes, however, "freedom" became a term of therapeutic transgressiveness, "culture" became identical with the pursuit of pleasures, however refined, thus to test the limits of those structures of enactable possibilities into which their pursuit of pleasure, as culture, led them.

The democratization of modern culture consists mainly, I think, of the spread downward, in the social structure, of the cultivated pursuit of pleasure, stripped of the disciplines of delay once thought necessary to acquire "culture" itself. Modern culture is something for which one can shop around: there are bargains to be had and the new ideal is that no ideal should be priced beyond the reach of anyone who wants to have it.

Every culture is an order of ambivalent drawing powers, of interdicts and remissions (mild transgressions, without severe penalty and perhaps even with reward) from those interdicts. A revolution may be said to occur when the most significant remissions and interdicts by which a culture is constituted change places in the established order of demands. No culture is immortal. The reciprocal functions of interdict, remission, and transgression are never so firmly fixed that they are not alterable under the pressure of conflicts within the political order itself, for example. Just such pressures in the political order gave rise to those culture revolutionaries, those true charismatics, the canonical prophets of ancient Israel. There had long been cultic prophets in ancient Israel, and official court prophets, and "war prophets," who actually gave the command to attack. In any society, the symbolics of interdiction and transgression may grow banal; the guiding cadres lose a certain drawing power; laities, who may include the ruling specialists in power, may lose their sense of direction both in private and public. But ancient Israel, in all its distress, was a credal society , definitely so since the victory of the Mosaic movement over Baalist and other competing cults. Not that the victory of the Mosaic movement was ever complete. But under the terrific pressures of total war, facing "merciless conquerors" such as the Assyrians, who practiced against the Israelites, warriors and "civilians" alike, a "mad terror," the canonical prophets rose to do their kind of battle, to save Israel in ways other, and more often than not, opposed to military. Certainly, ancient Israel was caught in the demonry of power politics. "Blood fairly drips from the cuneiform inscriptions." One specialist in the business of man-killing, probably not "charismatic" in Weber's terms, by the ordinary quality of his achievements, has recorded, in a "tone of dry protocol," that he "covered the walls of conquered cities with human skins."[7]

Only with the dulling of the transgressive sense can that sublime horror, innocence, be achieved. Where the transgressive sense remains keen, all are guilty and suffering achieves a certain sanction—a kind of universal random punishment, a sortilege. But with the transgressive sense diminished, suffering becomes the more intolerable at the same time that the inhibitions against inflicting pain are also diminished. This is not to say that suffering, as punishment, is not produced where the transgressive sense is sharp; on the contrary, men then inflict suffering righteously, as protectors of the interdictory order, and yet with a certain consciousness that they, too, are criminal. As Joseph de Maistre put this general sense of guilt, in his criticism of Voltaire on the historic earthquake, when Voltaire had written: "Lisbon is destroyed, and they dance in Paris!," to which de Maistre replied: "Good God, does this man want the Almighty to convert every great city into an execution chamber?"[8]

The potential of pity, in any order, depends on how commonly and sharply those in that order share the transgressive sense. The dulling of the transgressive sense, just as it achieves innocence, kills pity. D. H. Lawrence could argue for innocence and against pity. Neither he nor Mellors have pity for Sir Clifford, who is the image of weakness. It is not surprising that an intelligentsia devoted to dulling the transgressive sense has made *Lady Chatterly's Lover* a didactic novel of some importance, one that must be available universally, as one little instrument of healthy amorality. Can the transgressive sense survive without a godhead? The authority of any godhead derives from its ostensible unchangeability, and that unchangeability can only be preserved by orders which constantly so reinterpret their godhead that it appears to them against their dearest hopes—and not only to them, but through those interpreters to those who are not members of the interpretative cadres; it is in a chain of interpretation that what is not to be done achieves its grip on the possibilities of human behavior. When those interpretative cadres become devout proclaimers of some symbolic of "change," however unspecific, a major condition for the existence of any godhead is subverted. Just this subversion has occurred, as both the scientific and literary intellectuals of modernity have adopted symbolics of change; such symbolics, especially where they appear technological and "problem-solving" or merely erotic, are the prime subverters of the transgressive sense. Scientific symbolics constitute a paramount dissolution of all symbolics, for the interdictory part is constantly suppressed, thus inventing the entire normative structure of culture. Under such an inversion, cruelty and kindness become strangely mixed; the antiseptic of the hospital comes to smell like other, less obviously helping, institutions.

Remissive behavior is the more compulsive, much more so than interdictory, precisely as it seems more impetuous. The impulse is a highly structured release, a particular and specific breach. No transgression can be random. Failed authority is the father of rebellion.

Without godheads, interdicts in person, whom we fear to disobey, every remission, however trivial, has a fighting chance to grow into a transgression. Men will kill for no reason at all—and be acquitted because there will be no reason to convict them. Precisely the "best" will lack all conviction. It is for this reason that the revolution to end all revolutions is occurring among the revolutionary rich, among the educated, among the youth; these are the categories who have been most typically without godheads.

The alternative to this permanent, blank terror—the blankness of William Burroughs's *Naked Lunch*—is not tyranny, but authority. So long as authority is credal, its absolute character is such that no man or vanguard can wield it unconditionally. The remissions built into it are of an order that permit even the least authoritative in that culture to see that they are no more subject to the creed than its highest member. The early Christians understood the profound difference between power and authority. Bishops prostrated themselves with sinners, in public penance. So long as every man is a sinner, then an elite man can only weep with the transgressor, and understand him only too well. To be marked off as someone higher, in authority, was only to show that one was even more sharply observed by an even higher authority. Such vulnerabilities, in authority, sharpen the transgressive sense; they do not dull it. Absolute power does corrupt absolutely; against such power there remains, known to us, only the defense of absolute authority vested in the godheads. A dulling of the transgressive sense occurs precisely when the "spiritual power," as Henri de Saint-Simon and Auguste Comte still called it, our guiding cadres, deck themselves out in body imageries that all but displace the godhead himself, invisible and communicating from behind a concealment of creeds. These creeds are sacred symbolics; under them, an order of moral demands, that constantly resists being made convenient for the cadres who come to administer the creed, has a chance of developing, for a time, into a genuine community. In this opposition to becoming the ideology of its own adherents, the magic power of their office, lies the sacred character of the officers of a creed. Office charisma can never hide the absence of personal devotion. The interpreters must be responsible, first of all, for interpreting themselves; it is always a chastening responsibility, one that is bound to produce laughter at themselves, by themselves. Responsible guiding interpreters can never be pompous; they are too truly critical of the creed, as a proclamation of their godhead. So the most authoritative order, by training interpreters, should prevent righteous tyrannies.

Of course, when it happens that the interpreters of an order, its demanders, identify themselves too closely with the credal motifs, the result is some form of cultic tyranny, which needs absolute outward conformity. Such secularizations of the creed usually take on a theatrical character, with the authorities resplendent in what remains of the creed: their uniforms and robes of office. The nineteenth and early twentieth centuries were preeminently the age of authoritarian body imageries, of both church and state, military and ecclesiastical, precisely as credal contents were evaginated. Nationalist ideologies are a perfect evagination of credal motifs into cultic authoritarianism, a mass worshipping its own image, usually concentrated in one "leader." The entire fashion industry, with its rapidly communicated cycles of emulation, is a parody of credal authority emptied and externalized into body imagery. The Nazis were snappy, even impressive, dressers. Like the English, in their most imperial manner, the Nazis knew how to cut a tunic and how to put on a show of massed, deindividualized force. Our liking for such shows is a version of the most secular longing: for a closing of the saving distances between individuals. I recall feeling sudden satisfaction of that longing, during my years in the military, when we all marched, in perfect step. Marching, all distance would close. I would experience a terrifying satisfaction at my own mergence into one body, and at the thud of it. In uniform, in our office and its insignia, clerical or political, we are in fact functioning in a way that dulls the transgressive sense. Themselves constrained less by credal motifs than by the interests of the uniform itself, those men in uniform can—and have—demanded that their subordinates do everything in their name and image. Such transgressive behavior was once called idolatry. The revolt of youth against the uniform is a revolt against a type of anti-credal order, against a thin ordination of order, against a buttoning-up that does not straighten what is crooked. But this revolt against the uniform has adopted a bizarre uniform, a fantasy of the savage and uncultivated.

Organizations and uniforms may become more rigid than creeds; by their externalizing functions, they may hide what is no longer there. The entire rationalist revolt against creeds opened the way to the tyranny of anti-credal organizations and uniforms, in which all that matters is outward conformity—the inner left having been evaginated. Hermann Broch put the invulnerability to credal tension of the organization man very well when he said that when a man "has fastened up his uniform to the last button, he acquires a second and thicker hide."[9]

Both rationalist and romantic attacks on the absolute authority of creeds led to that far greater horror: the absolute authority of man. Against this anti-credal authority, no creed can prevail, for it is an authority that is identified with will, that is untied to any constraint except self-interest. The rationalists and romantics who have closed, for the present, the possibility of creeds mistook their object of attack. They knew and asserted that the orders, their creeds abandoned, were committing suicide; from this suicide they have felt a schadenfreude that they have mistaken for a freer emotive vivacity.

How shall we explain those periods in Western history when men did practically everything? The cruelty of the tenth century, outdone by the murders of the fifteenth, that outdone by the mass murders of the twentieth: how and why, and among which groups, was the transgressive sense so dulled?

The beginnings of an explanation, perhaps, are in the tie between specific interdicts and remission. We need sociological histories of styles of cruelty, the inflicting of pain in both interdictory and remissive modes. Scarcely a start has been made in this field of study. Is it the case, for example, that war is always and everywhere a remissive motif, a massive dulling of the transgressive sense? London, during the Blitz? In war, men are obliged to kill the innocent, and this killing is considered both honorable and glorious, thus reversing the entire moral demand structure of civil existence. The "glory" of war is precisely in this complete reversal of the interdictory-remissive order at its most fundamental level: of who is to take another life. The terrible and mysterious persistence of the organized and systematic effort to take (and the honor in that taking) of human life is built into the very structure of action, as the ultimate possibility. The drama of every society hinges on the possibility of murder.

Performing such a fundamental subversive act, it is small wonder the modern soldier has been decorated in way to make him up as an image of rectitude—of man in society, upon whom one can depend to act so and not in another way. This basic, visible rectitude of the killer helps us understand the significance of the uniform and also the conservative surface of the soldier. Underneath that surface, at which the soldier has always the role of defending things as they are, there is the most revolutionary of all roles—of killing.

Thus warriors are still hedged around with symbolics of security; soldiering becomes a parody of faith. A soldier needs no explanations, but only obediences. The best discipline leaves no room for interpretation. Warfare is not a hermeneutic art. Institutions of explanation, convervators of war as the greatest organization of remissive activities, grow up to disguise the subversive character of warfare. From the military situation the subversions spread, threatening the entire structure of culture, as in our own present case. The military is license in uniform, a regular way of launching fundamental, if not conclusive, attacks on the civil interdict against killing.

In an anti-credal society such as our own, permanent war is the real alternative to the authority of interpretation, by guiding cadres of interdictory teachers of what is not to be done. The alliance between the military and any moral demand system is only apparent; in due course, the technical needs of the military will break any moral demand system. War, as an institution, is by far the most powerful dynamic of anticulture deeply embedded in the structure of modern society, the supreme expression of its dynamism. Because it is the most fundamental and transgressive of all social activities, moderns have loved war and have gone to war with feelings of exultancy and the "something different" about it, only surpassed by the feeling of life experience by bored young killers in the act itself. All the inferior excitements, of the credal life and its tensions, have been evaginated. Good terrorists, like apathetic killers, have no godheads; they must produce their own excitements; that is why they are terrorists.

Terror is transgressive activity for its own sake; with politics as its sphere. A terrorist is a man totally devoid of manners; he is free of all respect, including respect for self. What the humanists called "manners" are really interdictory complexes. Manners and technology are linked; new weapons shatter more than opposing bodies and towns; they shatter whatever limits have obtained in the technique and effect of conflict. Innovative technology is one important element behind the transgressive totality of modern warfare. No theory of transgressions can escape the necessity of considering how to limit our innovative technology, not only in relation to nature, but to culture. Manners are not techniques. The modernist transformation of manners into personal management techniques is yet another expression of a society hostile to culture in any form.

FIFTEEN

THE REVOLUTIONARY NATURE OF THE THERAPEUTIC

THERE IS A QUESTION WHAT KIND of innovator the charismatic is, even in "traditionally stereotyped" periods of history. This problem of the nature of an innovating personality is linked to Weber's assertion that there is another force, equally innovative, and distinctively modern, which he calls rationality or rationalism. Rationality is the opposite of charisma. It "works from without," an objective or external reorientation of the individual, while charisma is a subjective or internal reorientation. Moreover, reason "intellectualizes the individual." In Weber's opposition of two revolutionary forces, charisma and rationality, we have the very basis of the shift of the dominant character type in modern society from the charismatic to the therapeutic. For the equally revolutionary force of reason is not a force born out of naïve enthusiasm as such or out of naïve suffering or out of naïve resolution of conflict: therapy as a mode of action, as an orientation to all action, occurs after individuals grow conscious of enthusiastic attitudes and of movements of enthusiasm. They may still be enthusiastic but that "enthusiasm" occurs in quotation marks. Just as they can be anything else in quotation marks. The question whether the charismatic must be a revolutionary, must have a revolutionary effect, must be answered somewhat differently in the era of the therapeutic. The revolutionary force is even more revolutionary, for it destroys the centrality of any particular system of attitudes and permits an infinite number of changes in the direction of action. This is what therapeutic revolutionaries, like Herbert Marcuse, are after (cf. his *Reason and Revolution*). Charisma is revolutionary by its new particular centrality. Charisma is the medium and message, a certain shift in the direction of action. Now this therapeutically new orientation of all attitudes is constituted by a capacity to keep making new orientations of all attitudes toward the different problems and structures of the world.

The therapeutic has emerged at the climax of a rationalistic culture, and as its living contradiction. Our culture is unlike the pre-rationalist types preceding it; in those types, tradition and charisma between them may exhaust the possibilities of action orientations, as Weber thought. The therapeutic is he who rides loose to all symbolics. Thus the therapeutic can include tradition and charisma within his new orientation. The therapeutic must be considered to be a new type, one who no longer has that peculiar kind of deference as regards any figure as particularly exemplary, precisely in the new direction he gives. The charismatic constitutes new authority. The therapeutic is an experiment in the permanent subversion of authority as such. The capacity to keep making new orientations of all attitudes implies that there are no fixed lines beyond which action becomes transgressive. At the present climax and contradiction of the rationalist era, there is an end of inwardness. A basic change is taking place in the institutional matrix within which we live. That change can be seen in the form of early education, which no longer is intended to facilitate the deep installation of interdictory-remissive contents. The education of the therapeutic is no longer a moral form. The merging of formal education and the mass media has succeeded in democratizing the aristocratic search for pleasure that was characteristic of the transitional period from church to secular civilization. The classical ideal of the good as that which involves a sacrifice of self is not only obsolete but a kind of sickness that must be stopped before it infects our children. How limited was the revolutionary force of the charismatic. A revolutionary type, the therapeutic is far superior; his innovative capacities can be infinite, never-ending; the symbolic being installed is not self-limiting. On the contrary, like science, it is a perpetual opening of possibilities. The therapeutic empties the term "revolution" of its original meaning, which was of a circular and self-closing process—like the revolutions of the stars and planets in the heavens. The progressivist conception of a nonrepeating evolution has completely displaced the classical meaning of revolution, as it was understood in an era in which charisma was still a possibility, however remote. Now, revolution is no longer constituted by a specific and determinant shift in interdictory remissive contents.

In this light, the Weberian conception of charisma as a revolutionary force within a traditionally oriented, or stereotyped, period of history takes on a different meaning from his own. For Weber, revolution ends in routinization—Weber's pejorative conceptualization of the new interdicts established and settled as the character of the culture in its changed direction. The dynamics of routinization are in what might be called the "traditionality" of the revolutionary force of charisma itself. Charisma is not the opposite of routinization; more precisely, routinization is the perfectly logical historical working out of charisma. The key to understanding charisma, beyond the pathos with which Weber clothed it, is its specifically interdictory-remissive motif structure. "Routinization" is a pejorative term for that thrust of charisma into the social order which is implicit in the revolutionary mission itself.

Is the distinctively modern revolution "democratic"? Freud implies that the new height of rationality which gives individuals their freedom both from inward and outward tyranny is limited to an elite, while the majority must continue to be routinized in the charismatic mode. My own conclusion is that, on the contrary, the therapeutic is a most democratic character; in fact, what Jean-Jacques Rousseau meant by the achievement of man's "natural" freedom. The "natural man" is a therapeutic. The culture of the therapeutic represents an end of the historical force of charisma working itself out in newly established and deeply installed interdicts and remissions, and in a highly differentiated cultural structure. This is because there are no superiorities; all "values" are equally entertainable. No great man will appear in such a radical democracy. An interdictory figure is not possible within a culture dominated by the therapeutic. In its evagination of deeply installed interdicts, therapy functions as a prophylaxis against greatness.

SIXTEEN

WHAT GREATNESS OWES TO GUILT

GUILT IS THE RULING EMOTION of every credal culture; those inside such a culture are compelled to responsibility for themselves. This is to say that they must act entirely within the enclosing symbolic. Any other action is transgressive. The enclosedness of the symbolic is not separable from the sense of responsibility. A society too "open" destroys the sense of responsibility, for then men lose confidence in the limits they actively defend against transgressive behavior. Such a sense of responsibility against the transgressive expressions of self or group, in defense of the enclosing symbolic, constitutes the guilt without which culture has no alternative except to engage in its destruction; all of what we now call "aggression" are really the amoral forms of cultural auto-destruction; all aggression is transgression, loosed from its true constraining sense. In such a cultural condition, the only possible form of greatness is transgressive. Stalins and Hitlers are more than possible.

Perhaps the most imaginative and ambivalent expression of the centrality of guilt in the literature of Western culture occurs in Franz Kafka's masterpiece "In the Penal Colony." The officer rightly declares his guiding principle, which, even after the remissive episode of Christ, men could never doubt—and here only in our own time have we learned successfully to doubt: "My guiding principle is this: guilt is never to be doubted." What a great man is the officer. In his own test of self, he defers to his creed. In the case of conflict between self and creed, the officer has the rarest of understandings: that his own ultimate crime would be to place self over creed. Moreover, in that case, he knows that he would lose not only creed but himself; he would cease to be the officer, adjutant to his own dead and absent old commandant. Thus the sociological equivalent to the crime of superseding creed by self is "disobedience and insulting behavior to superiors." That the entire creed is a mere scrap of paper, indecipherable to all except the officer, is Kafka's brilliant and hopeful nightmare of a culture without creedal authority—and without father figures. But the officer is faithful even to the enactment of his own death, which is the ultimate act of faith in credal cultures. Our exploring sense of the meaninglessness of death—and our efforts to outwit it with science—is the supreme expression of a culture characterized by a positive faithlessness. We have shed all acceptances of death just as we lack the grace to defend any particular motif of our culture. The changed meaning of death, and the absence of grace or authority from our actions, are so immediate to Kafka's story that the verdict of his imagination is given in the very second sentence: "Death for disobedience and insulting behavior to a superior." That was what once happened, in an ideal typical case, in a credal culture. Punishment for guilt was the true guiding principle, the enlightenment of death the final sanction of that principle. Weber knew what death once meant, and cannot now mean, in his remarks on father Abraham dying satiate, his life complete and death a judgment. But for judgment there must be a judge, and the distinctive feature of our modernity is that we will not even allow the fiction that nature is to be the judge; de Sade turned that enlightened substitute for God into yet another competition against self, a vast weaponry to be used in the permanent revolution of self asserting its dominance over any other assertion. De Sade's dream figures of dominance are charismatics shorn of grace—i.e., of any shadow of submission to anything except the logic of their own efforts at domination. De Sade grasped the principle that greatness could be a total transgressiveness, if it could be divorced from the inhibitory credal stratagems of guilt. De Sade's heroes are virtuosi of guiltlessness, free men in a free world. The only submissions that remain, in a free world, are the submissions of defeat. In contrast, the old submissions were those of membership inside a hermeneutic circle; within that circle every man could feel himself at liberty and none were prisoners. Kafka had the genius to make the "prisoner" of the story "In the Penal Colony" a figure of invincible stupidity; he is incapable of understanding the sentence. His stupidity is the normative condition of anti-credal intellects, of the explorers; though himself no explorer, the prisoner is outside the circle. Yet there is, at the end of the story, more than a hint that the prisoner and his guard sense the only alternative to life in what has become a penal colony—at once penal and a colony in the moment its members lose faith, their old commandant. Both men seek to jump into the boat of the explorer, as he departs to explore other possibilities for the conduct of life. But the explorer beats them off, as he must; they would have faith in him, and authority is the one qualification he cannot accept for himself, on their behalf. The Kafkaesque implication is that these ordinary men are incapable of relating themselves except to a figure of authority—and that the explorer has only just escaped becoming their new leader. Whenever a culture ceases to be credal, its rank-and-file will be constituted decisively in terms set by those critics of the culture whose authority then becomes identical with their criticism; that is the case of the explorer, who has the arrogance not to allow ordinary men into his boat. The explorer is a purely selfish figure, an authority who rejects a following, a charismatic who cannot transfer or even begin to permit the transference of his particular quality into institutions. Thus his hostility to culture as such, matching perfectly the incomprehension of the ordinary, now free of old authority and eager to follow their emancipator. Those who break old circles are the makers of new ones, whether they like it or not. Others, less clear, will leap into their boat; they, too, would sail forever, touching Byzantium, now and then, to light up what dark corners remain on earth. Soon, however, the entire world will have been visited—even colonized—by explorers; there will be no places worth an emancipatory visit. Kafka's explorer is practically an obsolete type. He has already sailed deep into the last Byzantium (which was also the first): the family. Obsolete, Kafka's type of liberation, the explorer, has already given way to the therapeutic, the virtuoso of hostility to any *compelling* form—which is tantamount to hostility to culture in any form, for there can be no culture without authority, or moral form.

Beyond the literal epoch of permanent criticism of culture—the utopian land of the modern intellectual—there is the epoch of permanent hostility to culture; in that epoch, I suspect, the intellectual explorer will be quite as dead as the old charismatic authority of Kafka's commandant.

Kafka's explorer is thus not quite so ideal or compelling a figure as he first appears. Indeed, it is the distinctive mark of modern idealizations that they be uncompelling; what could be less compelling than Weber's ideal type of charismatic?

SEVENTEEN

THE CURE AND PREVENTION OF GREAT MEN

CHARISMA OCCURS, I HAVE SUGGESTED, as a new form of submission to fresh interdicts. The pathos of modernity is driven to contradict charisma by giving it a transgressive character. By charismatic domination Weber is driven regularly to intend a transgressive figure; his indifference to interdictory figures reveals what is distinctive in modernity, at the end of its Protestant tether.

> Charismatic domination means a rejection of all ties to any external order in favor of the exclusive glorification of the genuine mentality of the prophet and hero. Hence, its attitude is revolutionary and transvalues everything. It makes a sovereign break with all traditional rational norms: "It is written, but I say unto you."[1]

None of this meets the major empirical cases. Charismatic "domination" has not meant a rejection of all ties to any external order, nor the transvaluation of "everything." Not true in the case of Jesus, nor in the case of Moses—the organizer of the Exodus, reorganizer of the tribal polities. More important, this domination means a rejection in favor of the "exclusive domination of the genuine mentality of the prophet and hero," and thus puts the emphasis entirely upon a figure who seeks essentially to enlarge himself. Weber may be talking about Kurtz or Hitler; he is not talking about Jesus or Moses. Weber has confused interdictory figures with transgressive; and so changed charisma into an amoral form.

Notice Weber's exact language of the charismatic: "revolutionary and transvalues everything," sovereign of a "break with all traditional rational norms." This is Nietzschean.

Like the Jews of his imagination, Weber, at the end of "Science as a Vocation," is a watcher and a waiter. Yet he believes the wait is futile, that true messiahs cannot truly come again but only false ones. The horror is that as a sociologist, Weber destroys the difference between true and false messiahs. All modern messiahs have to be false, and yet they are false precisely because of their domination for the sake of self. His science is so impoverished that he could not imagine a true one, and not being able to imagine a true one, he reduced the true ones to false ones. Instead, he constructed as a type of the true charismatic, that type's own killer, the ambiguous combination of transgressive and therapeutic. In the distinctively new social order thus emerging, all inhibitions are themselves transgressive, for what is to be de-inhibited are the transgressions themselves. In such a new order as Kierkegaard saw coming, his charismatic was bound to be the exact opposite of Weber's: the unrecognized one. Greatness must be poised against publicity. The celebrity machines are engines of prevention, by which great men may be "recognized." In such a cultural condition, the main question, against that condition, and before any great man may achieve his unrecognition is: how create again the possibility of inwardness? Surely the first discipline of greatness, in modernity, is to avoid becoming produced by publicity.

Elaborately disguised, first of all from his own critical acumen, from his refusal to be taken in by greatness, Weber's identification of the charismatic moves without his permission toward the transgressive type; the charismatic is a creature of domination, a man of power. Charisma is transformed by Weber into its opposite: a political category. What, then, in politics, is this proto-Nietzschean revolutionary transvaluer of everything? Is he not a Hitler? Weber's own doctrine of charisma in a time of crisis must lead to grim prognoses of what kind of hungry beast will be satisfied by those seeking surcease from their own hunger. Weber liquidated the interdictory figure as surely in theory as modern society has liquidated the possibility of his emergence in fact.

After the interdicts have been destroyed, the figure of charismatic domination transvalues himself into a therapeutic for whom even power is no god. Thus even the great man in the terrific sense—of a Stalin or a Hitler—may be cured and prevented. Still, there are a considerable number of charismatic dominators, junior grade, still in the field, urgent in self-publicity. The therapeutic is not a great man, for he can no longer prevent himself or us from doing everything; his revolutionary innovation is in the name of nothing.

Therapeutic criticism has turned the great man into a neurotic—the hero in the history of the sick soul. In contrast to the romantic notion of great men, Freud's middle-class neurotics are not candles burning themselves down to the wick for the illumination of mankind or humanity; rather, only the anti-heroic therapist, the central character type of emerging society, can develop a democratic culture of anti-heroes: only a self-critical democracy of the guilty is truly democratic. Only those who are inside a symbolic can be constrained by it. Once outside, riding loose to all symbolics, once outside the hermeneutic circle that encloses him in conviction, every person tends to become an explorer, the scientific version of the therapeutic, a culture of one, subdividing oneself infinitely against all other selves equally so divisible. A therapeutic culture is a contradiction in terms, for it is one that does not enclose its members, as a circle encloses its center. It is in this sense that Yeats truly realized that the center will not hold. The center will not hold because it is not enclosed in a circle; Yeats spent a certain part of his poetic energies trying to create new circles. Every person, as a therapeutic, is to be free at last to be his or her own prophet without a message. Meanwhile, there must be therapists—doctors—to the imperfectly therapeutic. But so long as there are therapists, there can be no democracy of the therapeutics.

EIGHTEEN

THE GIFT OF GRACE, AND HOW IT HAS BEEN TAKEN AWAY FROM US

HOW IS THE GIFT OF GRACE GIVEN? Weber is a symbolist of anti-charismatic culture; he cannot tell that this gift comes only through obedience to renunciatory command. Although Freud too, is an anti-charismatic symbolist, he understood—or at least reinterpreted—this gift of grace into an aberrant inwardness; what may have been the gift of grace is now the burden of neurosis. There is no salvation through obedience to renunciatory command; what may have been salvation is now sickness.

The structure of Western culture once worked through obedience to renunciatory command; it was charismatic in its ordinary state. Yet, in his late Protestant pathos, Weber makes over charisma into an extraordinary state. By making it a very special condition, in an interpretative effort that has led inexorably from this special condition to spuriousness, our understanding of the commonality of charisma has been lost; and with this loss, the very foundations of Western culture are lost. Our culture depended, for the creative energies of its oppositional ideality, upon the charisma of which all of us, in our ordinariness, are capable.

Micah puts the commonality of charisma, under the renunciatory command of authority, with a stunning and simple brevity. "Yahweh seeks nothing from you except that you do justice, love faithfulness, and walk humbly with your God" (Micah 6:8). To walk humbly with your God once carried the full discipline of obedience in a single phrase. The faithfulness sought was precisely the rejection and denial of what Schleiermacher and others, with sinister intelligence, called the "Infinite." By the nineteenth century, the Protestant God was not Micah's.

Rather, the Protestant God became what Micah's God sought and what men deny: what came to be called, by the theologizers of transgressive behavior, the Infinite—which is only the human capacity for doing everything, or at least thinking it. For ancient Israel, this dangerous infinity, this endless possibility, belonged to the supreme authority figure himself, and to nothing else; by the twentieth century that infinity, still deified, was rediscovered in two very different places: first, in Science, which could deny nothing permanently; second, in the psychoanalytic doctrine of the Unconscious, which lacked the gift of denial from which our understanding of charisma derives. With the end of charismatic authority, in the age of science and psychoanalysis, justice, love, and faithfulness lost their meanings as elements in any discipline of obedience. Society now truly shakes at its foundations; hostility to society becomes more than conceivable; such hostility becomes popular. The traditionalist ascetic doctrine of man's animal nature against his "higher" nature gives no defense against this distinctively modern attack. "Animality" can no longer account for modern transgressive behavior. The new ethologists remain lost in their traditionalist analogies between animal aggressiveness, which somehow is necessary to the moral order of animal kingdoms, and contemporary transgressiveness. Konrad Lorenz can make nothing of Dachau and does not even condescend to mention the Nazis in his book, *On Aggression.*[1] The key to understanding the distinctive modernity of human aggression is that the category is spiritual rather than biological. Doctrines of animality hide the failure of charismatic authority, as once such doctrines justified the renewal, with fresh interdictory energies, of the prototypal series. In animals, "aggression" is rarely transgressive. The aggressions of modern men, caught between creeds that wove violence into the interdictory remissive motif structure, and a violence that is the release from all such structures—anti-credal in its dynamic—are uniquely beyond good and evil. The practice of interdictory violence, as in Calvinist, Catholic, or utopian socialist modes, finds no echo of personal devotion. On the contrary, in modern violence, in "left" and "right," breaking the interdicts is our therapy against all disciplines of obedience; it is our most dangerous scientific experiment—with moral disorder; more precisely, with amorality, not only as science and art, but in the name of Life itself.

To establish charisma as an amoral category of authority is to deal a critical blow to the very basis of authority.

When humans act in their God-given limitation, charisma becomes a common phenomenon. When they reject that limitation, the organizations of culture are destroyed, institutions become confused. Out of the confusions of those travelers along the way of transgressions who now lead our culture, that culture is itself displaced by motifs of hostility to culture as such. The professionals of moral liberation, in various colors and at least three sexes, teach the new way with less and less fear of the old. The new teaching, not least in the new arts—film, television—actually inhibits our understanding of (and, indeed, any hope of achieving) that universal and common phenomenon of inwardness, through disciplines of obedience to renunciatory command, upon which depends the constant re-creation of culture.[2]

Modern Christians are now totally confused on this point. Although Kung sees that charisma is, in plain fact, an ordinary, rather than an extraordinary, event in our lives, even he, in his modernity, can only speak of this ordinary event as a form of "service"—without indicating further what "service" means. "Service" need not refer to any discipline of obedience to renunciatory command; it could mean—and has meant—the opposite, a calculated indiscipline, denying all renunciatory commands, as in our youth movements.

The analysis of disciplines of obedience as forms of transference-love may or may not be brought to support therapeutics of indiscipline. Freud himself was no therapeutic, and commended no freedom for ordinary men and women, doubting the possibility of collective therapeutic recognitions. Yet he is a great figure of transition, between neurotic and therapeutic organizations of our culture.[3] The central object of his analytic attack is a fixed inwardness, graven and therefore to him unable to cope except symptomatically with the mediocrity of reality and constantly in need of an authority figure of love. That inwardness, now aberrant because we know that no one merits such personal devotion, but depends upon our childish need, continues to express itself through mechanisms of obedience to renunciatory commands that are obsolete with the triumph of critical insight into the nature of all credal organizations, which began as a struggle within the dominant credal organization itself—the church. This he considered the systematic structure of both neurotic and normal action. Yet the thrust of therapy is toward the destruction of disciplines of obedience to renunciatory command.[4] The entire system is analyzed toward dismissive effect, as "neurotic." As a theorist who is at once a therapist, Freud puts the anti-charismatic symbolic on a new basis. While the Protestants, and their sociological offspring, argued that charisma had been defeated, Freudian theory implies the standard (cf. Durkheimian) belief that charisma is a historical condition which has lost its structural organization, an extraordinary condition in the sense that there are now not so many charismatics with charisma as neurotics with symptoms.

In Freudian implication, the internal agency of this too common phenomenon, this charisma gone wrong, is the "superego," which is constituted by renunciatory commands to oneself derived from external authority—the father figure. Moral disciplines are, in the first place, external and against "instinct." Yet instinct is strangely allied to superego, against ego. Freud's instinctualism is a biologizing mystique; what he refers to by "instinct" or "impulse" is a transgressive range of possible acts. Instinct is thus defined as that biological substratum of the psyche in which nothing can be denied. Against unconsciousness, the charisms, interdictory as they are, and renunciatory in effect, have become too costly, because, in the graveness they impose upon character, the movement of "life" is arrested. It is the superego which must be newly limited, while the ego, which is not a renunciatory agency, must be strengthened. Freud is no advocate of instinct, or of the unconscious; he is no worshipper of the infinite. He understands and accepts the interdictory structure of culture. Freud himself cannot be called a therapeutic; even less can he be called a symbolist of charismatic authority. Rather, Freud is one of those transitional figures obsessed with the prototypal survival of authority. There is a sense in which Freud prepared the way for the present phase of the therapeutic movement. For therapeutic reasons, he tried to diminish the intensities of an aberrant inwardness.

Interdictory authority can exist only as the agency which itself is engaged in creating renunciatory disciplines of obedience to god-terms beyond the figure of the charismatic himself. Both Weber and Freud, but especially Freud, broadcast the old suspicion, not unknown to charismatic theory, that authority was not disciplining itself, first, as it must, in obedience to renunciatory command. Both Weber and Freud suspected that authority had become too enlightened for its own good, no longer believing in any part of its old symbolic, largely Christian, but that it had become a mere disguise of narcissism. Only where authority engages itself, first, in its own discipline of obedience to renunciatory command, even at the risk of losing power, there only does authority become charismatic. This implies a confusion fatal to the "neutrality" of Weber's theory: Weber is perfectly able to conceive of charismatic authority that is not itself renunciatory. In this way, he destroys the oppositional tension between authority and power; the destruction of this tension has been fatal to the meaning and working of authority in Western culture; nowadays, even the possibility of authority is enough to elicit a preventive therapeutic response. This is, in sum, how the gift of grace is prevented, nowadays, from reaching us "from above." Moreover, we are acquiring a fatal incapacity to reproduce authority relations at the same time that we recognize them for what they are. That would be the ideal way.

NINETEEN

THE REPRESSION OF MEANING

CHARISMA OPPOSES THE LIFESTYLE of transgressiveness, not in the infinite, but in the finite. It is for this reason that the true charismatic is always an interdictory figure, closing down the openness of possibility, narrowing the human passion for the infinite into a particular culture or way of life. Kierkegaard's doctrine of the absurd is a subtle way of stating the ethic of the therapeutic. His subtlety is limited, however, by a certain terrible simplicity to which Kierkegaard submitted, the historical paradox of truth eternal precisely in its militant opposition to other possibilities equally attractive: the very historical religion, Christianity. The therapeutic takes the next ethically logical step after Kierkegaard: he becomes a non-Christian without becoming anything else. Like the emancipated Jew, all the affirmations of the therapeutic are critically negative: he no longer goes to synagogue in order not to go to church. Thus the therapeutic maintains the absurdity of every faith, including his therapeutic faith.

But therapeutic faiths, precisely in their absurdity, become more, not less, enactable; for they are precisely ways to keep acting, and yet without "being on." The therapeutic, as an order of interpretation, is not a sum of doctrinal propositions; that is to say, the therapeutic interpretation is not an objective faith, to use the Kierkegaardian language; nor is the therapeutic interpretation a kind of inwardness. For the therapeutic interpretation poses no eternity, no heaven, no salvation, no anchor, no depth; the therapeutic aims only at polishing his acting talent; he is an actor, impure and complex, like all his predecessors, but purified by his specially amoral form of self-knowledge. His greatest mythic efforts are to thrust the individual away from himself as a neurotic entity, and toward action. In that way there lies not salvation but living itself.

The great movements of modernity are therapeutic in character. Neither the liberation movements that denounce the opposition as fascist, nor the fascist movements, are in any way a sum of doctrinal propositions. Neither side is engaged in the construction of an objective faith, and those critics of both fascist and liberation movements who accuse them of not having an objective faith miss the meaning of those movements; they are *modern* in the sense that they aim not at anchoring ourselves, without all the consequent risks of inhibition, but untying us from anchors—so that, whatever our condition, we can *act*, keep up our interest in living strenuously and ardently, but also coolly; even rage is thus manipulable, opportunistic. We are in the age of pseudo-sensibility, not least because our moral revolutionaries are bound, according to their own implicit theories, only to amoral forms. Pseudo-sensibility is easily comprehended; it is the modern talent for acting out the condition of being deeply touched—hurt and/or healed—when in fact nothing can touch the actor deeply; he is continually retraining his sensibility from the outside in, for every moral form is a form of inwardness. The pseudo-sensibility of the modern moral revolutionary, based as it must be on amoral forms, constitutes what used to be called "hypocrisy," raised to the status of a science of self and other.

This is not to say that the therapeutic cannot cry aloud and rage and display the most shaking anger and sincerity. On the contrary, like the best actors, a therapeutic knows his roles by heart and yet can shift from one to another without self-confusion. Between a conservative or reactionary therapeutic, on the one hand, or a radical and revolutionary therapeutic, on the other, not to mention a liberal therapeutic, there are no lines hard and fast. The traditional political lines are destroyed by the colossal presence of the therapeutic as the performer of power plays. The therapeutic feels free to manipulate history by consciously asserting this fragment or that fragment in order to gain a particular advantage at a particular time. Historical materials are manipulated and everything is done to set forward a particular contemporary interest as legitimate by virtue of the fact that it is housed in one or two amoral forms: either self-interest or scientific neutrality. But neither form supports things as they are. Such supports are "systematic rigmarole,"[1] defenses of things as they are by their beneficiaries. Attacks on the "system" began early in the transitional period and culminate in Hitler's famous instruction to his followers, in a Munich speech, on the eve of becoming Reichschancellor: "If anyone should ask you: 'What is your program?,' you answer: 'Our program is against you [*gegen ihnen*].' " A therapeutic aims to be like the fluidity of living itself.

Neither Nazism nor current libertarian movements can be rightly interpreted as systems. On the contrary, the therapeutic proclaims that all systems are "rigmarole": they are against *all* systems.

It is from the systemizing authority of the charismatic mind that systems develop. What Weber refused to realize was that the system is there, from the beginning, in the discipline of authority that constitutes the presence of the charismatic. Against all systems, therefore, the therapeutic opposes all truths that are not one's own and inherently self-serving.

The problem for transitional figures like Kierkegaard is that he made an exception in the case of such an authoritative truth as Christianity, not in its institutional or doctrinal forms, but in its *personal*, moral form—in relation to Christ. But this is paralleled by therapeutic truth in relation to the therapeutic process itself, so that Christianity may be considered, in the Kierkegaardian interpretation, as the unconscious model and predecessor of the therapeutic movements. The difference between Christianity and its successor, the sex therapeutic movements, may be said to be the difference between coming to a decision and learning to be decisive—a condition in which many opposing decisions may be made.

There are certain sociological preconditions of the therapeutic: first, the therapeutic arises in a late phase of bureaucratization; and second, in periods of extreme disenchantment, in the Weberian sense; third, there is a very high educational level among therapeutics; i.e., many opposing symbolics are presented to them, cooked and ready for their peculiar digestive interest; fourth, the therapeutic generally has a middle-class experience in both the Marxist and the Weberian sense, the middle classes with their addiction to middle-class principles and self-criticism; finally, the therapeutic arises in a condition of widespread delegitimation of the social order. They develop at the higher ranks of social structures and are rather like aristocrats who have lost discipline and have their pleasures remaining.

In therapy, all thought is free, indirect, and negative, and as such, thought tends toward a decision to change oneself, to eliminate the fixed points around which one's ideas have become rigid with fear precisely of what they may express. But therapy does not permanently resolve all difficulties—it is not a cure-all. The therapeutic remains in a difficult situation all his life. He is attracted to the charismatic condition, or, if not to that, then to the neurotic. Therapy is constituted by the constant effort to remove the attractions of both charisma and neurosis. Therapeutic thinking is intensely personal, even among those who would sacrifice their individuality to a movement. That sacrifice itself is understood as the best way beyond certain personal difficulties. Marlow, in the *Heart of Darkness,* may be said to have sought a resolution of his personal indecision by pitting himself against the great transgressive Kurtz. Marlow must try to understand not only himself, but also Kurtz. This places a tremendous burden on his knowingness. Such knowledge is always personal and never indifferent to the object known. What is known is altered by being known: that is the point of the therapeutic's involvement in reality and the satisfaction he exacts as the investigative member of it. The therapeutic demonstrates, as Pirandello's Leone did, the sheer personality of his knowledge. Leone knows nothing that is not related to that essential problem: filling up his emptiness. If, as a man entirely of knowledge, he does not occupy himself constantly with finding new truths for his use, then Leone knows he would cease to exist. This danger of suicide as an act of self-ignorance characterizes all of the great therapeutic theorists: Kierkegaard, Nietzsche, Freud, Marx, and also the lesser ones. In this respect all oppose the naïve position of the positivists, for whom knowledge is tested for its truth precisely in the degree to which it becomes impersonal on the model of the Cartesian dichotomy between subject and object, in which the subject addresses an object and demands its knowledge from it, as if quite autonomous from the object; but the object, through the process of knowledge, must submit to the investigating subject. The one question that the positivist tradition never raises is about the relation of scientific explanation to that which it purports to explain, and about the understanding of the response of the investigator to the object itself, which is the true interest of the therapeutic. His true interest is in his response and only indirectly in the object to which he responds.

There is a stylistic question about the therapeutic writers that is most interesting. The question is simply, "Does the therapeutic writer generally or typically edit himself, polish his writing? Or does he repeat himself rather indulgently?" Certainly the evidence in Kierkegaard is that he repeated himself rather indulgently. There is evidence to suppose that Freud rarely, if ever, rewrote; rarely submitted himself to that kind of discipline, and, of course, unless the writer is in a particular phase of the strictest stylistic inspiration, the consistency necessary to a polished statement on first effort is usually difficult to achieve. I think there is also evidence that Kierkegaard never rewrote, but simply issued different works, making varied statements on the same theme. In this sense, the therapeutic writer is rather like the artist, whose varied pictures, finished as they are, really do represent, very often, drafts of the same effort, constantly repeated, so that one can conclude that the stylistic mark of the therapeutic writer is, in fact, *repetition.*[2] Certainly, no more indulgent case of repetition could be conceived. This self-indulgence may go with the particular depth of the therapeutic writer's effort. In Kierkegaard's case, for example, if we eliminate his submission to the Christian truth, then we are left with the therapeutic. For him, the fact that objectively there is no truth is inseparable from the fact that the truth of Christianity must be subjective. Thus, for him, an objective knowledge of the truth of Christianity, or of its truths, is precisely untruth. But a subjective knowledge of the truth of Christianity is only possible for the therapeutic if it may also be said that he has a subjective knowledge of the truth of that which opposes Christianity. Thus the therapeutic is constantly transforming his truths into untruths, his subjective knowledge into objective, and depending upon that objective knowledge in the therapeutic process to keep him going. The beginning point, then, at which Kierkegaard and his therapeutic successors agree is that objectively there is no truth. The end point at which they disagree is in Kierkegaard's assumption that Christianity is truth, its particular and historical subjectivity.[3] For the therapeutic, any number of possibilities may become subjective truths, while none become objectively so. Therefore, it may be said without exaggeration that the therapeutic is a Christian who has discovered that his own truth needs multiplying and dividing. The therapeutic is that kind of supreme Kiekegaardian Christian who can, for long periods of time, do without Christianity, since there are so many other subjective truths to which he may adhere for a time. The inner relation between the Christian and therapeutic movements is clear in the attraction that therapeutic lifestyles and the therapeutic mode of explanation now have for Christians less willing to be encapsulated so exclusively within their Christianity. "Decision," if it opposes others to be made, becomes the authority of neurosis rather than of charisma.

To achieve and install charismatic authority is to achieve and install new repressions; this is the sociological meaning of what Kierkegaard called "decision." Such repressions, and their maintenance, can only be achieved by interpretative preparations of guilt. *Guilt* interpretations are main elements of the charismatic mission, the deep reinstallation of interdictory structures in the midst of transgressive situations. Thus, all powerful charismatic movements add certain tension of guilt, as well as its resolution, to the ordinary tensions of workaday transgressiveness. Charismatic guilt builds hermeneutic circles within which the individual can be reenclosed. In his interpretation of charisma, Weber is already a permanent outsider, convinced, above all, that the religious root of modern economic humanity is dead. The killing of this "religious root" is in part to be ascribed to the interpretation of the charismatic, in which interpretation itself is no longer part of any charismatic effort at the intensification and resolution of guilt. Without the interdependency of guilt, no hermeneutic circle can be drawn around individuals; particular repressions, personified and exemplified in the interdictory figure, have no animating focus. This failure to assert and install interdictory remissive contents is itself a key to understanding the difference between the charismatic interpretations of the premodern era and the interpretation of the charismatic, of which Weber himself is an outstanding example.

A charismatic enacts his subjective truths, first and last, to and for himself. Made objective and institutional, these subjective truths of the charismatic become untruths. Charismatic beginnings lie so deep in subjectivity that Weber could never reach them. The "gift of grace" becomes, in his theory, mere mystification.

The charismatic remains an obscure figure, the new beginning his inwardness creates falsified by history. The historical fate of charisma is to become untrue, its inwardness falsified by the institutional history created under its sign. That is the late Protestant pathos of good beginnings and bad endings on which Weber built his theory. By his own untenable objectivity, by his assertion of what he calls value-neutrality, Weber elaborates an interpretation opposed to the charismatic. So in Weber we are already engaged in a post-charismatic mode of interpretation. Weber's language, his style, leads to analytic isolation, to the repression of meaning.

TWENTY

CRIPPLED IN OUR CAPACITIES TO PERCEIVE THE SELDOM-APPEARING THING

WHAT SHALL WE MAKE OF this absurdity, the charismatic? He is the tail we blind guests at a no-host party have pinned to the donkey of our history. Charisma, Weber told us, has a brief and yet incalculable effect. It is a revolutionary tail that wags the dog of ordinary life, bidding us come sniff, follow close behind, in personal devotion. Charisma is the one effervescence of the sociological imagination that has kept not only we professional sniffers on the trail of incalculable effects running after it; more important, if the scent be there, then some significant group of the unprofessional must be moving in the same direction, and by that movement, herald some change even more basic than a redistribution of privileges and deprivations in their society. Yet, for so important a concept as charisma, is there not something absurd when that concept is so heterogeneous that it can refer at once to the canonical prophets of Israel and to the blond beasts of Byzantium; to Jesus and an "Arab berserk" who bites his shield like a mad dog—biting around until he darts off in raving bloodthirstiness?[1] There seems to me something especially absurd about the "creative power" of certain individuals to mobilize what are after all only "short-lived mass emotions," even though these have their "incalculable effects." The charismatic is a figure who successfully demands personal devotion to himself and for his message; yet the concept has passed into popular use during a time in which we free spirits know that there is nothing worthy of our worship, that worship itself is a shortcoming of the unfree. It was Weber who transformed the nineteenth-century backward-looking religion of criticism into the twentieth-century forward-looking discipline of sociology, by reminding us of the existence of *charisma* as one of the two great and equal revolutionary forces in world history—the other being the force of "Reason." Until Weber put the concept forward again, it had been all but forgotten, except by a few historians of early Christianity; or it had survived under a variety of different names, and with a confusing welter of implications.

How questionable, first of all, are Weber's twin revolutionary forces, charisma and "Reason," precisely in their oppositional relation; for "Reason" is the highest of the passions; intellect will serve its affects. Weber locked "Reason" inside quotation marks and set charisma free for its current popular use. There is personality behind the impersonality of science. The two positions that have been offered to us for so long still remain unsatisfactory for the transforming of our unhappy consciousness, our failed social and skeptical attitudes.

If "Reason" is a world-changing force, then it might be summarized, in Weberian as well as popular usage, as *situation-changing:* if charisma is an older and equally revolutionary force, then it might be summarized as what Keats called *soul-making.* The younger force is thought to work, somehow, from the outside in, the older form, the inside out; the younger force is impersonally transferable, the older force is nothing if not transference of personal authority. My interest is in quoting the great question: what the transferences of personal authority can mean to us, here and now. I write unashamedly from the standpoint of my cultural situation. In that situation, all personal authority appears more and more questionable—and with it charisma, too, appears only in questionable forms. I have some extraordinarily tentative notions of the type that is succeeding the charismatic in our culture; I have tried to sketch the main features of that type in the course of this volume. I have already introduced my premonitions of that type, and his main carriers, in an earlier book, *The Triumph of the Therapeutic.*[2]

As Keats wrote in his letter of April 1819, it was while reading two very different books that he discovered the condition of soul-making. He began that famous letter with a poem:

> Or at thy supreme desire,
> Touch the very pulse of fire.

Keats had the sharpening experiences of reading, intermixed, William Robertson's *America* and Voltaire's *Age of Louis Quatorze.* "It is like walking arm-in-arm between Pizarro and the great little monarch," wrote Keats. Then he jotted down his great conceit on soul-making, and on our world, like his, as the "vale of soul-making." In the vale, "Reason" plays a small part. Souls are not made by force of "Reason."[3] How, then, are souls made? Keats's beautifully intuited alternative to the revolutionary force of "Reason" is worth quoting in full, I think, if for no other reason than that soul-making is not a condition easily summarized. Moreover, I consider *"soul-making"* a synonym for *"charisma"* that has the rare virtue of revealing more than it obscures, for *"soul"* is nothing to us, I suggest, if it does not represent an internalization of personal authority. Because we, in the here and now, appear to me almost entirely finished with those forms of self-respect, and of social organization, that found issue in authoritative theories of soul, and of morality, and begin to find issue in theories beyond that of neuroses[4]—I say, because of this movement away from soul, Keats on soul-making needs to be remembered. In my culture, as in my scholarship, it remains dangerous to forget the dead, or neglect the dying. If soul-making, or charisma, is a dead or dying theory of how we overcharged ourselves, then all the more reason for this present act of remembrance. This book I may offer as a life-act, a rattling of dry bones in what is probably a losing war against the radical contemporaneity of our culture; that contemporaneity is the mark of a true barbarian. For barbarism is not some primitive technology and naïve cosmologies, but a sophisticated cutting off of the inhibiting authority of the past. Keats belongs to the authority of the past. I depend upon him now, to help us out of our own lamentable case. He writes, of primitive America and sophisticated France:

> In how lamentable a case do we see the great body of the people in both instances: in the first, where men might seem to inherit quiet of mind from unsophisticated senses; from uncontamination of civilisation; and especially from their being as it were estranged from the mutual helps of society and its mutual injuries—and thereby more immediately under the protection of Providence—even there they had mortal pains

to bear as bad; or even worse than bailiffs, debts and poverties of civilized life—The whole appears to resolve into this—that man is originally "a poor forked creature" subject to the same mischances as the beasts of the forest, destined to hardships and disquietude of some kind or other. If he improves by degrees his bodily accommodations and comforts—at each stage, at each ascent, there are waiting for him a fresh set of annoyances—he is mortal and there is still a heaven with its stars above his head. The most interesting question that can come before us is, How far by the persevering endeavours of a seldom appearing Socrates mankind may be made happy—I can imagine such happiness carried to an extreme—but what must it end in?—Death—and who could in such a case bear with death—the whole troubles of life which are now frittered away in a series of years, would then be accumulated for the last days of a being who instead of hailing its approach, would leave this world as Eve left Paradise. But in truth I do not at all believe in this sort of perfectibility—the nature of the world will not admit of it—the inhabitants of the world will correspond to itself. Let the fish Philosophise the ice away from the rivers in winter time and they shall be at continual play in the tepid delight of Summer. Look at the Poles and at the sands of Africa, whirlpools and volcanoes. Let men exterminate them and I will say that they may arrive at earthly Happiness. The point at which man may arrive is as far as the parallel state in inanimate nature and no further. For instance, suppose a rose to have sensation, it blooms on a beautiful morning, it enjoys itself—but there comes a cold wind, a hot sun—it cannot escape it, it cannot destroy its annoyances—they are as native to the world as itself: no more can man be happy in spite, the worldly elements will prey upon his nature. The common cognomen of this world among the misguided and superstitious is "a vale of tears" from which we are to be redeemed by a certain arbitrary interposition of God and taken to Heaven. What a little circumscribed straightened notion! Call the world if you please "The vale of soul-making." Then you will find out the use of the world (I am speaking now in the highest terms for human nature admitting it to be immortal which I will here take for granted for the purpose of showing a thought which has struck me concerning it) I say "soul-making" soul as distinguished from an intelligence. There may be intelligences or sparks of the divinity in millions, but they are not souls till they acquire identities, till each one is personally itself. Intelligences are atoms of perception—they know and they see and they are pure, in short they are God. How then are souls to be made? How then are these sparks which are God to have identity given them—so as ever to possess a bliss peculiar to each one's individual existence? How, but by the medium of a world like this? This point I sincerely wish to consider because I think it a grander system of salvation than the Christian religion—or rather it is a system of Spirit-creation. This is effected by three grand materials acting the one upon the other for a series of years. These three materials are the intelligence—the human heart (as distinguished from intelligence of mind) and the world or elemental space suited for the proper action of mind and heart on each other for the purpose of forming the soul or intelligence destined to possess the sense of identity. I can scarcely express what I but dimly perceive—and yet I think I perceive it—that you may judge the more clearly I will put it in the most homely form possible—I will call the world a school instituted for the purpose of teaching little children to read—I will call the human heart the hornbook used in that school—and I will call the child able to read, the soul made from that school and its hornbook. Do you not see how necessary a world of pains and troubles is to school an intelligence and make it a soul? A place where the heart must feel and suffer in a thousand diverse ways! Not merely is the heart a hornbook, it is the mind's Bible, it is the mind's experience, it is the teat from which the mind or intelligence sucks its identity. As various as the lives of men are—so various become their souls, and thus does God make individual beings, souls, identical souls of the sparks of his own essence. This appears to me a faint sketch of a system of salvation which does not affront our reason and humanity. I am convinced that many difficulties which Christians labour under would vanish before it. There is one which even now strikes me—the salvation of children. In them the spark of intelligence returns to God without any identity—it having had no time to learn of and be altered by the heart—or seat of the human passions. It is pretty generally suspected that the Christian scheme has been copied from the ancient Persian and Greek philosophers. Why may they not have made this simple thing even more simple for common apprehension by introducing mediators and personages in the same manner as in the heathen mythology abstractions are personified. Seriously, I think it probable that this system of soul-making may have been the parent of all the more palpable and personal schemes of redemption, among the Zoroastrians, the Christians and the Hindoos. For as one part of the human species must have their carved Jupiter; so another part must have the palpable and named Mediator and Saviour, their Christ, their Oromanes and their Vishnu. If what I have said should not be plain enough, as I fear it may not be, I will put you in the place where I began in this series of thoughts—I mean, I began by seeing how man was formed by circumstances—and what are circumstances? but touchstones of his heart? And what are touchstones? but provings of his heart? And what are provings of his heart but fortifiers or alterers of his nature? And what is his altered nature but his soul? and what was his soul before it came into the world and had these provings and alterations and perfectionings? An intelligence—without identity—and how is this identity to be made? Through the medium of the heart? And how is the heart to become this medium but in a world of circumstances?[5]

I have quoted Keats at length because, accepting the world as it must be, in its distressing circumstantialities and yet restating the most ancient device for our living in it, by soul-making, Keats discovered how we have driven ourselves through one damn thing after another, beyond the despair of mere endurance. Keats knew, at least as well as Bertrand Russell, or as well as any man suddenly surprised by circumstance, that nothing will save us, not "all the devotion, all the inspiration, all the noonday brightness of human genius."[6] We here had our "seldom appearing Socrates" and other spirit creators. They have left us with some "creative power" of our own, some identity with which to resist change of circumstance. Yet, for all of its incalculable effects, there is something at once terrible and weak about this "creative power" that Weber recalled to us, far more ambiguously than Keats recalled to us, far more ambiguously than Keats recalled soul-making, under that old Christian rubric for soul-making, "*charisma*." How swiftly, after his appearance, the opposing authority of the charismatic to the world as it is "recedes in the face of domination, which hardens into lasting institutions"; how the privileged of "existing political, social and economic orders" take over this creative power, so to "legitimate" their positions.

Nothing seems to fail like the success of the charismatic.

It is equally wise to say that nothing succeeds like the necessary failure of a charismatic. Do not the hierarchs of the party know that out of Lenin, out of Marx, even out of Stalin, they are "thus sanctified," as Weber put it, not even troubling to put the old theological word between quotation marks, as he should? In Weber's simplest meaning, the powerful and the privileged, the always alert, scent the new opportunities opened up by a soul-maker; the mantle of new offices drapes his words; his unique shroud becomes another flag among flags they convert the soul-making organizations, as they are converted to it. The charismatic survives as an effigy. He may even be mummified; even as the body remains in this sense creative, the soul has departed. New and old opportunists, along with the genuine hero-worshippers, "wish to see their positions transformed, from purely factual power relations, into a cosmos of acquired rights"; this wish operates, among the converted to the charismatic organization, as much to persuade themselves of their sanctification as again to resign those who are to live under their somewhat altered rule. New bishops divide up the old provinces of empire, and a second Rome is established. New to authority and joined by interests earlier established, allied, "these interests comprise by far the strongest motive for the conservation of charismatic elements within the structure of domination."[7] Thus, charisma "remains a highly important element of the social structure."[8] Despite the vale in which even the most genuine soul-making must occur, Weber insists that "*genuine* charisma is absolutely opposed to this objectified form. *It* does not appeal to an enacted or traditional order, nor does *it* base *its* claims upon acquired rights."[9]

But this *it*? is so heterogeneous that it can include not only the berserk and saintly, vulnerable to an infinite number of "transformations," charisma can attach to the American presidency—acquired by election, stimulated, as Weber tells us, by "the power of money" and the "charisma of rhetoric." But in these quotation marks, charisma expands into technique and manipulation.

Weber did not invent charisma, and I doubt that he has the soul-taking power that would accompany its destruction. I cite Weber, as often as not, for his destructive neutral uses of the concept, so to do my little to defend it against this giant destroyer. His formulae of legitimation translate too easily into professional sales techniques, with leadership as the product.

Of course, Weber would deny such a charge. There is something about *genuine* charisma that takes it beyond its own heterogeneity, and beyond its modern degradation, as publicity. Weber understood, perfectly well, the acute opposition between the charismatic situation, on the one hand, and publicity (or the buildup of a personality) on the other hand.[10]

This opposition is not altogether modern. Hermann Broch states it beautifully in his great novel *The Death of Virgil.* To confuse charisma and publicity is already to state the condition of modern consciousness; and this condition is the ultimate object of Broch's masterpiece. That the condition is examined in the context of ancient culture and politics, in the relation of poet and Caesar, is an irony necessary to the author, in his address to the modern reader. The point remains that much of what moderns call charisma is really publicity, and therefore the opposite of charisma. It was Kierkegaard who insisted most thoughtfully on the opposition between charisma and publicity; in the face of publicity, and that reflectiveness of which sociology is one formal discipline, Kierkegaard sees that the charismatic must be, in the present age, more than ever before, not the "recognized," but the "unrecognized one." Of course, Weber recognized the limits of recognition. He, too, lived in the age of publicity and celebrity. Yet his use of charisma damns itself by its neutrality. Educated to neutrality in the context of a social science that must help make the world as a vale without soul-making, are we not crippled in our capacities to perceive the seldom appearing thing bearing "specific gifts of body and mind that were considered 'supernatural'?"[11]

NOTES

1. SPRAY-ON CHARISMA

1. Weber asserts three pure types of legitimate authority—the three pure types are well known. They are the type of rational authority that rests on a belief in the legality of patterns of normative rules and the right of those elevated to authority under such rules to issue commands, thus this type operates on rational grounds; there is the traditionalist type of legitimate authority that rests on an established belief in the sanctity of immemorial traditions and legitimacy of the status of those exercising authority under them, thus traditional grounds; and finally, there is the charismatic type, which rests on the devotion to the specific and exceptional sanctity, heroism, or exemplary character of an individual person and of the moral demand patterns or order revealed or ordained by him, thus the charismatic type. But these are all forms of the construction of legitimate authority. What we need is a typology that helps us understand the destruction of legitimate authority, its dissolution, and for this, I am suggesting a fourth type, which would help us understand the dissolution of legitimate authority under the critical concept of legitimation itself.

   This character type would no longer be given to devotion to some specific and exceptional sanctity, but would be beyond the compulsions of the interdictory motifs. In a vision of this type, there would be no normative rules revealed and ordained or accepted on the basis of the sanctity of usage, except such rules as may be convenient to that person in his analytic capacity, or in the capacity of those who are his doctors, and, moreover, legality would itself be a most fragile construction. The whole doctrine of convention would itself be a constant constraint upon the grounds of legitimate authority in legality. All of these character types issuing from the grounds of legitimate authority, rational, traditional, and charismatic, make judgments. In the dissolution of legitimate authority the therapeutic makes no judgment; he is value neutral.
2. Franz Steiner, *Taboo* (Pelican), p. 64.
3. Ibid., pp. 63–64.
4. Ibid., pp. 64–65.
5. Ibid., p. 65.
6. Ibid., p. 65.

7. Ibid., p. 66.
8. Ibid.
9. Ibid.
10. Ibid., p. 67.

2. THE FIRST VANGUARD OF OUR INHERITED CULTURE

1. Mazim Gorky, *Reminiscences of L. N. Tolstoy,* trans. S. S. Koteliansky and Leonard Woolf (New York, 1920), p. 48.
2. Martin Buber, *Moses: The Revelation and the Covenant* (New York: Harper & Row, 1958), p. 102.
3. Ibid., p. 55.
4. Ibid., p. 20.
5. Ibid., p. 22.
6. Ibid., p. 57.
7. Ibid., p. 57.
8. Ibid. Buber disagrees with this interpretation, but does not argue against the opposition between ritual acts and acts of power, which reconciles the conflicting anthropological and religious arguments on the rite of circumcision.
9. Ibid., p. 57.
10. William Hamilton, "The Jesus Who Keeps Coming Back," *The New Republic,* 158, 14 (April 6, 1968): 34.
11. Søren Kierkegaard, *Fear and Trembling,* trans. Walter Lowrie (Princeton: Princeton University Press, 1954).
12. Ibid.
13. Ibid., p. 11.
14. Søren Kierkegaard, *The Journals of Kierkegaard,* trans., selected and with an introduction by Alexander Dru (New York: Harper & Row, 1959), pp. 5–8.
15. Buber, *Moses,* p. 138.
16. This problem of confidence is beautifully elaborated in the story of the great captain—great through the divine gift of confidence—Gideon. The story of Gideon, and the fight he led against the Midianites, is a teaching on credal individuality. The Midianites were especially powerful foes because they had camels, yet Gideon, who was not at all a professional soldier, leads a handful of Israelites to victory. But the real struggle is not between Yahweh and Israel on the one hand, and the Midianites on the other; rather, the real struggle is between Yahweh and Gideon.

    This struggle is brilliantly developed in the credal (i.e., teaching) story. Yahweh orders reduced the number of Gideon's army. When the victory is won, it is won without a blow being struck; the victory belongs to Yahweh and not to the Israelites. In this way, the true relation between self-confidence and ultimate authority is taught. Moreover, the spoils of war belonged to Yahweh. In this way, the ego of the man of power, the warrior, is constrained by that credal order which is the real constitution of Israel. Pride is tempered by the fact that these victories and the spoils of victory are Yahweh's doing and responsibility, and not the doing and responsibility of men. This is equally clear in the story of Achan's theft, in Joshua 7. In that story, the spoils from Jericho were dedicated to Yahweh in advance; nevertheless, the soldier Achan took for himself "one good Babylonian cloak, 200 shekels of silver, and a bar of gold weighing 50 shekels," and concealed them beneath the floor of his tent. In the next battle, Israel was defeated and lost thirty-six men, which terrified the people. "So Joshua tore his tunic and lay down on his face on the ground until evening, both he and the others of Israel, before the ark of Yahweh, and they put dust on their heads. And Joshua said, Oh, my Lord Yahweh, why? Then Yahweh said, Get up. Why in the world are you lying on your face? Israel has sinned, indeed, they have transgressed my covenant, which I imposed on them." Thus, transgressions, all remissive behavior, is related to the covenant, which indicates the meaning of discipline in such a society, and the reasons for both disaster and the transgressions are sought out at the most holy object, the Ark of the Covenant, where Achan's guilt is discovered, and he and his family executed by stoning. The pact with God has been broken. Ordinarily, Achan's crime of theft would not have been so severely punished, but Achan's crime was in a totally different sphere. He had put Israel in the position of having broken the covenant with Yahweh. This was a fundamental and complete breach of discipline, and challenged the whole meaning of human discipline. He had brought the curse of the covenant into operation and this can be averted only by directing it onto the responsible party with all he has, which includes his person, his wife, his son, his grandson, his house, his land, together with everything he owns. For by breaking the covenant, he has transgressed in every respect and about everything.

17. *From Max Weber: Essays in Sociology,* trans. and ed. H. H. Gerth and C. Wright Mills (New York: Oxford University Press, 1946), p. 252.
18. Of which a monopoly of sexual gratification is the main fantasy.

3. COVENANT AND CHARISMA

1. *From Max Weber: Essays in Sociology,* pp. 256–57.
2. Not to mention the ancient casuistries by which the covenant, in a credal order, was made into laws.
3. See Harold Pinter's *Old Times* for a clever pastiche of acts that mean nothing whatever; the last thing in the world this play does is express the problem, or dramatize an analysis of emptiness; rather, the play itself is empty and meaningless. It does not grapple with being empty, or with meaning. For a masterpiece that does grapple brilliantly with being empty, and its three characters, with rules that are meaningless; for a portrayal of the therapeutic that is a work of genius, see Luigi Pirandello's *The Rules of the Game,* preferably with Paul Scofield as Leone. Pirandello makes Leone the perfect type of anti-charismatic and therefore complete master of those who cannot get free—i.e., empty—themselves of both interdicts and remissions. Cf. George Bernard Shaw's *Man and Superman.*

4. PROPHETIC CHARISMA

1. Buber, *Moses,* p. 63.
2. Johannes Pedersen, *Israel: Its Life and Culture,* vol. 1 (Oxford: Oxford University Press, 1959), p. 178.
3. Max Weber, *Sociology of Religion* (Boston: Beacon Press, 1963), p. 48.
4. Ibid., p. 59.
5. Max Weber, *Ancient Judaism,* trans. and ed. H. H. Gerth and D. Martindale (Glencoe, Ill.: The Free Press, 1952), p. 336.
6. Sigmund Freud, "Dostoyevsky and Parricide," *Selected Essays,* vol. 5 (London, 1950), pp. 222–42.
7. *Concilium,* vol. IV, New York, 1965, in a volume of Council speeches at Vatican II, the Paulist Press.
8. See his discussion of the charismatic structure of the church, ibid., p. 50 of previous citation ff.
9. Weber, *Sociology of Religion,* p. 46.

5. THE PSYCHIATRIC STUDY OF JESUS

1. The references here are to Timothy 3:5 and to St. John 3:5.
2. The mystical purification as indicated in 1 Corinthians 6:11 and in Ephesians 5:26 and especially the participation in Christ's death and resurrection, especially in Romans 6:1 and following.
3. 1 Corinthians 10:16 and thereafter, and in 1 Corinthians 11:23 and thereafter, and in John 6:51 and thereafter, and in Revelation 3:20 and 19:9.
4. Albert Schweitzer, *The Quest of the Historical Jesus* (New York: Dover, 2006), p. 369.
5. *From Max Weber: Essays in Sociology,* p. 357.

6. THE CHRISTIAN MEANING OF CHARISMA

1. Friedrich Nietzsche, *The Anti-Christ,* section 28.
2. *The Story of a Soul: The Autobiography of St. Thérèse of Lisieux* (L'histoire d'une âme) trans. John Beevers, Image Book (New York: Doubleday, 1957).
3. "To receive you is to receive me, and to receive me is to receive the One who sent me" (Matthew 10:40–41).

7. FAITH AND FANATICISM

1. Sigmund Freud, *Therapy and Technique,* p. 138.

8. MAX WEBER AND THE POST-PROTESTANT ETHOS

1. Ludwig Feuerbach, *The Essence of Christianity* (New York: Harper Torchbooks, 1957), p. 320.
2. Ibid.
3. Ibid.
4. Ibid.
5. Ibid., pp. 322–23.
6. Ibid., p. 323.
7. Ibid., pp. 320–21.
8. Weber, *Sociology of Religion*, p. 120.
9. Ibid.
10. Ibid., p. 122.
11. Nietzsche, quoted in Kaufmann, p. 82.
12. This is from *Luther's Werk*, the Weimar edition, Vol. II, p. 404.
13. This is from *Luther's Verker*, the Eirlungen edition, the 15th Vol., p. 145 and thereafter.
14. *Werker*, the Weimar edition, Vol. II, p. 18 and thereafter.
15. In the Werker, the Eirlungen edition, Vol 62, p. 311.
16. Friedrich Nietzsche, *Twilight of the Idols*, "Morality as Anti-Nature," section 3, in *Viking Portable Nietzsche* (New York: Viking, 1959), p. 92.
17. In Nietzsche, "God-consciousness" is psychologized into a *need* for both good and evil: "One has as much need of the evil god as of the good god" (*The Anti-Christ*, section 16, p. 126).
18. Sigmund Freud, *Beyond the Pleasure Principle* (New York: W. W. Norton, 1961), p. 4.
19. Ibid., p. 5.
20. Nietzsche, *Twilight of the Idols*, section 5, p. 45.
21. Ibid., section 6, p. 46.
22. Ibid.
23. The most convenient summary of Sohm's position is in Rudolf Sohm, "Die Charismatische Organization," in Part III, "Der Ursprung des Kathologismus," in *Wesen und Ursprung des Kathologismus*, 2nd ed. (Leipzig: Toebreu, 1912), p. 50.
24. Ibid., p. 103.
25. Theordor Heuss, *Friedrich Neumann, der Mann, das Werk, die Zeit* (Stuttgart-Berlin, 1937), p. 195.
26. Harnack, p. 177.
27. Ibid., p. 185.
28. See Adolph Harnack, the 2nd vol. of his *Didacha*, his *Sources* of the Apostolic Canons, etc.
29. S. E. O., p. 364.
30. When those purely factual power relations could have existed, I do not know; Weber does not say. Those power relations are never "factual," I suspect.

31. *From Max Weber: Essays in Sociology,* p. 262.
32. Cf. Frank Hardie, *The Political Influence of the British Monarchy* (New York: Harper & Row, 1970).
33. *From Max Weber: Essays in Sociology.*

9. THE MEANING OF LEADERSHIP

1. *From Max Weber: Essays in Sociology,* p. 246.

10. THE THERAPEUTIC WORLD IS WITHOUT DISCIPLINE AND WITHOUT DISCIPLES

1. Joachim Wach, "Master and Disciple: Two Religio-Sociological Studies," *The Journal of Religion* 42, no. 1 (January 1962): 1–21.
2. *From Max Weber: Essays in Sociology,* p. 254.
3. Sigmund Freud, "Observations on Transference," in *Therapy and Technique,* p. 179.
4. Albert Schweitzer, *The Quest of the Historical Jesus,* p. 400.
5. Nietzsche, *Anti-Christ,* pp. 57, 177.
6. *From Max Weber: Essays in Sociology,* p. 357.
7. Ibid., p. 261.
8. Ibid., p. 262.
9. Cf. Gershom Scholem, *On the Kabbalah and Other Essays* (New York: Schocken), p. 181.
10. Ibid., pp. 180–81.
11. Ibid., p. 199.
12. Ibid., p. 202.
13. Emile Durkheim, *Moral Education* (New York), pp. 33–35.
14. Ibid., p. 51.
15. Ibid., p. 52.
16. Ibid., p. 52 (my italics).
17. Ibid., p. 53.
18. Ibid., pp. 53–54.
19. Ibid., pp. 35 and 36.
20. Ibid.
21. Ibid., p. 42.
22. Ibid., p. 43.
23. Ibid.

12. THE MYSTIQUE OF THE BREAK

1. Max Weber, "Science as a Vocation," *From Max Weber: Essays in Sociology,* p. 78.
2. Steiner, *Taboo,* p. 100.
3. R. R. Marett, *The Threshold of Religion* (London: Methuen, 1914).
4. Cf. Steiner, *Taboo,* pp. 104–5.

5. Cf. ibid., p. 105.
6. Ibid., p. 108 (my italics).
7. Ibid., p. 113.
8. Note how Talcott Parsons uses the term "break through" in his long and thoughtful, but essentially uncritical, introduction to the English translation of Weber's *Sociology of Religion.*
9. Steiner, *Taboo,* p. 116.
10. As Parsons describes Weber's theory, at one point (see introduction to *Sociology of Religion*) without yielding to the irony of the theory.
11. Alfred North Whitehead, *Symbolism, Its Meaning and Effect* (New York: Macmillan, 1927) (my italics).
12. Weber, *Sociology of Religion,* p. 2.
13. Ibid.
14. Ibid.
15. Ibid.
16. Ibid.
17. Weber, "Politics as a Vocation," *From Max Weber: Essays in Sociology,* p. 79. Weber's emphasis.
18. Ibid., p. 123.
19. Weber, *Sociology of Religion,* p. 2.
20. Ibid., p. 6.
21. Ibid., pp. 6, 7.
22. Ibid., p. 7.
23. Ibid.
24. Ibid., p. 7.
25. Ibid.
26. Ibid., p. 10.
27. Ibid.
28. Ibid., p. 15.
29. Ibid., p. 20.
30. Ibid., p. 22.
31. Harnack, *History of Dogma,* vol. 2.
32. Weber, *Sociology of Religion,* p. 22.
33. Ibid., p. 25.

13. EVIL ANGELS HAVE ALL BUT SEIZED CONTROL OF THE WORLD

1. *From Max Weber: Essays in Sociology,* pp. 123–24. In a curious way, Weber, in "Politics as a Vocation," repeats the renunciatory motif of this Christian rhetoric: that, inwardly, a politician must take power as if he took it not, maintain an inner distance, avoid "vain self-reflection in the feeling of power." The alternative is that "sudden inner collapse" of the "mere 'power politician,' " when we can "see what inner weakness and impotence hides behind" all the "ardently promoted cult . . . to glorify him." But how can the striving for power by a political leader, and the renunciatory demands of an interdictory figure, first

against his own strivings for power, come together? The notion of "political religions" derives from the Catholic doctrine of structural charisma, from which Weber derived his concept of office charisma. This theory belongs to the analysis of how charismatic authority is transformed into organizational controls.

2. Ibid., p. 116.
3. R. G. Collingood, *The New Leviathan* (Oxford: Oxford University Press, 1942), p. 73.

14. WHEN THERAPY REPLACES CHARISMA

1. Lévy-Bruhl, *Primitives and the Supernatural* (New York: Dutton, 1935), p. 206.
2. Being a good Comtean, Lévy-Bruhl is quite ambiguous about the psychic depth of these defenses—against dogs copulating with pigs and other worse monstrosities.
3. Lévy-Bruhl, *Primitives and the Supernatural,* p. 219.
4. Ibid.
5. Which, on Freud's account, moves purposively, in certain directions, sexually, for example, to genital eroticism and procreation; to the preservation of the species, though never without the possibility of a "fixation" somewhere along the line.
6. Evans-Pritchard, p. 91.
7. Weber, *Ancient Judaism,* trans. and ed. by Hans G. Gerth and Don Martindale (New York: The Free Press, 1952), p. 267. What boring recitals these tales of ancient woe make. I have more recent recorded events to tell. Indeed, I have even visited a place where, not long ago, lamp shades and other useful articles had been made, by a few excellent at their rare craft, from human skins. Such an aside as this is not entirely irrelevant to the particular cultural situation from which I am obliged to make these notes in defense of culture. I, for one, cannot read Weber on ancient Israel without thinking of modern Israel. I draw dubious but affecting analogies and contrasts between the ancient and the modern settings, of internal weakness and external threat. Although modern Israel is a bureaucratic state, free public prophecy is not prohibited. But the age of prophecy is long gone. Only those "entirely new types of prophets" are rising, under the modern condition, and they will be marked between quotes, where no "genuine" charisma can survive.

   The canonical prophets of ancient Israel were the resurrecting figures of old ideals; sociologically understood, they renewed Israel as a *credal* society. It is in this specific sense that they were true charismatics; their gift was the fight of an extraordinary energy of conveying the established but failing interdictory motifs. It is a nice question—for sociological theory, as the study of ideals and their social structures, or social structures and their ideals—whether social structures can survive without creeds that are compulsively authoritative; that have tutors, who can remind those they have re-created how near they are to being the worst.
8. Lively, *De Maistre,* p, 219.
9. Hermann Broch, *Sleepwalkers* (New York: Grosset & Dunlop, 1960), p. 21.

17. THE CURE AND PREVENTION OF GREAT MEN

1. *From Max Weber: Essays in Sociology,* p. 250.

18. THE GIFT OF GRACE, AND HOW IT HAS BEEN TAKEN AWAY FROM US

1. See Konrad Lorenz, *On Aggression.*
2. Culture can become too "honest," and thus, auto-destructive. There is now a large popular literature in which transgressive conditions or acts actually function as once credal acts did. Charisma becomes the function—even the business—of an array of "creative deviants"; this is "grace from below." It functions to undo the established renunciations—indeed, renunciation as such. Thus directed upward, "charisma" functions to relax the discipline of those who are subject to the experience of "delegitimating" the culture. The legalization of the illegal must follow.
3. Freud himself was almost aware of this. See Sigmund Freud, "Reflections on War and Death," in *Character and Culture* (New York: Macmillan, 1963), p. 132.
4. Cf. Sigmund Freud, "The Resistances to Psychoanalysis," in *Character and Culture,* p. 259.

19. THE REPRESSION OF MEANING

1. Kierkegaard, *Concluding Unscientific Postscript* (Princeton: Princeton University Press, 1992), p. 194.
2. There is an example of repetition in Kierkegaard, pp. 200 and 201. First passage: "Whether speculative philosophy is right or not is another question. Here the only question raised is how the speculative explanation of Christianity is related to the Christianity it purports to explain." Now the passage on the very next page, 201, of the *Concluding Unscientific Postscript:* "Whether speculative philosophy is right is another question. Here we merely inquire how its explanation of Christianity is related to the Christianity it purports to explain."
3. This particular and historical subjectivity is precisely what makes Judaism a lie, according to Marx.

20. CRIPPLED IN OUR CAPACITIES TO PERCEIVE THE SELDOM-APPEARING THING

1. *From Max Weber: Essays in Sociology,* p. 245.
2. Philip Rieff, *The Triumph of the Therapeutic* (New York: Harper & Row, 1968).
3. Rousseau had already stated the limits and implications of "Reason," in his first ambitious essay, "The Discourse on the Sciences and the Arts," when he

insisted on the new forms of evil that must spring up from the vast material and intellectual advance of science.

4. See, further, Sigmund Freud, "Reflections upon War and Death (1915)," in *Character and Culture*, pp. 107–33.
5. *The Letters of John Keats*, ed. Maurice Buxton Forman (London: Oxford University Press, 1948), pp. 334–37.
6. Bertrand Russell, "The Free Man's Wish," in *Philosophical Essays*, p. 59.
7. *From Max Weber: Essays in Sociology*, p. 262.
8. Ibid.
9. Ibid. (my italics).
10. The opposition between charisma and publicity points up the anti-charismatic functions of the modern communications and knowledge industry. In both structure and function, the mass media constitute the most powerful of all prophylaxes against charisma. The mass media destroy the time required for inner preparation both by the charismatic and his followers.
11. Max Weber, "Charisma and Its Transformation," in *Economy and Society*, vol. 3, p. 1112.

INDEX

ABOUT THE AUTHOR

Philip Rieff's other books include *Freud: The Mind of the Moralist, The Triumph of the Therapeutic: Uses of Faith After Freud, Fellow Teachers: Of Culture and Its Second Death,* and *Sacred Order/Social Order: My Life Among the Deathworks.* Philip Rieff died July 1, 2006.

ABOUT THE EDITORS

Aaron Manson is associate professor of clinical medicine at Columbia University.

Daniel Frank is the editorial director of Pantheon Books.

Both are former students of Philip Rieff.

A NOTE ON THE TYPE

The text of this book was composed in Trump Mediæval. Designed by Professor Georg Trump (1896–1985) in the mid-1950s, Trump Mediæval was cut and cast by the C. E. Weber Type Foundry of Stuttgart, Germany. The roman letter forms are based on classical prototypes, but Professor Trump has imbued them with his own unmistakable style. The italic letter forms, unlike those of so many other typefaces, are closely related to their roman counterparts. The result is a truly contemporary type, notable for both its legibility and its versatility.

Composed by Creative Graphics,
Allentown, Pennsylvania

Printed and bound by Berryville Graphics
Berryville, Virginia

Designed by M. Kristen Bearse